ARUBA VACATION WITH ARUBA JOE

Story as told by Aruba Joe at the Café to Jan and Rob

ARUBA VACATION WITH ARUBA JOE

Story as told by Aruba Joe at the Café to Jan and Rob

By

Barbara E. Ringrose

DEDICATION

This story is dedicated to those people who are either young or young of heart. For those that travel to learn and share experiences with friends, family members, or people they have never met. People wishing to interact with others in the pursuit of dreams, visions, or a much-needed vacation-where caution is sometimes thrown into the wind and a rejuvenation of ones' spirit emerges. This story is also for those that dream of sharing an experience without any regrets and embrace the memories into eternity.

Here's to the extension of family and their collective uniqueness and contributions to create the whole experience of 'vacation': Lindsey-her intensity, Tara-her genuine heart, Anthony-his gift of conversation, and of course: Aruba Joe-his joy in giving. And Debi and Panos, true survivors and victors of life's challenges; their generosity-for without it, the family vacation to Aruba would not have occurred.

ARUBAN VACATION WITH ARUBA JOE

Story as told by Aruba Joe at the Cafe to Jan and Rob

This story is dedicated to those people who are either young or young of heart. For those that travel to learn and share experiences with friends, family members, or people they have never met. People wishing to interact with others in the pursuit of dreams, visions, or a much-needed vacation-where caution is sometimes thrown into the wind and a rejuvenation of ones' spirit emerges. This story is also for those that dream of sharing an experience without any regrets and embrace the memories into eternity.

Here's to the extension of family and their collective uniqueness– contributions in part to create the whole experience of 'vacation': Crystal-her intensity, Jade–her genuine heart, Vincent–his gift of conversation, and of course; Aruba Joe–his joy in giving. And Debi and Panos, true survivors and victors of life's challenges; their generosity–for without it, the family vacation to Aruba would not have occurred.

CHAPTER 1 – JOE

While sitting on that horrible hard, plastic chair I had time to think about our trip. The situations that emerged. The days flipped through my mind as one would hold a paperback book in one hand while using the thumb of the other hand to fan through the open pages. I looked out the huge plate glass windows of the airport in Charlotte feeling a chill from my lower limbs to my arms; the air conditioning was not the cause. The sky was just as dark as my mood. I should have been somewhere else; not here.

Was it my fault our trip had not been the fantasy vacation of a lifetime? From the inception of the travel plans my intentions had been easy enough. I would take Alex and her three children to the arid, tropical island of Aruba, show them around a bit to explore the vast nakedness of the bulk of the island, and have some romantic evenings watching the sunset. I had planned on winning the hearts of all four of them. I am, after all, a romantic. Simple right? Not so fast. I rewound that vacation plan in my head and infiltrated parts of it with the actual events during those ten days with Alex. Kind of like that old saying–'the best laid plans of mice and men often go awry.' I can assure you I am the man that made the plans and as for the vacation experience-well, you will determine the rest for yourself.

I had gone to Aruba so many times before-primarily with family. For the life of me, I honestly could not recall having any problems while vacationing in the past. There was one time; my sister got violently ill after eating at one of the restaurants. The doctor claimed it was caused from eating fly shit in her food. My sister is a girly-girl if you can relate. A Gucci kind of person if you know what I mean. But, she also has a keen sense of humor-I like to tease her now and then and often tell her to go eat shit. It's kind of a family joke now. There was one time when I did miss a plane. It really wasn't my fault. The cab had picked us up late from my family's time share. In Aruba; the residents live by island time. They don't live at the pace the typical American does. Actually, they may have a lifestyle similar to people of the southern part of the US-only slower. I haven't traveled all over the world yet but, I have accumulated quite a few frequent flyer miles which, provide many benefits to me. I am, what you may call, a seasoned traveler and thoroughly enjoy my miles.

I only wished the airline was to blame for my late departure earlier today instead of the rental car company's idiot-of-an-employee. Then, I would have gotten a free trip out of this miserable ordeal. I lose track of time; so I'm told. I don't necessarily agree with what I am told. I have been known to support my behaviors with well thought out justifications. It's a skillset actually. I can justify any situation to suit me. I remember someone once said I

2

was 'arrogant'. And I know that is simply an untruth-ask my mother or any of my sisters for that matter. They will set the record straight.

I had some time to think–hours to think about everything. An inner transition of thought began taking place as I waited for my home flight. I kept looking at the flight schedule board waiting for the times and flights to change. I began to brood and became immersed in a self-attack mode. I was second guessing myself. At least I could play a bit of solitaire on my cell phone while I waited for my flight; something to occupy my time for the next hour and a half. I found it difficult to focus on the game. My mind kept drifting back to my situation with Alex. My battery was running low anyway. I shoved the phone back into the pocket of my shorts. That's when I found them–the keys!

Good grief! I slapped my forehead with my open palm at the sudden realization of my stupidity. I was sure I had slipped the keys into her purse that morning. Surely, Alex had to know about the missing keys by now. I envisioned her ripping through every bag and compartment looking for the keys. She was an organized woman; I cannot claim that trait for myself. Now, I wasn't sure what was going to happen when I met up with her. Hell, I was even more worried about what was going to happen far beyond tonight-my life and future were hanging in the balance-my expectations for the past six months were dashed to bits.

I had been unlucky at love my entire life. I started dating far later than anyone in my family. I was considered a 'late bloomer' in high school. Everyone in the entire dorm in college had dates planned months in advance for all of the social formals. Sports and studying were my primary objectives. I was also way too scared of girls and women. I had been raised around a lot of estrogen driven females in my family–a lot of constant gibbering and drama–and didn't get much of a chance to talk while growing up. I tried. Those women were louder and talked faster than I could. Perhaps, that may be the reason I am not much of a conversationalist today.

After college I thought long and hard about getting married. I started dating–a whole lot. I lived with a woman for a couple of years; she eventually left. Out of familiarity we still dated on and off for a couple more years. My second long-term relationship resulted in a long-distance relationship. Her primary residence was on one side of the country and mine on the other. The second relationship was with a woman that became a workaholic, dedicated to the latest anti-depressant, and had the most severe, violent mood swings. I truly think she had some sort of inner pain that was never diagnosed like fibromyalgia or something. In our own ways we constantly strived to make it work. Sometimes, I think I may have brought the worst out in that woman. Nonetheless, I felt doomed to live out the duration of my life labeled as the world's number one hopeless romantic.

I was a seasoned, mature male now. I may have been unlucky in my youth but, I felt compelled to find my love—with *the* woman that would love and want me as much as I wanted her. Alex was less than a couple of hours from me in another airport. They had to be tired. I know I surely was. It was getting late. Alex had a nine o'clock business meeting in the morning. Another thought struck my brain like a bolt of lightning-she hadn't prepared for it. She had mentioned it the other morning over breakfast. Even though the trip to Aruba is usually laid back there is always time to get a little work done. I guess Alex just didn't know how to embrace the vacation/relaxation thing and went somewhat overboard on the vacationing and relaxing. Anyone, including a hard-working woman like her, could be challenged by the Aruban fun and sun.

Man, I wanted to get to her as quickly as I could and at the same time, I also dreaded seeing her beautiful, disappointed face. What was that saying she had? Oh yeah-how could I forget: 'if it starts out gooly, gooly never gets better.' In the early planning stages of our vacation Alex told me she didn't want to return home on Sunday. She had emphasized, rather strongly I might add, how important it was to return on Saturday and have a day to get organized before her work week. Naturally, I pressed the issue and scheduled the return flight for late Sunday afternoon. I wanted her to take in as much time in my beloved paradise as possible, to be intoxicated by the salty air she breathed in each morning, and to soak

5

in the Caribbean sunrays as they tanned her slender body. I wanted her to feel the same way about Aruba as I did.

Images floated through my brain, images of those months prior. I had begun counting the days for our July departure as early as January. We would spend languorous afternoons sizzling in the sun around the pool; rum drinks in hand, my free hand massaging her soft skin with SPF 50 suntan lotion. The sun there is intense. Alex's skin would have fried like Hahn's country bacon if I didn't make sure she was lathered in lotion. Perhaps another man would not have given this the slightest of thought. Experience prevails; reddened and swollen sensitive body parts can ruin Caribbean vacation nights-if you know what I mean. Plus, I prefer watching the serene, pink hues of the Aruban sunset sipping red wine and munching on my favorite Irish white cheddar cheese and fresh fruit with a sun tan-not a sun burn.

The vacation had turned out to be an adventure teetering on the brink of bizarre; a series of events. It seemed I just couldn't do anything right for very long while we were in Aruba—at least not with Alex—not this time. Good golly; was I a total failure?

The grand finale of the vacation was my present situation; the debacle that would surely eliminate any chance of my future with Alex. She was probably wondering how someone so handsome and intelligent could do so many downright stupid things. I was feeling down—even lower than that first night I spent away from home after my graduation from college. Missing the flight home earlier today was unforgivable after all that occurred. That S.O.B. at the rental car company had gotten me so hot under the collar. He was the reason I was late to the airport. He charged me an additional six hundred dollars when I checked out. I had never had any rental car company do something that absurd to me. I used that same company for years. I stood my ground and argued my point with him. Notably, there are times when I will defend my position until I am virtually breathless–no matter the cost. I was right and he was so wrong! Sometimes, Arubans can be so stubborn.

My head hurt from thinking. My chest hurt from the tension of the last couple of hours. *And*, my butt hurt from the stupid hard plastic airport chair I was sitting on. A deep, heavy sigh voluntarily escaped as I closed my eyes. The aroma of the pine-scented cleaning chemicals used by the airports late night crew filtered through my nostrils. One of the crew brushed his cart carelessly against the edge of my chair thrusting me out of my deep thoughts. I longed for the smell of Alex's Estee Lauder perfume. I imagined her sitting next to me with her head resting on my shoulder enjoying the intense blue lights on the runway.

I would have to admit to Alex that I plain screwed up. Begging for forgiveness after the fact was my motto. I would have to rely on my justification skills to get her to see how much we still shared in common–perhaps a little humor could help. It was time to seize my thoughts to plan what I would say to her when we met later. I would remind her about how we were brought together yet again by fate. I would remind her of the many years we had known one another–the times our lives had crossed–we were destined to be together. I could make her understand. I would play the card of emotion and let the hand of fate win. This was my chance–maybe even *our* last chance–to be together as I knew we were intended.

As I relaxed my strategic thoughts for a few moments I smiled as I recalled the night we sat on the pier bar sipping tequila–alone–and just talking. Conversation flowed freely as we spent the evening catching up from the many years we had been apart. The sky had darkened as the sunset lit the western sky in a muted yellow with pale pink altocumulus clouds forming in the afterglow-a backdrop of pure nature and beauty. I would have not known the difference between clouds if it hadn't been for my college biology class-that intense studying in college had paid off. The memory of a fleeting look from Alex's gorgeous blue eyes and dynamic smile against the Caribbean evening sunset was killer.

I looked down at my RE/MAX travel bag laying by my feet; its stark contrast to the blue carpeted floor. The bags primary colors red, white, and blue were the trademark of the company. For a moment I thought about my career; the career I so deeply loved and the one that had first brought Alex and me together many years before. I removed the tan suede Australian-made hat off my head and slowly turned it over in my hands. The outback hat had been a gift from my brother-in-law from his trip to the land down under. I remembered the morning of our departure-when I first put the treasured hat on. Aruba Joe was the name Alex's daughter, Jade, had dubbed me in the morning of our departure. "Aruba Joe," I softly spoke out loud to myself. What the hell–no one was around to hear.

Soon, I would be left with nothing less than what I had prior to our reuniting-memories. In a few hours, I would return to my life before Alex-more lonely nights. I sat overlooking the tarmac of one of the busiest airports in the world. At least I had managed a later flight on the same day instead of tomorrow. The blue lights rotated on their posts along the runways. I would not have any brilliant blue colored lights flashing along the perimeter of my life's pathway. Blue simply painted the color of my mood. My pathway shade was more like a steel blue dimly lit street with an unknown destination.

I wanted Alex so badly. I wanted her to be right beside me in retirement. When we were thirty years younger, I had literally envisioned us that far into the future. My stupidity and awkwardness allowed her to slip through my fingers repeatedly. Therein lies the summation of the adage, repeating the same thing over and over and its equivalence to insanity. Yes, I was feeling a bit mentally challenged to say the least. Good God: it is amazing how all of this stuff just keeps coming into my head. It's like a free flowing, endless river; bouncing around, splashing against all objects in its path while disbursed particles reunite as they travel quickly downstream in a violent turmoil.

CHAPTER 2 – ALEX

I should have known from the very first mishap on the morning of our trip-when Joe took that first-class seat–grinning from ear to ear and waving his ticket at me. His smile had been as broad as the Cheshire cat in Alice in Wonderland; from one side of his handsome face to the other. I could not believe he chose to sit in first class rather than sit with me. It was my birthday vacation for God's sake. He kept emphasizing how this trip was all about me. He has no clue what I am all about after all these years. To me, a birthday is just a number. To him-it should be a national holiday. Aruba Joe–the romantic-my foot!

Joe could sit in Charlotte for all she cared. He could stay alone for-ev-er. Alex hoped the air conditioning was making him as cold as she was. Alex hated air conditioning. She could never understand why people in the US had the air conditioning temp set so low. But, not in Aruba she quickly thought. In Aruba the temperatures were set higher. The Arubans embraced the heat and the outdoors. For a moment her mind slipped back to the island. It appeared she was either going to miss her meeting tomorrow morning or appear to look like an ill-equipped fool; all because of Joe's selfishness. She felt pure dread and anguish as she envisioned facing the committee in the morning. Alex went to work even when she had a migraine headache. The meeting had been planned for months and Alex had been instrumental in the preparation of the agenda. She needed to give herself some credit–she knew the material.

How could a family vacation in the Caribbean become so complex and crazy? For decades the island of Aruba had been a destination she held only in her dreams. She had thought the island would be more tropical than arid. The surrounding water hues of greenish blue did not disappoint her. The beach sand was a whitish cream and had been soft under her bare feet as she walked along the ocean–not coarse, dark, or burning hot to her feet like other beaches. There was nothing worse than yearning for that perfect spot to place your beach towel and then hop across it while wincing at the unbearable pain on the bottoms of your feet.

Alex reminisced about the Joe she came to know so long ago–B.C.–before children. During that time, they had confided in one another and talked freely. There were no walls or barriers between them–they were too young to have developed any. There were no social filters–they hadn't yet learned about those. She remembered many afternoons and early evenings in the real estate office; when the two of them were alone and shared so much together. They had been so young. Alex's life had vastly changed since those days. She was no longer young and carefree and certainly not the party girl. She had gone twenty years without a drop of alcohol preparing for a family; then raising her children. Her

12

once waist long brown hair was now shoulder length and layered. She was a mother of three young adult people–all were survivors of their father's death-at age fifty by his own hand.

She didn't know what she had been thinking when she accepted Joe's invitation to go to Aruba. She rarely vacationed; she was too busy raising her children, going to college, or working on her latest career. Her life was both full and financially rewarding. Her eldest child had once commented; 'mom, you seem happiest when you are single.' Why in the world did she even consider another relationship-another chance at love? Those ridiculous thoughts were for younger people–not a fifty-two-year-old woman for God's sake!

Hadn't she learned some valuable lessons throughout her past? Why hadn't she recognized how complicated her life was now? When a situation started out wrong there was just no righting it. Wasn't she quick to point out to others one of her much-spoken quotes: 'goofy doesn't get better–it just stays goofy.' It was through much personal trials and many errors to uncover that one. Her motto was 'rebellious by nature and a non-conformer.' She was silly to think she could add romance to her full life just because Joe made his grand performance once again. He had made it clear from their first off-chance meeting what his intent had been–had always been. That was something she never knew. Strangely, he had not once let on about how he felt about her those many years ago. She was too engrossed in her life to detect any of his subtle indicators. It seemed Joe was more of a listener. She often wondered why he didn't speak much. She did most of the talking. She vaguely remembered he was quite supportive when she told him she was going to live with her boyfriend.

Work, home, and her career had become all that mattered to her now. Admittedly, Joe's re-entry into her life just a few months ago did provide some pleasures. She needed to re-focus on those three things: not a man. Her world–her way-had been far safer psychologically than dabbling in the silliness of the emotion Joe taunted her with. Joe had told her Aruba would be the vacation of a lifetime. Some vacation-ha! Her emotions had swung like a pendulum–to the left, center, and right and back again. Alex had not experienced anything like that since her early days when dating the children's father. She had learned many a lesson of life, love, and hardship with him and as a result she just wanted peace. She and her children were fine before this Aruban vacation. Truth be told: if it weren't for Joe's financial generosity, they would never have been able to go.

Her little family had come a very long way. All of them were happy before. They had managed after their father had passed although some emotions were still quite raw. It had only been a year. She glanced over and looked at her children in the way only a loving mother could. Their bodies were curled up on the hard,

14

plastic covered metal chairs–much like they did when they were mere toddlers in bed. They would have to wait here for Joe on the lower level of the airport–by the baggage claim area–in absolute exhaustion. It had been a long day. Their last day in Aruba turned into a vacationer's nightmare. Some of their luggage had been lost. She dreaded the thought of being tired tomorrow. At least she had thought enough ahead and had cleaned both house and laundry prior to their departure. She sighed at what she would need to do tomorrow afternoon. This would make her first day back to work so difficult; so stressful. But she would just have to call the airline to locate the two lost bags and travel back to the airport in the evening. One could only hope they could locate them that quickly.

Details from earlier that day crept into her mind as she let out a low sigh. Joe had told her she had his keys to the van. He said he had put them in her purse. When they arrived at the airport, she searched her purse four or five times looking for them. Alex began wondering if the keys were in one of the lost luggage bags. She also wondered if he had left them at the house and just *thought* he had put them in her purse. She had discovered something about Joe during the past ten days. One thing was certain; his mind was like the absent-minded professor. He was very bright and knowledgeable and yet he would forget a lot of things. And he was clumsy. Like when they had prepared to go to the beach one day. Alex had prepared a cooler filled with food and drinks for an entire

15

day. Taking control in a rather authoritative manner (much like her father would) Joe had insisted he would get the cooler to the car–he preferred to pack everything himself. When they arrived at the beach and unpacked the car the cooler was not in the Jeep. Joe had to drive back to the house wasting an entire hour and a half of their day. As incidental as this may seem, Alex simply hated having someone else in control of her life for that very reason. She liked doing things on her own. She didn't like someone offering help, then when she declined, they would do something that wasn't wanted or needed. She wanted ease and a good flow; good ju-ju. She thought ahead–thought things through–to avoid minor if not major preventable challenges.

The thought to hire a taxi to drive them home right now suddenly flashed through her mind. She sighed as she dismissed the idea. How many times had she said she was a team player? They began this trip as a team and would finish the trip as a team. She had no other alternative but to wait for Joe. She let out another much longer, deeper sigh of submission–the way she had learned to reduce anxieties and control the debilitating migraines during turbulent times in her younger years with her children's father. Those times of enormous conflict and changes required some noteworthy self-help solutions which, became life-long lessons. She watched the gentle rise and fall of her oldest daughter's chest as she slept beside her. Tendrils of blonde hair partially covered her tanned, beautiful

16

face and fell over her shoulder. Her daughter's face was relaxed and radiated the youthful glow of life.

Alex had to think strong and assessed the extent of the negativity from events of the past ten days. After all; no one had died. From her perspective, they had arrived on the beautiful island with few plans and no expectations. The hot sun, warm trade winds, and mixture of the island smells of salt, ocean air, and hot cement and asphalt greeted them as they walked through the glass doors of the airport. The street in front of the small airport had been a busy flurry of people, taxis lined up along one side of the curb, and luggage of every color and size on the other. Admittedly, they had a lot of laughs in Aruba. She knew she needed to think long and hard about what to do about Joe. She also knew she didn't have a long time to make up her mind about him and the sooner the better. His flight would be arriving in less than ninety minutes.

Wrestling with her inner turmoil, Alex was determined not to let it overwhelm her—not now. She noticed how tanned all of the children's skin had become from the Aruban sun. Her skin was now a deep brown. Her cheekbones still held some heat and were tinged a bit red from the intense tropical sun. She would have to focus on what was best for the good of the traveling group now. She was quite capable of working through issues and problems. Her past had been a series of surviving challenges that most people would not—could not-have endured. Years of financial hardship, the loss of a home, a brutal divorce, and the children's fathers' sudden death the previous year had been overwhelming.   With time, she had successfully conquered each problem-ultimately survived rather than choosing to be victimized by any of them. Each devastating situation, every arduous life changing event, had ultimately led Alex to embrace a life anew. Admittedly, she was tired of making mistakes; life had just begun to change. Alex brushed the few lonely tears from her cheek as they sprung from her eyes.

CHAPTER 3 – ALEX – HER STORY

The most horrific of all those situations was when her children's father left them in December–just three days before Christmas. He had walked out on them when the children were only 2, 4 and 5 years old. Their office bookkeeper had looked up at Alex when she walked into their home office that morning. Her bookkeepers face appeared full of anguish while her furrowed brow deepened as she spoke; the bookkeepers face grew flushed. 'Alex,' she began in a quivering voice, 'I was told to tell you your husband packed his suitcase for good.' Alex stood still searching poor Doty's eyes and mouth as she looked for more. More of an explanation of why Doty could speak to her like this. 'It's true. Your husband said he is not coming back.'

For support, Alex leaned against the wall. Her legs gave way as she slumped downward until her knees met her chin. Her chest became tight as her heart pounded against her ribs; her throat seemed to cave in and she couldn't breathe. A pounding sound in her head became deafening. She had felt so victimized, so betrayed, and very lost. Days turned into nights without conscious thought. The enormity of the impact of that day was still with her; only the somatic effects were much more subtle. More than two decades had lapsed and time had thankfully minimized the pain surrounding his departure. At least three or four weeks if not months vanished from memory of that time. She wasn't certain. An involuntarily shiver grasped her as she remembered those harsh wintry days of that year- a few memories remained vivid. The winter was so cold; the day was January 19, 1994. She remembered carrying Vincent–the girls stumbling by her side–as they trudged across the snow and ice in the front yard toward the family car. It had been parked the previous afternoon along the top of the driveway to avoid the downward sloping of the ice-covered driveway. She still remembered slipping and falling with her beautiful baby boy in her arms. She remembered sitting on the ground and crying in absolute defeat that early evening–both from the ice causing her to fall and their father's sudden, pre-holiday departure. She remembered how she staggered to get her footing on the ice crusted snow and secured each child safely into their car seat of the oversized hunk of metal. It was a heavy, solid vehicle. Walking around to the passenger front door, she slid across the cold, cracked leather seat to sit behind the wheel. She remembered the bone chilling cold temperatures and the way she felt. Most days, the driver's door had jammed, and she was unable to open it. She had to stay normal she would tell herself-her life was anything but normal. Somehow, she managed to get the girls safely to ballet class on time that evening with tear stains streaked down their little faces.

That winter would stay icy adding daily challenges. During those icy weeks, she pulled the large trash cans up the sloping

20

blacktop driveway-a dangerous task-walking one step-at-a-time along the crusted path she had created alongside it. She had barely been able to afford food. Several times, she had visited the local food pantry just to get some canned goods and cereal. The original family car, a jet black-colored Chevrolet with burgundy leather interior, had been sold to reduce the family debt and replaced with a twenty-year-old Mercury at a cost of $700. She pawned off some jewelry to buy the heavy older car. Its exterior color was a muted worn brownish burgundy, matching the interior. The back of the driver's seat was slightly tilted from someone's larger body leaning against it over many years. The roof lining was a greyed muted burgundy color and hung loosely in some areas; dusty particles fell from it when she closed the doors. She didn't have many choices when she lost her husband, the home, and the bit of income he once gave her was more like an allowance. She knew those past travesties may appear to be a shocking discovery to some that did not know her present day. Those circumstances and the enormity of it were barely imaginable now. For years, she could not view the entire situation-only fragments of some days. She had once feared if she had focused on them, she would have died; literally.

In the year of 1994, April had been the harshest spring following a nasty winter. She filed for bankruptcy. The entire house had been practically emptied. Furniture, oriental woolen carpets; the ones she had spent countless hours shopping for on the Atlantic

City Boardwalk with their father were auctioned off. Even the children's toys went to the auction that spring. Her two young girls never played again on the Play School kitchen set used for making delicious faux meals. They wouldn't eat their lunch on their small table and chair set ever again. As the weather broke, Alex had a yard sale to sell other items—mostly, precious baby and toddler clothing. The family dog, a beautiful black Doberman named Bruno, was given to one of the neighbors. Walking through the house from room-to-room she had practically nothing left to represent the eleven years with their father. All that remained were some of their clothes, a few stuffed animals, some books, and family pictures. And, boxes of cloth, sewing supplies and sewing machines, and countless spools of thread.

They followed the separation agreement verbatim. Alex learned quickly she had to or else he would become quite volatile in his behavior. The children's father came over every Wednesday to pick them up. His voice was venomous and filled with hatred as he regularly spewed profanities at her. He had burned the photographs of their romantic Miami wedding for two—her tiny baby bump hadn't even shown then. In a fit of rage one sunny spring evening, their young smiling faces were reduced to smoldering gray ashes in the charcoal grill. She remembered watching him from the rear kitchen window as some tiny pieces of their wedding photos rose and then fell to the ground as the subtle wind carried them in the back yard.

Images of them casually posing for the photographer in a Miami park still burned in her memory. She had worn a white shirt and midi-length cotton skirt, and he wore a white polo shirt and navy twill cotton pants. He always bought the pants with elastic in the waistband. He hated wearing belts. She remembered his shoes, black Adidas Sambas with white strips. He seldom wore anything but those Sambas. He hated shoes, too. Bad memories. Good memories.

One early September morning of that same year of that icy winter, she stood on the county courthouse steps-the final loss of their family possessions–their forever dream home-went to the highest bidder. At a distance from the crowd, she listened as the auctioneer stood on the cement steps bellowing loudly. She heard the familiar street address-her ears keenly tuned to words spoken by the short, portly man with the bald head. He spoke with a bit of a lisp. Then she heard the auctioneer bellow the word 'sold' quite clearly. She froze. There on the sidewalk-her body and mind went numb. The auction was so matter of fact and so-final. In defeat, she hung her head and turned away from the twenty or so people in front of her-she wept only a single tear. On that day, she felt as though she had aged nine years in those nine months leading up to the public auction. Losing her home–the home she thought they would age together in love and joy and ultimately die in–had been so demoralizing yet humbling. In a sense, Alex did die in that house.

She had left her soul there. The previous year of mental and emotional pain and torture from her children's father had created a different woman. Almost a total stranger. She also lost her joy.

From the day the house was sold, she yearned to have her own home again and yet she was afraid to buy one. She lived in shame, fear, and was penniless. One person, a total stranger at the children's day care, had learned of her situation. He mentioned to her she was indigent. Alex didn't even know what that meant. She had to look up the definition. He was such an ass. She couldn't buy another home for the first seven years because of her bankruptcy. She knew what it was like to have, have plenty, and lose everything. She had yearned to be able to paint her walls a sunset yellow-a tequila sunset. She longed to add granite to the counter tops in her kitchen and bathrooms. You couldn't do those things in a rental property.

The time finally presented itself; all four of them moved into a modest house four months after the children's father had met his maker. Almost 14 years from the date she lost their previous home. She was now the second owner of a thirty plus year old house. She made it 'home' as best she could for all of them. A twisted set of circumstances, his sudden and untimely death, had led her to a level of confidence she had not experienced in years.

She always knew his death would happen sooner rather than later. She wasn't certain whether someone else would do the deed

24

or he would succumb to his own deep, depression. He had many enemies. His creative and inventive cruelties toward her escalated over time. She witnessed him doing the same thing to others over subsequent years. He never tired or waned from inflicting his cruelties on others. He seemed to enjoy a euphoric sense of pleasure with his cruelties toward them. In his end, he endured extreme pain and suffering all alone-just him and God-in the moments leading to his death. His heart literally exploded in a massive heart attack by his own hand. Knowing he had lain for days in temperatures above one hundred degrees before his body was discovered was disturbing. Alex felt no comfort or satisfaction about his death. There was no love left for him. No hatred. In those last few seconds of life, she wondered if he begged the Lord for forgiveness or was he just too incapable to see the errors of his past. She never knew him to show any signs of remorse for his cruelties; primarily, to his own family. Perhaps God knew he was incapable of either and called him home to secure a different job for him-a job where he would not hurt anyone ever again.

Another of life's milestones had occurred. No longer was she living in the shadow of a man torn with raging manic depression with the intense desire to control and destroy her or their children. Amazingly he had managed to cover his depression for years-some say he had a split personality. Others would never know or had not been exposed to his emotional instability. She had remembered thinking he was a prince arriving on a valiant white steed–his sole objective was to save and embrace her in his loving arms. He had bought her expensive jewelry–including a gorgeous one-and-a-third carat diamond ring. A marquis cut with three smaller emeralds on either side. He had given her red roses; just because. No one had done that to Alex before him. And then the rage began. She had lived in fear of him for so long she could not remember when prince charming left and the possessed demons from within emerged. What she knew now was certain–she would never live in fear of anyone or anything ever again-or let the romantic persuasive antics of another man lead her to misery and self-destruction.

Her three children had mourned and were emotionally devastated with the death. Like a tigress she had raised them to survive and thrive much as she had learned to do. They would fight the death's residual effects of loss and anger and sorrow and learn the supportive collaborative strengths of one another. They had adapted well–they were not just a family–they were a team. Something they would understand with time. The thoughts of her past exhausted her. She prayed for them–every day. *Her* children would make choices–far better choices than she.

CHAPTER 4 – ALEX – FROM HERE TO?

She was unsure how long she had been in a quasi-sleep. Opening her eyes to the bright lights overhead made her realize how much of her past still occupied her mind. Why at that moment had she reflected on so much stuff? 'Wow, I really did need to get back to practicing meditation,' she thought to herself. Still amazed such deep and old memories welled up and still spewed from the depths of her brain. She would practice and re-route her mind-to sweep the dirt of the past from the present. She wanted those thoughts to go away forever. She didn't like the hurt they instilled within. Her shoulders shivered -she didn't like thinking he still had any control over her.

There was a lot to be thankful for. So much had happened in the past year. She was proud of what she had accomplished. She was proud of being able to give the children what they deserved; mainly, another family home. The home was older and rather plain and yet it provided tranquility and peace in their lives. The yard needed some changes to the landscaping; particularly, close to the house. The scraggly bushes and deep ruts in the yard would be taken care of with time. Most visitors frequently commented on the peaceful feeling of the home or the back yard. Even the children's pets, the black cat and Lhasa Apso dog, behaved differently in the new home. No longer did the cat chase and torture the dog like he had done in the rental house. Perhaps the higher altitude played a role in all of this-they lived atop one of the highest elevations in the county-or maybe it was just, plain Karma. In a couple of months her family grew in a new, cohesive way–a truly remarkable recovery from the sudden death. Perhaps the recovery had been another of God's gifts to them-so blessed in so many ways.

The brightness of the overhead lights in the airport continued to strain her eyes and yet they made this small part of the world so clear; so absolute. Why could she not see the answer she would be forced to make soon with such clarity? Joe was as nice as he was selfish. He was a gentleman, but he also seemed to possess the need to be the center of attention in a strange sort of way. And there was a bit of a concern about him wanting to have control over some things-little things-in a narcissistic kind of way. And, he always had to be right. What was that all about? He was intelligent and handsome as well-she could never discount either one of those two traits. Perhaps the former of his personality traits stemmed from being coddled during his lifetime from within the confines of his immediate family structure. She didn't know that much about his family yet. He had been raised around a lot of females; from what she had learned-a dominant matriarch and sisters that jockeyed with one another to be heard by all that were within earshot. She had heard firsthand; they were loud.

The strain of the lights after the long day caused her to close her eyes again. It was almost comfortable to tilt her head on the back of the hard, plastic seat. She began envisioning the warmth of the trade winds crossing the back patio of Joe's house in Aruba; her body comfortably supported by the beige colored mesh lounge chair alongside the pool. Joe was by her side, holding her hand. The scenery included overlooking the ocean–the other white and cream-colored houses covered with clay tiled roofs, lots of barren land with thorny bushes and cactus. Palm trees around the house swaying in the breeze.

Old cacti and sparse long field grassy clusters grew in a disheveled manner throughout the back yard. Their muted gray-green colors blended well with the reddish-orange dirt. Black and orange colored birds visited periodically and expertly clung to the cacti, sucking their juices through their narrow beaks. The troupials would sing to us as they hung around the back patio–their voices were quite distinct as if calling out to pay attention to them with their presence. She had called them Oriole birds as they are similar in appearance to the well-known bird of Baltimore.

Lime-green feathered wild parrots had flown overhead in small clusters chattering to one another as if to beckon the parrots in the rear of the flock to hasten their pace. They appeared to be in some sort of bird flight race from the side of the house, arcing over the thorny cactus, and disappearing around the farthest side of the neighbor's home. The sights of the vivid and vibrant   beautifully feathered creatures are not just appreciated by ornithologists.

Joe had welcomed the children and Alex into his vacation home. He introduced his long-standing family traditions such as watching the Caribbean sunset poolside and traveling to the island's landmarks. Alex and Joe had sampled glasses of different wines and ate sliced fruit with a variety of imported cheeses. Alex had laughed at Joe when he purchased imported cheeses from the local grocery store. The label read 'cheese from Wisconsin'. Joe had to remind her that everything was imported to the island of Aruba. She noticed something else about him. He was kind of like a paternal teacher; always educating or correcting about anything and everything she said or experienced.

Most nights they sat beside the pool talking in subdued tones in total contentment. The sunset in Aruba is so different from the sunsets back home. The myriad of colors in the sky form muted delicate shades of yellow and the palest of pinks. The water sparkled in the early evening light like little diamonds rising and cresting. At the farthest end of the pool along the edge, five dolphins sculpted of metal made a serene trickling sound as the seemingly endless water filtered through their five rostrums aka beaks. The formation of the five mammals was representative of the vacationing party-different sizes much like their group.   As darkness would fall–usually by seven due to the close proximity of the equator–the pool lights beneath the water surface reflected a gorgeous periwinkle blue. The vacation had provided many such moments. Why couldn't she just capture those moments forever and bottle them much like wine-to savour and pour as needed? There were times when they bonded and had felt so special; so right.

During the very first sunset, she felt as though she had found the right man to spend the rest of her life with. Being with Joe had felt so comfortable; even his house made her feel welcome. The house had been inviting, accommodating, and pleasantly decorated. Her children had settled into the house with ease. One morning as Alex walked down the steps, a rather strange thing happened. While briefly pausing on the landing in admiration of the crystal chandelier overhead she felt a sensation. A soft, emotional surge penetrated her body. A few of the crystals tinkled together although there was virtually no breeze in that area of the house. She listened intently and knew the air conditioning had not been turned on yet. No windows were open. The house seemed to send a soft whisper inside her mind that said; 'you are the mistress here.' She knew the sprawling cement-built house accepted her; even though several strong-minded women had slept in it before her. The sun kissed cement structure was warm with its desire for her-she felt it.

But now, things appeared rather different. Alex was torn between what was then and what was happening-right now. She also could not wait to climb into her queen-sized sleigh bed and get some rest. She needed the comforts of her newly acquired home. After this long journey the pillows and her pink fuzzy blanket would provide a welcoming sanctuary to her travel wearied body. She longed for the opportunity to stretch out her legs and melt into her mattress. She would sort through the barrage of these complicated thoughts another time.

CHAPTER 5 - JOE – HIS STORY

Sometimes, Joe felt truly amazed by the things that happened in life. Life was full of unexpected situations. He knew he had been blessed with both a wonderful family and a very good mother. His mother has been there for him through all the times–good and bad. She knew he was a bit different-an awkward child from the start of life. He constantly spilled his milk at the dinner table and tripped upon the loose shoelaces of his sneakers. His siblings were relentless with their verbal jabs while his Mom made light of his constant mishaps. She would stroke his cheeks with her delicate, manicured fingers and tell him, 'you are wonderful.' She used to call him 'her handsome little man.' She had always been reassuring to him about one thing or another; primarily, he just needed to grow out of his awkwardness. When he was quite young, he began wearing thick, dark framed glasses. We have all witnessed to this before-some kid with Coke bottle lenses. The other kids in the neighborhood used to seize every opportunity to make fun of 'little Joey.' He was known as and often referred as, the 'skinny four-eyed kid' in the neighborhood.

His uncle 'Grumpy' had accused him of peering at life through a pair of rose-colored glasses by. The man never spoke of anything pleasant and complained about his job a lot-although he was paid quite well to complain tirelessly from what Joe understood.

The girls in school would huddle together and giggle if he tried to sit at their lunch table. He had a few 'girl' friends. He knew romance would turn around; it was simply a matter of time. His mom told him; 'you are just a late bloomer.' During his more youthful times he kept active, and his day revolved mainly around sports; his mother made sure he was signed up for every sports activity and encouraged his participation. She provided transportation to make certain he participated. He ended up doing okay- 'above average' he often thought. Running had to be his best sport. In high school his siblings and friends were busy dating while he ran track or kicked a soccer ball around a field. What was missing or rather who was missing from his activities was his father. His father was always working late and couldn't attend the sports activities. Truth be told; his father's absence still bothered him to this day. Dad wrestled so Joey had to wrestle. Dad did the yard work-Joey had to do the yard work.

His first intimate experience with a girl was when he joined one of his sisters and her friends at the family beach house. The beach was always a great place to visit. As a young child, his fondest memories began with summer vacations at the beach. His family owned a vacation home with another family. There were four adults and eight kids. Visits to the beach were always crowded, cluttered, and full of excitement-as one can imagine. There was another benefit–beside the frantic chaos of two families sharing one

34

home-there was always someone to go body surfing with. Body surfing had become a favorite summertime sport. Joe thoroughly enjoyed swimming in the ocean with the boys in the other family. His sisters liked lying on the beach. Although he never understood why they liked going to the beach because, they always complained about the sand getting in the crotch of their swimsuits and they seldom got into the ocean. The parents-well they stayed in the confines of the house during the late afternoons sipping cocktails; leaving the kids unsupervised and alone to enjoy the oceanic view and beach pleasures.

One afternoon, Joe received his sister's phone call. He had absolutely no plans for the weekend. She had invited him—her oldest brother—to the beach to be with her friends; her '*girl*' friends. With one phone call, his typical lonely weekend plans spent studying in his dorm at college would turn into a weekend surrounded by feminine bliss. He longed for some fun. College was hard and full of stress and anxiety. He had become quite the lonely young man.

He drove alone down the familiar highways from college; unlike those many previous family trips to Ocean City, Maryland. His sister and her girlfriends had left earlier in the morning to avoid traffic. With the car windows down-the warm, fresh air circulated around the inside of his Honda Civic. The air conditioner was on the fritz and hadn't worked since last summer. He didn't care. He maneuvered the car through the usual heavy beach traffic in an effort to save a little travel time. It looked like it was going to be a fabulous beach weekend by the view of the high sun in the pale blue sky; barely a cloud to be seen. As usual, the thought of body surfing was foremost on his mind. Unlike the west coast board surfers, he was content to drift in the ocean even though the waves were only about three foot high. They were enough for Joe to body surf.

As he drove over Assawoman Bay Bridge into Ocean City, the smell of the salty air filled his nostrils. He breathed deeply to engulf the humid air into his lungs as he smelled the familiar aroma of the decaying crustacean remains–typical when entering the city. Their carcasses had been cast out the evening before in the restaurant dumpsters along the bay. Even if he were blindfolded and hadn't been to the shore for one hundred years he would have known he had just arrived to the eastern shore. Nothing had changed. Neil Diamond's song, "Cracklin' Rosie", blared from the car speakers as he cranked up the volume. His speakers weakened by prolonged use at high volume cracked a bit too.

Meeting his sister and her friends would prove to be an entirely new experience for him. For the first time since his youth there were no parents; just a bunch of young adults. In minutes, he arrived at his destination. As he parked the car on the hard, sandy driveway along the side of the house he felt home. Grabbing his duffle bag from the back seat he sprung up the creaky wooden steps– missing every other one–and entered the house much like he had always done. Like a good sister she had left the door unlocked. She also left a note on the kitchen countertop. Unlike his own, her beautiful script writing provided explicit details to meet them to the right, back side of the house. In comparison, his handwritten scrawl was more like some form of chicken scratch or ancient hieroglyphics.

The house was quiet and lifeless–a notably different aspect from his previous experiences there. It was decorated with the old, familiar beach furniture–nothing had changed since their parents had bought the place. The bedrooms and living room had matching white wicker furniture–the white paint was a little worn. Overall, the furniture was quite functional. The familiar wall hangings held the same beach scenes. Their mother had purchased them at the local five and dime to give the house a 'beachy feel' as she used to say. Notably, five and dime stores had been replaced with dollar stores these days-a relative term due to inflation. The interior was still in remarkably good condition. He would attribute that to his father's constant nagging and yelling at all the kids those so many years about taking care of things. Dropping his duffle bag, next to the sofa bed he quickly changed into swim trunks and grabbed a towel and sunscreen. Just as before, he took two steps at a time back down the weathered, gray wooden steps. It kind of made him feel free-youthful again-taking those steps that way.

Unlike some people, he really *liked* his family. He headed across the dunes to join the group of ladies. He stopped at the edge of the dune and peered up and down the beach looking for some familiar faces. He had never been good at distinguishing his right from his left–a mental flaw. He didn't know if her directions meant when he was standing at the back of the house looking toward the ocean or standing from the beach looking toward the house. He finally located his sister before she noticed him. And that was all that mattered. Walking toward them, the sand had already become heated by the intense midday sun. The bottoms of his feet were tender, and his skin was pasty white. He immediately felt the burn from the sand on the arches of his feet and leapt across the sand taking three-to-four-foot strides at a time. He hopped in pain; alternating one foot forward to reduce his plantar exposure to the intense heat. To the beach observer he looked more like the dude in one of those karate movies with his hands and legs extended in those weird poses.

Finally arriving at his destination, he recognized every one of the scantily clad young ladies lying in a cluster; except one. Considering himself a nice guy but, like any other young, virile man he couldn't help noticing the amount of exposed skin. Their bodies might just have been totally naked. The bikinis they wore were just threads covering their nipples and pubis area. His focused landed on the petite built blonde haired girl lying farthest away. The one he did not know. She wasn't the prettiest girl he had laid eyes on but, she wore quite the flirtatious string bikini. She had a good tan, too. Ms. Flirt turned toward him; her body supported on her right elbow. Or was it was her left? Her round tan breasts practically popped out of its yellow fabric like two grapefruits. His sister looked up at him just at that time and said, "Hello, Joey!"- disrupting his thoughts–a good thing because his mind was going in the wrong direction. The other girls turned and greeted him with huge smiles. Waving in response he spoke an excited 'hello, girls' in a cracked voice. They had been sunning for a couple of hours and their skin was a bit red from the intense sun.

He perused the area for a fleeting moment; looking for a place to lay the beach towel down on the sand. Suddenly, he didn't seem to mind the heat of the sand. He figured he would get to know the flirt a little better. Being careful not to fling sand on his sister or her friends, he walked around the maze of mostly naked girls and positioned himself next to the flirt. The flirt immediately sprung up from her position and watched him with a look of curiosity. Removing his shirt and dark-rimmed glasses he squinted from the bright sunlight-carefully tucking them under the shirt. He lathered his arms with white suntan lotion. He was not going to get burned and suffer later like these girls certainly would–he was smarter than that.

Completely outnumbered by the opposite sex he figured his position as the only male in the group provided a rather unique opportunity. He eagerly accepted when the flirt offered to lather his back. Her small hands and fingers busily stroked his skin. Her touch was like butterfly wings-so light it gave him goose bumps on his arms and legs. She slowly massaged his back in circular, penetrating patterns with her fingers and used the palms of her hands across his dry skin. He could feel the difference as the lotion penetrated his shoulders and lower back. The flirt proved to be a good choice and worthy of his selective process.

His sister had quickly turned her attention back to her friends; she was busy talking as usual. He listened to the girls chatter about their high school graduation and the after-prom parties. By Jesus! Those girls could talk, and it wasn't long before the conversation switched to comments of other sun worshippers lying nearby. Then, they started talking about something else. He decided to tune them out; there was no keeping up with their perpetual change of topics. Their babble bounced around much like the beach ball between the little kids playing next to us-back and forth and up and down. Jeez!

In the past there had been an awkwardness when meeting or being around females. He was not confident enough to walk up to a strange girl and start a conversation. There was something different that day from those days of his past. He felt somewhat

40

macho–all grown up-sitting on that beach with all those ladies-for all other males to envy. Stretching his long legs outward with his arms supporting him from behind, he took in the various sights. A massive display of body shapes of every shade of tanned human flesh dotted the cream-colored, sandy beach. Most of the bodies faced the ocean; some of them faced the sun. He compared the maze of bodies on the beach to his companions. Undoubtedly, his sister had some very nice-looking friends. He also realized he was surrounded by bosoms. There was a vast assortment of bosoms; bouncing as they walked or turned over, hanging as they sat, or flattened when they laid on their backs. The bosoms were small, large, round, and some were long and hung rather low like elongated water balloons. Boobies!

Amazingly, he quickly relinquished his earlier thoughts about body surfing and decided to strike up a conversation with the flirt. It wasn't long before he recognized the flirt didn't really have a lot of topics in common with him. Nonetheless, he enjoyed listening to the flirt's stories. Perhaps, it was the silkiness of her voice when she spoke with a slight increase in pitch as she shared her interests and family. Naturally, he had acquired keen listening skills from growing up with the women in his family. The flirt talked a lot about money and her extravagant shopping trips to the mall–she came from a well-to-do family-somewhere along the Newtown Creek in Pennsylvania. He hated shopping. He further learned her mother was a plastic surgeon and her father was a trial attorney. They could afford to let her shop all the time and probably enjoyed the peace in the house when she left. Or maybe, her parents were never home, and she got bored-a disadvantage of growing up without any siblings. It almost sounded like shopping was a passion, her lover. His responses to her feminine babble were relatively simplistic. All he had to do was nod every once in a while, or say 'aaahhh' or let out a laugh from time-to-time. It didn't appear she even noticed the dialogue was one sided or that he did not speak more than a word or two the entire afternoon. Women. Simply said. But oh; he adored the human species with those boobies.

Lying back on the beach towel his eyes eventually closed and his mind drifted away from the flirt's chatter. She did not appear to notice. The intense sun rays penetrated his pale skin. His body had warmed from head to toe. His curly, dark hair was hot. The methodical sounds of the waves hitting the surf delighted his inner ears. Hearing the crash of the waves was much like listening to the low deep tones from the Baltimore Symphony Orchestra's huge drum; feeeeewwww....weecsh.... He could take in all the beach sounds as the familiar whistling from the beaks of the sea gulls floated overhead. The birds encircled the beach waiting for a handout; an occasional French fry or cracker from one of the neighboring sun worshippers made a great treat. Their wings spread wide as their bodies were suspended in the air riding the warm ocean breeze; their heads spun frantically from a long neck from side-to-side in search of the next morsel. The gulls soon fell silent from either being tired or the food resources ran out. The girls around him fell silent as well.

Suddenly his eyes opened, and he realized he dozed off longer than he had intended. Time slipped by quickly as the beach sounds lulled you into a slumber. The sun had reached its high point of the day and beyond. His experience told him it was well after three o'clock. The flirt was quiet and lying on her back-her breasts flattened against her rib cage. I wondered if she realized I had stopped listening to her shopping expedition tales or maybe the suns intensity had dried up her tongue. I was feeling a bit thirsty. I was also getting hungry. In my haste to get to the beach, I had not stopped for food earlier and was rather famished. Breaking the silence around us I asked, "are any of you ladies ready to go eat this evening?" Once the others overheard me speak there was instant chatter from the other girls, and they chimed in with their ideas. One of the girls suggested pizza while another mentioned fried chicken. My sister wanted to have dinner at the downtown boardwalk. One of the local all-you-can-eat restaurants boasted a range of foods to please all our palets and we unanimously agreed upon that destination.

For the first time, I noticed the beach house had never been remodeled or updated like some of the neighboring houses. There

43

was only one bathroom in the house. It had always suited our needs and sure did get a lot of use. Since it was getting late, my sister suggested taking showers together to cut back on time. There were seven of us. I did some quick mental math. We could have four different shower times: three for two girls at a time and one for me. Luckily, I was the first to shower. With a group that size, the shower water temperature always got cold after the first couple of showers. I liked a hot shower—even in the summer. The girls would get over taking a cold one. I was the first dressed and waited somewhat impatiently in the living room on the sofa; observing the flurry of girls while they hustled about. The puffy sofa's hidden bed would serve as my sleeping accommodations for the evenings.

Every room in the house quickly became a chaotic mess. The ladies rummaged through their suitcases and tried on multiple outfits—darting from bedroom to hallway mirror and back to bedroom-until each of them settled into an outfit for the evening. They chattered and complimented each other about their choice of clothes, jewelry, and shoes. Hairdryers, makeup, and towels were scattered on every surface, including the floors. The flirt was ready before the rest of the ladies. She sat down across from me in one of the equally puffy, over-stuffed chairs. Her long, blonde hair cascaded over her bare, thin shoulders showing off her newly acquired tan. I wondered if her pink tinged skin was painful—she made no comment one way or the other. I was glad I took great care

44

to avoid a sunburn and took above adequate measures to make sure I didn't get burned earlier.

"I'm glad you could come visit with us Joey," the flirt said as her hand twirled her blonde tresses in her fingers.

She crossed her legs; her short skirt hiked a bit higher up her thighs. In an effort not to look at her lower extremities, I deliberately forced myself to look at her face and locked my eyes with hers. A faint smile crossed her pink, glossy lips–she was quite aware of my discomfort. In her presence, all alone, I also felt a bit intrigued by the girl.

"I wouldn't have missed it. I love coming to our beach house." I wanted to sound confident and hoped I did. After all, I mused, what was there to be so uncomfortable about anyway? We certainly had more clothes on than we did lying on the beach earlier.

While everyone else finished dressing the flirt and I began talking about the evening and vacations from our pasts. I had become more relaxed by the time we were ready to go out. We decided to take two separate cars to the crowded inlet parking area. I offered to drive my Honda-the flirt jumped into the passenger front seat of my car calling 'shot gun' as she did so. Two other girls got into the back seat from either side of the car. I don't think anyone noticed the obvious advances from the flirt toward me during the ride to the inlet. She even put her hand on my hand as I shifted gears–applying pressure when I shifted to a higher gear.

The decision to eat at the buffet style restaurant turned out be a good idea. The food was cheap and suited our slim budgets. As we left, the line of newly arriving diners spanned a block or so-quite the popular place to dine I mused. All of us strolled along the 'boards'. If you have not experienced a boardwalk stroll in Ocean City, Maryland before it is rather memorable. The flourish of boardwalk activity provides a rare opportunity to observe raw humanity. Some people shed their inhibitions at the ocean along with plain common sense. Guys wore neon colored mesh tank tops sporting their muscular biceps–others had bellies larger than a pregnant woman in the last part of her trimester. Women wore low cut tops and shorts that barely covered their lady parts and derrière. Some of them bore way too much flesh consisting of rippling flesh in cascading layers with dimples and stretch marks. We sat for an hour on the benches looking, pointing, and talking before taking a last stroll of the inlet and returning to our cars.

The beach had zapped our energy. We were all very tired. When everyone had turned in for the night, I stretched out spread eagle style on the sofa bed. Normally, I would go out for an evening run while on campus but, I was content to just lay there as the cooler evening air drifted in from the kitchen window. Just as I was dozing off to sleep, I heard the soft sound of footsteps on the worn carpet. I had removed my glasses prior to getting into bed. Being somewhat blind without them, I could barely make out the face of the silhouette; the small body standing at the side of the sofa bed. Silently, the flirt slipped under the thin, cotton blanket with me. Her foot gently crossed over mine and slid up my shin as if to wake me. "Lay still," she whispered.

Her hand slid across my chest and then traveled south to my belly. She hesitated briefly accepting my silence as the unspoken approval she needed to proceed. My heart quickened as I started breathing heavier. I felt an unusual fluttering inside my gut. Even though I had no clue of what to do my body certainly did as she guided me through a couple hours of lovemaking. In the darkness of that warm, summer evening I realized something; I was no longer a virgin. The skinny, four-eyed kid grew up in the darkness. The flirt leaned over on one elbow and kissed me gently on my swollen lips. Just as quietly as she had arrived, she eased herself off the sofa bed. She retreated across the floor to her bedroom–the sound of footsteps barely audible. My ears strained in the darkness as I listened; I heard a door softly closing. The quiet and stillness of the night returned.

Every muscle in my body was relaxed. 'So, this is what it feels like to have sex,' I thought. Pulling the blanket toward my chin the smell of our lovemaking filled my nostrils. I liked it and I couldn't help but smile to myself. I stared for a moment at the ceiling. The low sound of the ticking of the kitchen wall clock was the only noise in the house. I turned on my side and drifted into a sleep–the best night of sleep I could remember in a very long time.

Even though I had lots of good times with my family at the beach, that weekend with my sister and her friends proved to be the most memorable. The flirt and I parted ways promising to stay in touch with one another–we never did. I could not imagine going shopping every week with her. From the time we conversed, I knew we really didn't have much in common, although we found substantial commonality in the darkness that first night. Neither one of us let on to the others about what we had done. Over the weekend we managed to exchange a secretive sparkled glance a few times toward one another.

CHAPTER 6 – SCHOOLS OUT

In the fall, I returned to college and roomed in a new dorm with a bunch of other sophomores. My dorm was a huge building and housed about fifty students. A local family had granted their spacious home to the college. The façade was a deep reddish-brown colored brick and brownstone with a gray slate roof. The interior boasted high ceilings and tall windows allowing more than sufficient natural light to fill each room. It was rather like most of the surrounding buildings on campus; also granted to the college by other affluent families.

The food in the dining hall was sufficient and plentiful. Initially, I was a bit homesick for a home-cooked meal as were most of the other students. The cooks couldn't hold a candle to my mother's home cooking. I wouldn't say her cooking remotely resembled gourmet dining but, they were always filling with ample leftovers for late evening snacking. I missed that while I was in college. The leftovers-there weren't any. One thing was certain; I had lots of company. There was always someone to study or hang out with or take a run around the track. And there were always plenty of distractions. Life in the dorm was far noisier than living at home but, I soon became accustomed to it. No matter how hard I tried to keep things neat there was always laundry and clothing strewn about the dorm. Now, if you asked my father, he would say

I am a total slob. By his high standards that statement would be correct. Admittedly, even I got confused and did not know which clothes were clean or dirty. I'd have to pick them up and smell them to know the difference. I know that sounds weird but, it is the truth.

College was harder and more time consuming than any schoolwork I had done in high school. I studied and read book chapters through the evening until my head hurt. There were times when the first hint of daylight met my tired, swollen eyeballs while seated at a wooden desk. During the day, I ran track to keep in shape and clear my head from the weight of the previous night's tension and anxiety. I worked my tail off writing papers for those professors and can still say to this day-I don't like typing. I was a pecker and a poker on the keyboard and still possess that same awkward talent. I received passing grades by the grace of God because I never did learn how to spell. I wasn't necessarily a good student in high school but, I was determined to graduate with a B average in college.

After four long grueling years of college, I packed my bags and began the three-hour long bus trek back home. I succeeded in earning both my sheepskin and that B average-much to my family's amazement. I excitedly returned to my parent's home to relish in the festivities of a well-planned large graduation party. My mom put together one helluva party for me. She was great at bringing the family together and used practically any reason to do so—not that my graduation wasn't a substantial cause for a celebratory gathering. She was an elegant hostess; regardless, of the reason for the affair.

After college I had planned to spend the summer hanging out with a few friends. I hadn't had much of an opportunity to see them while I was in college. My visits home during that four-year period were limited to holidays or working during the summer months at my grandparent's farm. I discovered my father had a different mindset than mine; he wanted me out of the house. The day after the lavish celebration, my father made it clear I was to evacuate the family domicile as soon as possible. To his way of thinking, a man had to go out on his own and make his way in the world. I voiced my lack of preparedness; that didn't matter to him. I soon left home to rent a small one-bedroom apartment for two hundred dollars a month. The apartment consisted of meager accommodations. It was located on top of a two-car garage behind a single family home; a short drive from my parent's home. A long wooden stairway led up to the apartment from the side of the garage. It included a small bathroom and kitchenette with equally small major appliances; a washer and dryer stacked on top of one another in one of the closets.

My mother made a few household purchases for me: a used floral print over-stuffed chair, walnut coffee table with a few dark cigarette burns on it, and a small black and white television with rabbit ears. Before she left, she ran out to her car and brought in a vase with a dozen red plastic roses in it. She placed it on the walnut

51

table covering the largest burn; we both nodded in agreement at her thoughtful touch. The living room was rather large in comparison to the other rooms. It looked a bit empty with my meager furnishings. My old wooden bedroom furniture: a twin bed, nightstand, and grandfather's old chest of drawers literally filled the bedroom. It wasn't anything elaborate–it was home. I will never forget my mother's words when she left that day; a bit of sadness in her eyes as she smiled at me. 'You know, your father wasn't raised by a kind man. The fruit doesn't fall far from the proverbial tree. Therefore, he never knew how to be kind to you.' She kissed me gently on the cheek and gave me an endearing hug before she left. I love that woman. She had such grace and managed to soften the effect of the most difficult situations.

I knew she did everything she could to make my father happy. The man was a hard worker-much like his father and my great grandfather. I also knew there was a male genetic pre-disposition to have a bit of a nasty streak on his side of the family. I swore I was never going to be like my dad; no matter how many of his generations of men had the crotchety syndrome. That's what my mom called it. I was going to break the streak of that syndrome. I wanted to be more like my mother: kind, supportive, and caring. I was generally a happy person. Everyone loved me–especially, old people. One particular person I refer to is my grandfather–my mother's father. Unpacking my clothes and belongings, I placed a family Christmas portrait on one side of the dresser and another of my mother's father's Irish setter on the opposite side. Duke had been such a good dog. My grandfather bred Setters and Duke had always been my favorite. After spit polishing the glass and rubbing it with the inside of my white t-shirt, I hung my well-deserved degree over my dresser.

People refer to a come-to-Jesus moment and I had never really given the saying much thought before. I kind of felt like I understood it as I sat in the small living room area–alone. Looking around I felt loneliness slip into the room beside me. There were no more loud noises of my fellow dormers. No high-pitched voices from my sisters chatter. Silence filled the air. I became cognizant of the sound of some cows mooing in the distance. Mentally I began tallying some numbers. I had saved almost three thousand dollars from working the past three summers and received another three thousand in gift money from my graduation party. The money would not pay my bills for too long but, at least I had enough to fall back on if I needed it.

The following week I was ready to find a job and began my search. Regardless of the number of applicants for any position I applied for–whether it was two or twenty-two-someone else was always selected. I thought a college degree would make getting a job easy; that is what I was told. Why was I now struggling to get hired? After a couple of weeks, I no longer perused through the classified section of the local newspaper with discriminating eyes. I was determined to work anywhere doing anything. Thoughts of my fathers' words ricocheted through my mind. I could not bear to hear his condemning words. I did not want him to look down on me or tell me I was not a man. I may have been given my father's name and half of my genome was donated by one of his sperm cells but, my heart came from my mother. I put every ounce of blood of that heart into a passion toward honoring my diploma, getting a job, and pleasing my mom. And of course my father deserved some tribute. It all happened because of his hard-earned dollar.

My spirit, so I believe, came from some old farmer of another generation. Perhaps that was why I pursued my degree in biology–particularly, botany. Rather than do absolutely nothing I took on a part-time position with a local landscaper. I learned a lot about trees and flowers and various details about every insect in the county. I knew it was temporary. Just as I felt my employment search was doomed an opportunity appeared. Sort of. A family friend suggested real estate sales. Selling anything, let alone real estate, was the last occupation I would have sought. I had a biology degree for goodness' sake! I had a sheepskin representing a full spectrum of facts imbedded in my head by mastering four years of rote memorization skills. How many times had I heard a degree opened more doors or paid more money? When was I going to live the aftermath of the American dream from a good educational experience and sample the fruits of my labor? Realizing my limited options, I figured I needed to seek another outlet. I was eager to start doing anything. I received my real estate license and went to work for a small, local brokerage. While relaying the good news over dinner one night, my mom was elated–my dad was totally unimpressed. He sat at his end of the table, chewing his food, and never once looked up at me as I spoke.

The introduction into the world of financing and real estate was a tough educational experience all by itself. Mortgage interest rates had risen into double digits. I was ignorant of what challenges that meant to a realtor. Despite the economy, and with so many indicators pointing in the wrong direction, I managed to sell a couple of houses. I finally had earned some money on my own! A couple of months later I purchased a small condo near the real estate office. I got a great deal because some poor dude couldn't pay his mortgage payments any longer and I was able to assume the great rate of five percent! A community pool was located centrally inside the development. By my standards I was living the good life; just beginning to get better. Before long a couple of other young agents moved in with me splitting the expenses. Mortgage interest rates went up another two percent. I didn't sell another house for six months. There was a large jar of peanut butter and grape jelly in the cabinet, a loaf of bread on the counter, and a gallon jug of milk in the refrigerator. Other than the metal ice cube trays, there were only a few tv dinners and pot pies in the freezer.

Using any method of measurement, the three of us didn't set the real estate world on fire with any real estate mega deals. All of us thought we would get into real estate and make lots of money. After all, our managers had told us that–we believed it even though money was tight, and we still managed to get by on the barest of life essentials. And, if we ran short on cash, one of our moms would shell out a hundred bucks to help pay the gas and electric bill. Don't get me wrong; the three of us didn't take advantage of our parents. When we got low on food and the cupboards were bare, one of us would call our respective female parental unit and ask what's for dinner? It was uncanny how our moms seemed to instinctively know when we needed money. That was a godsend; I was determined I would *never* ask my father for help. I was far too proud and a bit afraid at the same time to expose myself to that situation.

CHAPTER 7 – CHA-CHANGE

I was working and living like a dirt-poor man in a condo with my two friends. We shared much in common: we continually talked about making the big bucks and we dreamed of living a more lavish lifestyle. The three of us just wanted to lie by the pool during the day and work real estate at night and on the weekends. That's when my routine changed-when Alexandra came to work in the small real estate company's office as a part-time agent. That is how I formally met her although I think we knew each other when we were younger. We may have been in the same home room class in junior high school. If you would have asked Alexandra; I was barely a friend. Her real friends called her Alex. However, I considered Alex the type of friend I wanted to get to know better and to have more than a platonic relationship.

I was open for an intimate relationship. Alex's physical attributes were not to be overlooked. Alex was attractive. She was tall and slender. Her nose had a few freckles across it with these amazing large, blue eyes. Those eyes drew me toward her from the first moment I saw her. Her smile was rather exceptional. Every time she looked at me, I found myself captivated by her smile; it was engaging. Her smile began slowly until it gradually opened to expose her beautiful white teeth. Her lips were a light pink, full and tender looking, creating a framed picture all to itself on her face. It was a genuine smile–not one of those model type pasted-on fake smiles with clenched teeth at the jawline.

When I was in Alex's presence, it felt like it was just the two of us; even when there were others in the room. The world around me ceased to exist. For the first time in my life, I felt confident–I knew exactly what I wanted–I needed Alex. I didn't care how long it would take to have her; one of my well-hidden talents was my patience for such things. My happiness meter filled up just sitting across from Alex and talking to her while she was on weekend floor duty. All the newer agents were assigned weekend floor duty. The office wasn't one of those high-volume super busy offices in some swanky high-end area; quite the contrary. The office building was a former home in a small town in Baltimore County, Maryland. There may have been a total of twenty agents hanging their 'shingle' on the back wall. Shingle is a term frequently used in the profession for a real estate license. Most of them worked part-time and had regular full-time jobs doing something totally different than real estate sales. The office phones were relatively quiet in the small real estate office-a perfect place to engage in uninterrupted conversation with Alex.

There was another key factor that I viewed as a benefit. The owner of the real estate office was never around. He was more likely to engage his time in the local bar than overseeing his real estate office. It meant Alex and I didn't have a lot of interference by a manager, other agents, or disruptive phone calls. At the time, I was grateful to be in a low producing real estate office. I wasn't concerned about the money at the time. I was driven by my heart. Cupid had shot his arrow into it–bulls' eye! I wanted Alex to feel the same toward me. We talked for hours on those weekends. What am I saying here? *We* didn't talk–Alex talked. Most of the time I just listened to her.

I sat across from Alex in total contentment and fantasized about what we would do on our first date. In my fantasy I would take her to the Inner Harbor in Baltimore. We would walk around the shops on the red brick promenade; hand-in-hand. There would be a display of boats in the harbor consisting of everything from small whalers to speed boats to magnificent yachts hosting a bustling crew aboard. The Constellation floating in full view–the sailors tending to painting and regular maintenance of the once mighty ship. Perhaps I would take her to tour the tall ships when they came in to dock in the summer.

Sitting before Alex I ran my fantasy date over and over in my head. We would drive together– her head resting on my shoulder–*my* hand covering hers. I would take her to an expensive restaurant for steak; perhaps, even lobster! I had learned lobster was one of her favs. I was just too afraid to make the words audible, not unlike any other man in pursuit of an attractive woman. But I was willing to let go of that fear. I was gonna do it; I would ask Alex to go out on a date with me.

My plan seemed so simple. I practiced my savior-faire in the bathroom mirror in the morning. In real estate class, they called it 'role play'-only I practiced solo. Face it; my roommates–my fellow agents-would have laughed me out of the county if I asked them to role play 'how to ask out a woman for a date with me.' I even practiced when I drove my car. 'Would you like to go to the harbor this weekend?' I practiced when I stood in the grocery store aisle for God's sake. One time, I even started asking out the cashier when it came time for me to check out. I was that fixated with my fantasy date. I was in constant flux. I lived in sheer agony from thinking about this and began wondering if I was developing some sort of anxiety disorder. Every time I thought I had it down right– exactly what to say to Alex-I immediately chickened out when I saw her.

That frustration had grown when I pulled into the parking lot one afternoon. I sat in front of Alex with my legs crossed tightly; my fingers entwined over my knee. I did my best to control the swinging of my lower left leg–I think it was my left. That day, my nervousness seemed harder to control as I committed myself to take the plunge. I decided I was going to be straight forward and tell Alex how much I cared for her. Alex didn't seem to notice my nervous behavior. She possessed the uncanny ability to beguile me

60

to a level of comfort while in her presence. Nothing else mattered but, to sit and listen to her beautiful voice.

Yes, Alex was a worthy trophy for any young man, but rather hard to capture. Through our conversations, I discovered Alex was a little bit on the wild side. She liked to party and run with a group of her friends to local bars and nightclubs from Thursday to Sunday nights. One thing in particular; I discovered how much she loved to dance. I would have enjoyed dancing with her. She liked rock music. I thought about what her body looked like as she danced in time with the music. I envisioned her with her friends laughing and talking as the loud music blared from the huge amplifiers on either side of the stage. I found out a lot more about her, too. I learned she liked Estee Lauder perfume. She enjoyed reading–one of my favorite past times. She liked horror, romance, and mysteries; I liked history. She liked buying plants and it sounded like she had somewhat of a jungle growing in her bedroom. Alex had told me her mother was concerned about the plants growing in her room. Her mother told her they would suffocate her in her sleep. Alex said she tried to explain that the plants were a good thing–they gave off oxygen–not depleted it. I don't doubt that oxygen helped reduce her pain and suffering from a wild night out either.

My life was far less exciting. My weekends were rather mundane compared to the discothèques Alex frequented. At best, I was an in-home partier. Good grief! It's not that I was a snob or anything. I grew up in a home with my parents regularly entertaining the entire neighborhood, so I knew how to party. I saw a great deal of drunkenness in my youth and even prepared many a drink for my father and mother–taking an occasional sip in the kitchen before I handed the glass over to them. I rarely ventured out at night. Most nights, I worked late in the real estate office. Afterwards, I retreated to my condo and the company of my two real estate roommates. Now, that was a pair that could beat three of a kind. They did some serious partying of their own. I never had the urge to join them. One night, I pulled up to the front of the condo. Toilet paper streamed from the roadside oak tree limbs. The tree trunk was massive and covered the bare area between the sidewalk and curb. When asked how or why the oak tree was covered in toilet paper, they looked at one another and burst into a raucous laughter. I knew better than to ask anything more. Their pot filled minds couldn't focus on a question. It was apparent what they had been doing together all day. The smell and smoky living room told all.

During the day, Alex had a full-time job as a paralegal in Baltimore. She was living a far more exciting life than I. I remembered stating I was going to make a lot of money selling real estate but, I hadn't quite figured out how I would accomplish my financial goal. Alex just smiled at me. At the time, I wondered if she thought I was full of it when I had been dead serious. I knew several real estate agents making enormous amounts of money. Establishing wealth through real estate sales was an attainable goal although held by few and desired by many. The surrounding counties held the future promise of brand-new subdivisions with new home construction starts just on the brink of development. The 1980's proved to be a really bad time to become a new agent let alone aspire to become one of the wealthy, notable tycoons. Real estate sales were increasingly harder to come by. The lots would have to wait for the shovels and heavy construction equipment. The rapid rise of mortgage interest rates kept activity at a slow pace.

My mother didn't raise a stupid son. After all, I did obtain a bachelor's degree in biology. I wasn't working in the medical field as she and my father had envisioned but, I did have a job. I had spent two years in real estate sales and made about twenty thousand dollars. I was not exactly a high contender for real estate agent of the year.

And then it happened. A rather unique opportunity became available. The opportunity I had been silently wanting was within my grasp and just what I needed to gain my father's approval as a man of substance. I was offered a job to manage a different real estate office in another area. The offer had one negative aspect to it; I would no longer work with Alex. Thinking from the manly sided hemisphere of my brain I found myself eagerly accepting the challenge. At that pivotal point in time, I realized I just might be better suited to manage other agents rather than be one. My new job title was a better fit for my personality. The new job opportunity could also renew my confidence. I would have money coming in each week on a consistent basis–straight salary and no more commission. One other aspect of the position as manager of an office; I would be a more suitable partner for Alex and she would be proud of me. Now, I would ask Alex to go out with me and turn that imaginary fantasy date into a reality.

The time was coming soon. It was only Monday. I wouldn't see Alex until the weekend. I was bursting at the seams to relay my good fortune to her. Each day, I forced myself to focus my efforts on my new job. I felt I would never make it to the weekend. It helped to have a side job as a landscaper and help my old boss out that week. The time was right, and I could not have felt any more confident that Saturday. I didn't want to arrive too early, nor did I want to be too late–the latter of which I did with propensity.

As I walked through the front door of the office Alex looked toward me. She was radiant as the last bit of sunlight peeked through the front window and danced on her hair. I think I fell deeply in love with her just at that instant. It took me most of the day to prepare mentally to get there. And then it happened. Something that I did not even explore. I never gave it any thought. Our conversations never breached the topic.

"I'm glad you came in," Alex said. "I was hoping I would see you. I have something I want to tell you." I was bursting at the seams to talk to her–what I had to say was so daggone important. I began talking first. I just couldn't contain myself. I told her about my new job. Alex got up from her chair, walked around the agent desk, and gave me a big hug. Her silky shirt slid across the front of me. I felt her long brown hair cascading over my arms as I embraced her in return. She pulled her face away from me a little and looked up at me with those huge blue eyes. I could smell the subtle fragrance of her Estee Lauder perfume. Her voice was full of praise as she said, "you deserve a good job. You're smart–not to mention-handsome. You will go places, Joe. I am so very proud of you." She raised her hand and gently tapped my chin with her forefinger.

I wanted to land one right on her glossy lips right then and there. Certainly, there couldn't be a better opportunity-I hesitated. Although her excitement and the words Alex spoke to me were sincere, I detected something was missing as her eyes turned away from mine. Call it intuition on my part. I sensed a strange bit of a disconnection between us in that instant. Out of awkwardness I stepped back from Alex. Her fragrance clung to my sweater and rose to fill my nostrils. God, I was hoping she didn't notice the awkward look on my face in the same way I felt at that point. Alex got busy closing the office. I wondered if she had become nervous, too. It was a few minutes to seven. Just like any other evening, we closed the office for the day–I emptied the trash cans–she turned off all the lights and straightened the agent desk. I held the front door for her as she locked up. I had deliberately parked my Honda next to her Toyota being careful to back in so I could watch her face as I backed out of my parking space and drove away. As usual, there were no other cars in the parking lot. While walking toward our cars Alex began telling me about her news–the news I had interrupted earlier because I was so focused on giving her mine.

"I almost forgot," she began. "We were so busy talking about your new job. My boyfriend and I have been talking about moving in together. We're signing a lease tomorrow. Isn't that just wonderful?"

That was it–somehow, I knew something wasn't quite right. Boyfriend? Had I been so engulfed in my thinking throughout all those talk sessions; so self-centered? Did I miss something in our conversations about some guy she was interested in? I knew she had dated but, I didn't realize she was in an exclusive relationship. My heart completely sank, and my stomach twisted into a huge knot. I felt physically ill. I dropped my car keys and bent over to pick them up–glad I had a diversion from her eyes–I didn't want Alex to see the look of anguish and pain on my face. I felt a physical tightness in my chest much like when I ran ten miles on a cool autumn morning in college. The opportunity to ask her out had

66

instantly become extinct. An atom bomb dropping in the parking lot would not have had the affect her words had on me.

Deep down, I guess I really knew something was up when Alex had hugged me earlier. I had felt it then. Her hug wasn't like other times. She usually hugged with more force; tighter. Upon hearing her words-and it wasn't just the words-but the excitement in her voice. I lost any thread of confidence. Inside of my head I was chastising myself for being too late and too afraid to vocalize my true feelings to Alex. Since the instant I met her, I had been more worried about my fragile manhood being at stake and fearful of her rejection. What young man wouldn't be afraid of rejection from such a beautiful young lady?

I immediately wrestled the thought of congratulating Alex on her decision, but I chose to remain quiet. I simply didn't trust myself to say the right thing or fall apart like a blundering fool. Instead, I just smiled-a forced smile-nonetheless, a smile. There were times, such as then, when a smile is the only response one can give. Alex didn't seem to notice my anguish. I thanked God for that small favor!

Alex continued talking as she seated herself in the Toyota and tucked her short skirt beneath her; I stood opposite her-leaning against my car door as I listened. I probably would have fallen over if that Honda hadn't been there to support me; 'boyfriend' and 'signing a lease tomorrow' were all I heard. Everything else she said seemed to fracture into unintelligible pieces inside a fog in my brain.

CHAPTER 8 – CHANGED

That night would be the last time I would see Alex for a very long time. My energies became focused on the new real estate office. I felt I had no alternative but to succumb to my new role. Decisions were made by each of us; I needed to train myself to concentrate on my career and she would start her future in her apartment with her boyfriend. I hoped and prayed work and time would be in my favor and, ultimately, ease my pain and heartache. A couple of weeks later, I overheard someone mention Alex and her boyfriend-a confirmation of the inevitable. She had been just within reach and I let her slip into the grasp of another man. My opportunity to be with Alex was now obsolete; hearing the words out of the mouth of the town's latest gossip source provided finality to the situation.

Everything around me had changed–not just my new job. My roommates moved out of my condo and in with their girlfriends. I found myself alone-again. Fall had arrived. The brisk winds of late October reinforced the changing of the season. Over the past few weeks, the daily temperature had dropped suddenly. Leaves on the huge oak tree in front of the condo turned a reddish-brown; some had already sporadically fallen on the sidewalks. The toilet paper was now gone, too. A little grey squirrel adopted the tree as its new home.

69

One of the girls in the new office introduced me to her friend. Her girlfriend and I dated for a couple of months. Although the girl was a bit hormonal at times, we shared some commonalities. Basically, I felt she had two attributes of considerable importance although some would beg to differ on their uniqueness; she liked food and wasn't an expensive materialistic type. She was far different in the latter from my weekend encounter with the flirt in Ocean City years ago.

The girl had been someone to go out to dinner with and share quiet evenings in my bachelor pad. Evenings had become rather lonely and uneventful since my roommates had taken up residence elsewhere. She filled the void of silence within the condo walls with her conversation about her friends and family. I listened, as I always did, whenever she spoke. We enjoyed the fireplace warmth together during the brisk fall evenings. The studs were all that remained of the adjacent living room wall. A reminder of a particularly crazy time with my former roomies after one of our home remodeling ideas to have more open space for the next party. Without a verbal discussion between us the girl moved into my condo and into my bed. I also realized one other benefit to dating the girl-she took my mind off of Alex.

I never told anyone about my feelings toward Alex. Even though I made no solicitations directly, someone always managed to let me know what was going on with Alex. It was that type of

70

community. Within the next couple of years, Alex ended up getting married–unfortunately, not to me.   The girl I was with wasn't a lengthy commitment; quite the contrary. My new roommate of only three weeks decided she couldn't handle being in a serious relationship. Initially, I was driven to be with her to while away the time after my roommates' departure. I had primarily chosen her to console my wounded heart–the one cupid should have impaled with an arrow solely meant for Alex.

My roommate told me she wasn't as in love with me as I was with her. I thought about telling her about the actual chain of events in my life which led her to my bedroom. I thought about telling her about Alex–how lonely I had been–and how I would have been with Alex in a heartbeat. But I didn't–I wouldn't. I couldn't bear to see her face–the same face of rejection I once wore.   Those thoughts remained mine and mine alone; never to be shared with anyone. I knew I needed to move on with my life yet another time. I also knew something else-I would never forget Alex. She continued to have that much of an impact on me. My heart held a very special place in it; a reservation only for her.

I focused on making the best of my life and my career. I allowed thoughts of Alex to drift through my mind occasionally–not merely fantasizing, just good memories. I pushed them down and out of my frontal lobe and into the depths of the gray matter of my temporal lobes as quickly as I could. I immediately came to terms

71

with the realities of my short-lived relationship. The more time we spent together, the more I knew we couldn't work out. She was just better at vocalizing it than I was. I blatantly admitted we didn't share enough in common to survive our differences–the need for food and conversation just weren't a strong foundation to sustain a serious relationship.

Informing my family of the termination of my partner was a conversation I did not want to initiate. I held off making the announcement for as long as I could. Eventually, the inevitable time came at the holidays. My family voiced their varied opinions and were disappointed about how quickly the relationship ended. Admittedly, my parents didn't think that much of the girl in the first place; nor, did she of them. No more lying about her being sick every Sunday to attend the family dinner at moms. She felt they were a huge detriment to her independence. She hated the endless chatter about family things–places we visited and people we grew up with– seldom did anyone in my family ask about her. Nor, did she try to bring up any topics. If she did, no one engaged with her. At times, I truly felt sorry for her and was relieved when she decided not to go to family events.

There was no way I could talk to anyone in my family about Alex; especially, after our split so I refrained from sharing my feelings about her to them. I knew how opinionated they were–not that I hold that against them mind you-I just wanted to spare any further comments or questions.   Not one of them knew about any of my personal feelings about anything. I was too proud to divulge them to even my closest sibling.   That was the way things were. Moving out spanned over a month but, when my roommate moved the last of her possessions out of the condo, I was ready for the separation. I grew comfortable and resumed my life alone. I found tranquility. I felt like I had grown up a bit. I felt happy about being alone again. At least the routine of living alone held few surprises– I knew what I was or was not capable of.

Unlike a marriage, there were no separation papers to drag out the process or cause animosity. We were not in any rush to sever all our bonds. We eventually recognized we would never reconcile. We even spent a few nights together–mainly for coitus when my loneliness meter was low. I also realized I was happier with my feelings of loneliness than filling the emptiness of the four walls of my condo with just any woman.

This time, living alone was far different than I had experienced in the past. I once associated living alone with being lonely. I now welcomed the experience as I discovered solitude. I rather liked living alone with my thoughts. And, yes, I liked having my dirty laundry lying on the bedroom floor. The clutter made me feel comfortable somehow. It was quite familiar to me and had been since my youth.

For months, I enjoyed a rather typical bachelor lifestyle. I dated and went out to dinner with some attractive single ladies. Some had children. I even went dancing. I perused each venue; always searching for a familiar face–I never saw her. A couple of times a month, I welcomed meeting my former roommates for a drink at local establishments during happy hour. I had settled into a new routine–a new life. The managing job was going well–a good fit for me–and I became engaged in my managerial role in real estate. One night, I agreed to meet my old roommates for happy hour. I was just about to savor the final sip of my third drink and pay my bill when I realized I must have gotten either the wrong night or the wrong establishment. As I raised the glass to my lips, an unfamiliar face from across the bar caught my attention.

The next thing I knew I awoke in a most unusual place. Now, I knew how Dorothy felt when she realized she was not in Kansas anymore. I opened my eyes and looked at the strange surroundings; frilly white, sheer curtains hung at the windows in a bedroom. I certainly was not at my condo–I had thin, vinyl blinds with a few dented slats. I turned on my other side and looked at the attractive face as she lay sleeping peacefully next to me. She looked so sweet and innocent in the early morning light. Her skin was milky white. Her dark eye lashes rested against her high cheek bones. Her short, cropped dark hair was tousled about her head. I watched as her chest rose and fell–her ample bosom filling her night shirt-her breathing was ever so soft. It was out of character for me to make this type of mistake. I usually did not just jump in bed with a total stranger. I tried to jostle my memory of the previous evening. I remembered very little. Although, I did remember laughing a lot. Particularly, about the stories she told about her recent breakup. Something about the guy being a total airhead. Other than her favorite drink, merlot wine, there wasn't much I could remember. There was too much fogginess of that entire evening.

I lifted the silky, pink satin sheet and peered down below. I was relieved at the sight. I still wore my t-shirt and whitie-tighties. Looking over my shoulder I noticed there were no tell-tale foil wrappers on the bedside stand. I would usually discard my preferred form of birth control by the side of the bed. For the life of me I could not remember a thing after laughing at the bar. Relieved by the thought of my apparent non-performance the evening before I became more relaxed. I had no immediate desires to start a family. I did not want to have children–ever. Living in a somewhat small home with a large family had taken its toll on me. I wanted nothing but peace and quiet for the rest of my life. I had been making sure I was the one taking precautions. I heard too many stories from some of my other male friends. Some of the things I heard from them were akin to horror stories. The women they had slept with or dated had skipped a pill, became pregnant, and then like a ball-and-chain they were shackled to her side with a kid. No sir ree; I did not ever want that to happen to me.

I brushed my scalp with my fingers to untangle the drunken cobwebs from the night before. I couldn't remember driving. I wondered where my car was. Worse yet, I realized I couldn't even remember her name. Was it Joanna? Maybe it was Sandra. Somehow, I was thinking it was two syllables. Once again, my mind raced as I rewound through the foggy images and conversations of the evening before. Slowly, I started to remember a bit more. On her way to the ladies' room, she had introduced herself as she stood between a neighboring chair and myself. She was rather tall and slender–about five foot ten inches–just a wee bit shorter than I. She had ordered her glass of wine from the bartender. Suddenly, the visual fields began to link to the memory portions of my alcohol infused brain cells and I remembered her name. It was Gina.

I remembered teasing her and calling her 'Gina Lollobrigida' after a famous European actress from the 1950's and 1960's. Pretty Gina lay beside me. Her breath softly escaped through her partially opened mouth. Her deep rose-colored lips were curvy; her upper lip more plump than its bottom counterpart. Her breasts were full– but, not too large for her body. She was an attractive package wrapped in satin sheets. We made an attractive couple. As the morning light became stronger through the windows, my mind gradually became clearer. I guess the alcohol had loosened my

76

tongue. Or maybe I was just in need of spilling my guts to someone–anyone other than my family–about the women in my life to Gina. I remembered telling her some of the story about my short-lived marriage and the breakup. In turn, she had just broken up with her boyfriend. Together, we sat at the bar sharing stories of our past-mainly our lost loves. We laughed freely about being single again as we consumed our preferred libations of liquid courage; in rather excessive quantities I might add.

I also remembered Gina had a passion for cars. Red was her color. No matter what car she bought she had said it just had to be red. She also said she liked people to notice her. Red always drew attention. I was sure she was a looker behind the wheel of any vehicle. On the other hand, I did not particularly care about the vehicle I drove. Make, model, or color didn't matter a hill of beans to me. If it could drive forward and backward that was all I needed.

Thankfully, I didn't need to be to work until late that afternoon. A couple more hours of sleep would be far more advantageous for my health than getting out of a nice, warm bed and going to the office. I usually ran about five miles in the morning–the beginning of my morning ritual from my college days. I needed time to sleep off the gin and gingers I had consumed the night before. I couldn't even stand now and walk to the bathroom let alone run anywhere. It didn't matter. I would go back to sleep. The one last thought gently permeated my mind as I drifted off to sleep;

I wished Gina was Alex. As it turned out, we shared our separate beds on and off again for over twenty years. I just stayed with Gina out of familiarity and I built a new home with her input. I eventually heard Alex had married again, too. Knowing that she had married somehow made my second relationship seem copacetic. We were both doing what we should have been doing–pursuing our destiny– our future. Unfortunately, we had not done it together. That was solely my fault, and I would live with that mistake.

Not long after my relationship began something in my head changed. I began to think differently. I became entrenched with the construction process of my new home. I rarely visited my condo. I let go of my bachelor pad and rented it to a young man and his two, large German Shepherds. I became immersed in an entirely new life. My parent's sold the Ocean City home–the destination of fondly remembered family vacations of my youth.

Gina and I began vacationing several times a year-much like the long-standing traditions of my family. We traveled to Europe, Hawaii, Australia, Canada, and the Caribbean. I even found a new vacation spot on a little Caribbean island, Aruba. I worked and lived for our semi-annual vacations. I soon forgot all about Alex. Life eventually changed with Gina. She traveled for business more. As an attorney, her legal contracts in the energy sector led her to the southwest on many occasions. I thrusted my energies on gardening when I wasn't working. Our life became somewhat of a turbulent, ongoing battlefield; each of us vying to be the victorious General. Most of the time I lost. Gina was highly skilled giving me the silent treatment. On rare occasions I ultimately became the victor. Although, I admit that with tongue in cheek because I paid a price soon thereafter. Sometimes, she wouldn't talk to me for an entire week after one of our screaming episodes. I think women in general (no pun intended) are good at the silent game. Gina and I would always make up. Our promise– was always the same-to never fight again.

To justify the need to continue in this maddening relationship after those fights and silent times with Gina, I began mentally sorting through our accomplishments. The two of us were financially stable. Money was not an issue. We made plenty of that. Gina's monthly personal maintenance expenses and expansive wardrobe purchases of Gucci and Prada cost more than any other woman I knew. She could afford it We had all the luxuries and materialistic items we needed and our own homes. I had my golfing and annual membership dues to the club. Not close to the expense of her shopping expeditions. She could afford them too. We were both passionate about our interests; although mine were far less expensive. Together, we had built a relationship of convenience. – Using my architectural skills I learned at college, I built an addition to my home. Gina and I also traveled a good deal; mostly, because of our occupations.

On occasion, I would think about Alex and wondered if she was still married. I wondered if she fought as often with her husband as I did with Gina. And yes; I recognized our arguing had become a bit of a problem. I was actually worried I would one day act out on those deeply secretive desires toward Alex, when I would reach that pivotal level of frustration with Gina.

There was always the pressure from my family. My family periodically expressed their upset over my first relationship which, still stung a little. No one in my family ever divorced. Not that they did not believe in divorce, mind you, they just felt marriage was a series of challenges. Challenges were to be overcome–like a chess or bridge game-and solutions or compromise were the winning result. I knew I did not want to create any more strife in my life or theirs. Marriage was not for me. I surrendered toward finding a way to minimize the negative aspects with Gina and did my best to remain focused on the positive ones. When I became angry, I recited them silently to myself until I cooled off. It took a couple of days most times after our quarrels. I worked really hard at it.

Through an old mutual friend and just after one of those bitter battles with Gina I learned Alex had divorced for the second time. Her marriage had lasted only a few years. I wondered what Alex looked like. I wondered if she still danced. I wondered–did she still wear her Estee perfume? I was grateful I didn't make a fool out of myself by contacting her. I knew many a person seeking out

80

their high school friends–saying they just wanted to reconnect-and ended up ruining their marriage. Dialing ten digits to Alex would have been so easy and it may have brought instant laughter to my ears and a ray of sunshine back into my life–or, made me a fool. For the millionth time, I plunged Alex into the deepest layers of my mind.

I had discovered the pragmatic approaches I used in life were virtually useless when it came to Gina. My mind revolved around concepts of logic and thought. Gina's stemmed from a hormonal imbalance. Her emotions fluctuated immensely; the cycle was repetitive. Her emotions were like watching waves pummeling the sand at the beach; crashing, calming, and then building back up just to crash on the sand again. In public, she showed the grace of a beautiful butterfly in languor between vibrant colored flowers. Gina was beautiful. The adage 'practice makes perfect' surely does not apply to affairs of the heart. I know I tried to make Gina happy. Amazingly, flowers, wine, and romantic dining did not do the trick. I even tried buying her jewelry–expensive jewelry with real diamonds and pearls and opals. She loved rubies. Baubles and other romantic purchases surely salvaged other relationships. Other women appreciated them–apparently, Gina did not.

I realized making myself scarce from Gina's presence was the one thing I could do that minimized the fighting. When the construction of my house was completed, I turned to other challenges around the house. I retreated to the garage or to the yard as often as I possibly could and began practicing my post-college skills at landscaping.   During those horrid spats with her and physical   escapes, I spent hours landscaping and mowing the lawn until I felt it was safe enough to reach out to her. I worked my fingers into the dirt and grew some of the most spectacular gladiolas and rose bushes over the years. I had a vibrant rainbow assortment of colored glads in various strategic areas throughout the front and back yard. My roses–well, they eventually did not meet my expectations and became more like spikey, thorny bushes. I planted raspberry bushes along the back yard fencing.   Within three years I made some of the best tasting jam you ever put on a piece of bread. Over time, the lawn boasted a variety of different deciduous and coniferous trees. I mulched around the trees every spring. I raked the leaves and pine needles each fall.

Other aspects of my life were entirely different than those on the personal front. I was living life far different than what I had known. The real estate market skyrocketed. I was on both salary for the management position and commissions for making home sales. For the first time since I graduated from college, I had money in the bank and cash in my wallet; a phenomenon which thoroughly pleased my father. At last, there was something that made him smile and speak to me about. My father loved talking about all the money he saved and invested. Our common ground revolved around investment strategies.

CHAPTER 9 – SHE DROPPED A BOMB ON ME

As fate would have it, a rather uncanny sequence of events would bring Alex and me together once again. I was working in my office on the realtor annual awards dinner; an annual affair showcasing the accomplishments of the entire county's previous years' performance. The dinner was that very night. Being the last-minute coordinator that I was I frantically scurried around the office making sure all of the details of the event were covered by my staff and assistant. There was no mistaking that smoky, low tone. I looked up from my desk as I heard her voice. Suddenly, she had walked in my office–into my world. Of all the days, of all the realtor offices in the county, she chose to come into my office. I took in every feature. Her brown hair was much shorter than I remembered. She wore very tight tan colored pants and a loose fitting floral printed short-sleeved shirt. The neckline rested just above her bosom. A single strand of pearls hung around her slender neck. Matching pearl earrings with a small diamond studded each ear lobe.

She had gained about twenty pounds since we last parted ways and every ounce of it looked great. The weight went to areas of her body creating voluptuous curves where they were once rather slim and straight. We made eye contact, and I locked right into those familiar blue eyes and couldn't help myself from smiling. She possessed an elegantly casual look. Her air of confidence was still the same as I remembered. Pushing back my black leather office chair, I stood up to greet her. Alex walked over to me and stood less than a foot away. Neither of us made an attempt to physically embrace one another.

My God; it was twenty years since we last stood in that parking lot and those years felt like they had been days. Alex spoke just as casually to me as she had done so many times before. She began chatting. The familiar faint smell of Estee smelled so good. I had smelled Estee perfumes on other women but, on Alex it was a unique fragrance altogether. We spoke for only a few brief minutes. But even though it was quick, our conversation had a memorable impact on me. She still possessed a way of making me laugh and feel good. My heart began beating rapidly. I wondered how Alex could appear so at ease while I was not. I quickly reminded myself about the difference between us-one significant fact-our love affair had been one sided.

When she exited my office, leaving her business cards at my receptionist's desk, I bid Alex farewell. A squeakiness resurrected in my voice. The awkward sound was a dead giveaway of my discomfort to anyone within earshot. Alex did not appear to notice. After all these years she would never know what she would always mean to me. I couldn't even extend my hand before she left. I dared not touch her as I did not trust myself.

My associates knew me all too well. The office front door had barely closed when I was approached by two of the members of my team. My staff lost no time telling me what they had observed.

"Who was that?" my secretary Anna asked. She told me how they all saw the way I acted when Alex came in. I managed to brush them off with a wave of my hand. To say anything to them would have surely equated to an admission of guilt. Besides, I had no time to elaborate on my relationship where Alex was concerned; they would not understand. How could anyone understand my feelings? I quickly retreated to the safe confines of my office. I needed to finalize the plans for the evening. Some minor details required my undivided attention. There were only a couple hours left before the awards ceremony event started and I still needed to pick up my tux from the cleaners.

How could anyone understand the frustrations I had with Gina? With my closest friends, family, and business associates I was unable to hide my problems with Gina. Over the past couple of years, I was mainly hiding my problems from myself. I buried the sordid details of our explosive relationship. There were some things about my personal life I chose to share only with one or two people– I might add. I'm not necessarily known for talking about myself with others–even my siblings. I am a listener. I'm not even sure I like people enough to talk to them.

However, it was hard to keep anything a secret in this town. Especially, when your partner argues and complains outwardly at every function–business or personal. Everyone noticed we were always late arriving for every commitment; they knew. The comments from my peers were usually brief and empathetic. I had overheard their occasional tactful comments–they did not fall on deaf ears. I was even told my mood darkened while I was in the presence of my Gina. I was told I became quiet and dull when she was around. I guess I wasn't very good at hiding my anxieties about Gina from anyone; I just thought I was.

Perusing the agenda for the evening, all kinds of thoughts shot like little lightning bolts in my mind. I kept repeating to myself– 'focus.' The ongoing problems with Gina made Alex's unannounced visit simply a highlight in my day; hell, it was a huge lift to my spirit. It was a dichotomous sword if you will–I was deliriously happy to see her and yet felt fortunate the duration of Alex's visit was so short and we spoke so little. My internal conflict caused me to reach for a bottle of antacids in my desk drawer. The short interlude created a temptation. Our relationship had recently taken a turn far more serious than all of the fights Gina and I had combined. A couple of months before, Gina made an untimely confession to me; as if bad news from her could ever be timely or pleasantly received. What it did explain, however, was the intensity and constant anger she displayed. Damn her; I would not feel guilty.

While we were having dinner at my home one evening, Gina matter-of-factly told me about an encounter she had while on a business trip. She went on to tell me about her trip she took in January to Austin, Texas. She has always loved the food in that town. She reminded me about Tom; the attorney she worked with. Her pitch went a bit higher as she continued. She told me Tom became. ill right after they had dinner with these new clients of one company they had worked together over the previous year. She spoke of the many challenges and hours she spent providing them with updates and quotes. The company she had been working with to open their national franchises. Tom went back to his hotel room leaving Gina alone with the group of the company's business associates.

I had listened intently that night as I watched Gina carefully collect herself. Her demeanor suddenly changed from matter of fact to a little off beat. Gina cleared her throat as she looked down at her plate for a moment, raised her tiny face toward me, and continued speaking. Her cheeks became intensely flushed. Her neck and chest did the same. Her eyes became moist. For a moment, I thought she was going to cry. She shook her head and shoulders as if shivering from a chill and gathered herself once again. Was she in love with Tom?

She finished by justifying her stay in the lounge of the hotel until late; too late. She drank much more merlot than she usually

88

consumed. I knew firsthand what merlot does to her. Gina's voice cracked as her words were almost spoken in a somewhat apologetic tone; then, the bomb. Before long, it was just two of them sitting at the table. The next thing she said she knew; some guy followed her off the elevator and into her room. She literally stopped speaking for a moment as she watched for my reaction. I'm sure she recognized the look of betrayal and pain covering my face. I had felt a huge knot in my chest. I knew Gina could see the fear welling up in my eyes as she spoke. I had been totally unprepared for an admission of infidelity from her. We were monogamous. I hadn't wanted to hear any more and yet I had to know. I never thought my pretty Gina could betray me in this way.

Her face had become defiant. She didn't stop there. She confessed there had been others before him—mostly after we first dated—when her traveling had first begun. I had held my head in my hands just so I didn't have to look at her. I stared at my black Allen Edmonds shoes. Gina had given them to me for Christmas the year before. The conversation then took another bizarre twist. I had looked up at my Gina as the onslaught of words entered my ears but, I'm not sure I heard everything she said. It was as if I was in a distant tunnel—far away from the table-so far away.

I got the gist of the conversation though. Ironically, Gina blamed the affairs on me. She justified her sexual trysts by stating I didn't show her enough attention. She also claimed we had lost our romance. Even more hurtful, Gina confessed she was no longer attracted to me and she had actually said the betrayals were the result of our constant fighting. I remembered hanging onto a couple of words– 'no longer attracted'–I was about as handsome as a man can get! Everyone tells me so. How in the world could she say something so ridiculous to me? That evening was like body surfing in the rough ocean when I was a kid; one wave after another knocked me down. I tumbled in an ocean of disbelief and physical pain. Instead of sand in my shorts I must have had rocks in my head. I just never saw anything coming at me when I was a kid in the surf and clearly did not see anything going truly wrong with the two of us. Okay, we fought–what young couple doesn't?

And I couldn't seem to let go of that other thing; how could someone not be attracted to me? I had done everything to be more attractive for Gina. I even had laser eye surgery to rid my face of those horrible thick, black glasses she hated. I got some moles removed from my back that she complained about. Shoot–I even groomed the long nostril hairs so they didn't hang out. Gina hated hanging nose hairs. I was tall, slender, and was in top physical shape. I ran track in school and still enjoyed the morning oxygen running through my veins. I was popular–not just with the other agents–but old people even loved me. I didn't understand how my Gina could even do, let alone say, such things against me.

From that night forward, Gina's tone became even more hostile toward me. While she was there, we continued to live in the same house–just in opposite sides or levels from each other. She acted as if her admission of infidelity opened a once locked door to her abusive thoughts. Her tongue became the key to unlock them to flood our air space. She fought with me violently before any gatherings–most of the time she flatly refused to attend. She refused to do just about anything with me; came home late every evening after work and was out with friends most weekends. I was willing to forgive her for straying away from me; from even having thoughts of other men. I prayed I would not lose Gina and hoped we could find a way to work everything out. I wanted our life to go back to our normal–the way it used to be. I didn't care if it wasn't perfect. I would do everything I could to keep Gina. On the east or west coast.

During our entire relationship I justified her extreme hormonal fluctuations on bad genetics. Over the years, I noticed her temper quickly flared up and her dark moods lingered for longer periods of time. Most of the time when we were at home, Gina kept herself in her office above the garage–I stayed in the family room if I wasn't outdoors. All of this was fine with me. It had become our normal. I had become complacent.

So you see, when Alex had walked into my office, I was in an emotional transition and was experiencing so many feelings.

91

Gina and I had argued earlier that morning, before work. I was worn out from arguing before I even started my day. When I arrived to the office, I called Gina pleading with her to attend the awards banquet that evening. After a long silence between the two of us, Gina softly said 'okay' and we hung up. I know I may sound like I gave in to her but, I am a man of dedication. When I'm committed to a person I meant it. I wasn't interested in having an affair. I wasn't interested in splitting up either. Granted; accepting Gina's infidelity was something I knew I would have to work on continuously. I was willing to sacrifice my ego for Gina and I accepted the challenge willingly. The inner turmoil I felt was gut wrenching. I wrung my hands constantly and scraped my thumbnail with my forefinger. When I sat watching the television in the evening, I looked at the screen and became utterly consumed by a show or a movie. I needed to. I had to avoid thinking about my disastrous life.

My friends and associates told me to end my affair with Gina. They had noticed the further decline in our public appearances together. When we received invitations to holiday office parties or personal engagements with friends-I attended solo. I continued with the excuses for Gina's absences. I typically blurted out some comment about Gina having a headache or that she was traveling for her job early the next morning. Everyone knew why Gina wasn't with me. It took me a couple of years but, I became painfully aware there were far too many issues to resolve with her. As hard as I tried to talk with Gina, to let her know I wanted to salvage our relationship, my attempts were futile. Gina remained hostile and impermeable.

I arrived early to the awards dinner. Not only would I be the recipient of an award, but I was also the presenter of another award. I kept looking down at my watch as I waited for Gina to appear. That morning, I knew I had worn Gina down-she would be there for me. The cocktail hour ended; everyone seated themselves at their assigned banquet tables. Judging from the full tables in the banquet hall the painstaking details leading up to tonight's event paid off. As I looked up from studying the evening's brochure, I was absolutely taken aback by whom was seating themselves at my table. I hadn't noticed her during the cocktail hour. She wore a sapphire blue sequined sleeveless halter top and tailored black pants and looked stunning. The soft lighting from the crystal chandeliers hanging above reflected on her body; her blue eyes glittered in unison with the sequins. She hadn't mentioned going to the awards dinner earlier that day. While the announcer began introductions and made several event related announcements Alex and I seized the opportunity to catch up with one another. My heart was fully exposed. Twenty years of our lives spilled between us in a mere fifteen minutes. I was the first to begin talking about my personal life and the multiple properties I had acquired. Alex spoke of her three teenage children with undeniable affection. I spoke of my Gina. It was as though my tongue was on some type of automatic pilot; unleashing things about my life that were exactly the opposite of the present truth.

I could not fess up to the admission of my failing love life to Alex. I would rather not speak than lie about anything. I found myself telling Alex about my beautiful Gina. For some inexplicable reason I had to lie to her. Alex expressed her happiness for me and gently patted my knee. I had no idea why I spoke so positively about my situation. Alex radiated such happiness–just like when we were young and single-I didn't want to bring her down with my problems and did not want to worry her. I hid the truth from her like I hid my feelings many years earlier. I noticed there was no telltale gold ring on her left hand. Her hand certainly in plain view now. It didn't matter. The ceremony began and we continued conversing in subdued tones and laughing softly together. We spent another twenty minutes conversing–our eyes locked into one another.

Alex got up from the table to get us a glass of wine from the bar. She did not return. I didn't see her again that evening. Just a few minutes after Alex had left her seat, Gina came and sat on my other side; the only empty chair in the entire ballroom. Gina and I began arguing almost immediately. I never found out, but I wondered if Alex had started to return to the table, saw Gina and me arguing, and decided to leave. Thankfully, I heard my name as I

94

was invited to the podium to make an announcement for the special award. I was relieved for the opportunity to escape Gina's furious wrath. Her hostility from the morning flowed into the evening. As I spoke and addressed the packed room of people, I notice the entire table I just left was empty; except for Gina. I forced myself to finish the introduction of the recipient of the award, managed a smile as we shook hands, and sat down on one of the three seats facing the podium. The audience became a haze before me as I listened to the speakers' voice drone on for another painful hour.

When I returned to the banquet table, Gina was in no better mood than when I had left her. Of all times, Gina decided to drop the bomb on me; just after I had worked so hard for the award ceremony. She was done. We were over. She didn't even make a comment about the event–she had known how hard I had worked at putting it together. Gina knew it was the premier event of the year for the realtors. Historically, it was our one night of celebration.

Alex came smiling into my life earlier that sunny, April day only to vanish in the darkness of the evening. And Gina, with her wrath of anger and torment, made me realize just how dark the evening had become. That night I drove home in despair thinking about how complex my life had become over the years. The fifteen-mile drive felt like an hour. I was driving the speed limit but, it felt like I would never get home. The house was dark and still when I arrived. Retreating to the family room, I grabbed a blanket and pillow and turned on a movie until sleep stilled my overactive brain. I never heard Gina return home that evening–she could just as well have arrived in the early morning. She would do that on occasion– never explaining her whereabouts.

Over the weekend, Gina spent most of her time packing her clothes and belongings. For the very first time, I noticed there were a bunch of marked boxes stacked in the garage. I sat on the sofa in the family room–my eyes glued to the television in a state of paralysis. I had not shaved; the stubble was rather dense. On Sunday afternoon, Gina walked into the family room. It had been the first time we were in the same room in our home together in many weeks. Her parting words to the back of me were short and direct; 'you will hear from my attorney to close our mutual accounts.' I deliberately chose not to answer–I had nothing to say. I heard the heels of her shoes clicking across the ceramic tile in the kitchen and the opening and closing of the garage door. The subsequent silence was deafening. I stared at several items in the room; she was leaving my home for good. She chose every wall and ceiling color as well as the trim work. Gina had been the interior decorator and each room was filled from ceiling to walls and floors with pictures, furniture, and carpets she chose for me. Everything in that house was all about her. I think I may have picked out one chair in the family room–a leather recliner. The old furniture my mom had given me after college was still in a storage locker along with my grandfathers' wooden dresser. Gina refused to have any of the family furniture in my home. I paid a monthly fee for decades for that furniture; not knowing why I did that for so many years. I might soon need it.

I walked to the front of the house. I watched Gina's red Cadillac SUV exit the sloping driveway from the large front window of the family room addition I had designed and helped to build. The car was her treasure trophy–one of her many gifts to herself–the image she projected as she arrived on her appointments with her clients. Red; her preferred color. The color of every vehicle she ever owned. I could care less about cars. The addition to my house had been my greatest gift to Gina. Now, tears dripped from my eyes as the combination of memories of our past and her abrupt departure flooded me. Once again, loneliness came to visit and stood beside me. During the next few months, I became a hermit of sorts. I worked during the day and went home at night. I anticipated darkness and welcomed an end to the light of day. Rarely, did I turn on any interior lights-the darkness blanketed me. On weekends, when I wasn't in the office, gardening and yard work consumed my time. I sat in front of the television every night–my mind completely absorbed-entrenched in the people in the box before me. Instead of talking on the phone I communicated by texting. I would not dare take time to focus on my own life. On rare occasions, I went out with a few close friends, and did not really enjoy myself. They talked; I listened Solitude became my best friend, and I was realizing I was content with him as my new housemate.

CHAPTER 10 – TOGETHER AGAIN

Driving home from work one dark, November evening several of my business associates called and persuaded me to join them at one of those local networking events. Usually, a company in the area sponsored an annual 'meet and greet' for the real estate related professionals in the county supplying the food and drinks at a local venue. Against my desire to sit home in front of the television–alone with my microwaved meal-I drove to the restaurant. I rationalized the free good eats and alcohol sounded more palatable than the canned salmon and canned string beans I had planned for dinner. There was also something else underlying my decision to go out and it had started bothering me lately. I had become rather crotchety to my peers. Perhaps I had been staying home at night and on the weekends far too long. I justified a change of scenery would do a bit of good to my psyche. Besides, some of the people there were always up for a political discussion. Politics was a topic I thoroughly enjoyed.

Most of the real estate community was invited to the networking event including builders, insurance agents, and surveyors. The affair was to encourage people to interact with others; to get to know people related to the business community. There was always some social hour or networking function going on but, this event was usually well attended. Rarely does anyone 'network'. These people don't really want to meet anyone new–they attend for the free food and drinks. They stare at one another as they sip beer, wine, or other favored intoxicants; huddled in small groups with familiar folks. They consumed their poison of choice as egos magnified and inhibitions lowered. I must admit. I consider myself somewhat shy and do not like the thought of introducing myself to anyone I don't know. I knew how they felt. However, I greatly admire those that can walk up to a total stranger and start a conversation. That takes a great deal of effort, and I just don't seem to possess that sort of inter-human trait. Maybe I just didn't like people. I never felt like I knew what to say; even with those people I knew for a long time. I'm not sure why I am this way.

The upcoming holidays were adding a bit of stress. It meant more of these events; more frequently. Then again, maybe I was just getting older and less tolerant of all the formalities of life along with the same old business functions. I didn't know what the exact problem was; life had become a pure mystery to me, and I am unable to conjure any sort of self-analysis. Prior to my arrival to any function, I usually began planning my departure and inventing a reason to leave as quickly as possible. I responded differently to family invitations. All my family usually got together at our parents' house growing up and then at Mom's after her divorce. Family events were pleasurable to me–they were sheer joy. I was accustomed to the multi-generational gatherings engineered by my mother; soon filled with nieces and nephews. And believe you me, she started the invitations in the spring to make sure you were coming for the holidays. I could easily listen to my mother, the idle chatter of my sisters, and extended family members. They possessed the ability to talk endlessly–I suppose it was a possible genetic trait from my mother or another female in the family lineage. All I had to do was show up with a bottle of white wine or Bailey's Irish Cream.

The weather was unseasonably warm. It had to be 72 degrees. I peered through the large plate glass window toward the bar area as I pulled the handle of the heavy wooden door to the entrance. The bar was packed. People were standing like sardines in a metal can. I immediately saw her as I passed by the bar. But, instead of walking over to her, I looked for my friends and weaved through the crowd of people to the back of the restaurant. I searched the crowd looking for their familiar faces. Finding them, I sat in the last seat in the back; facing the bar where Alex stood. I was caught off guard by her presence. My happiness meter changed from grumpy to excite by a fleeting glance of her side profile. I needed some time to think. My associates engaged in their usual chatter of real estate sales which, ultimately led to a passionate discussion of politics. I listened; albeit half interested while the other half of my brain focused about what I would say to Alex. My eyes couldn't help but look toward the front of the restaurant. Looking, searching;

she kept moving around. I had to get away from this conversation as soon as I could; before Alex left me again.

I consumed a few glasses of my usual liquid courage; gin and ginger, of course. After munching on some fried chicken wings and tasteless cheese cubes I realized the time was now or never. Without saying a word to my present company, I walked toward the bar–Alex was at the end farthest from me. I was not about to allow frivolous conversation to interfere. I was confident in what I knew–as I had always known. I had absolutely nothing to lose this time. Pride had left me because of a woman and was suddenly reappearing. I was a man now. Not the young man of twenty something years ago but, a seasoned and mature male. Not to mention one other fact; I was darned good looking. Alex would see me differently that night–different than she had ever seen me before.

As far as I knew, Alex did not see me when I had arrived. I felt I had a slight advantage and planned to act like I just bumped into her. As I walked along the ornately carved, wooden bar, I quickly changed my strategy. Why was I going to play some silly game? I was not going to waste time acting. I was not going to waste any more time–period. Finally, and without hesitation or embarrassment and with a driven determination I had not felt in years, I wove my way through the crowd. I was within twenty feet of her when an old agent friend of mine grabbed me. I became wedged between him and the bar. The crowd had become even more compacted as the remainder of the happy hour waned and my view toward the front became   blocked by this super tall and rather large guy. The light wool sweater was a bit much for the night-too much body heat from within and surrounding me. Not to mention all of the hot air escaping from the crowd as the chatter grew more intense and louder.   I do not know why but, I accepted another drink. Instead of wasting more time talking with the agent I grabbed the drink, gave a thank you nod, and edged my way through the crowd until I was within an arms-reach of Alex. She was in a rather tight group of agents chattering and laughing. Her eyes found mine and her smile grew-that all too familiar smile. The other ladies moved back a bit as they turned to see who was approaching. My happy meter in my chest fluttered.

The other agents walked away and one of her co-workers approached us for a few minutes. "Well, hello, there" she said as she extended a warm hand "I work with Alex. I am Joann," she added.

"Nice to meet you. I'm Joe with RE/MAX. I think we may have done a deal together."

"Oh yes," she responded. "The New Windsor Road property. I remember." We exchanged some idle chatter about the real estate market and mortgage rates and then she moved on to another group of people. I finally was alone. With Alex. My brain was on hydro mode and my mouth just started spewing so many things. I told Alex about what I had been doing in real estate and my Aruba property and time shares and then, the breakup of my relationship. I had to fill in every second. She stood listening. It was role reversal between us. Like the game of truth or dare I played with my young roommates in earlier days-it was time for truth. It was time to converse and explore one another on an adult level. I finally took in a breath and became silent. There. It was done. I told her.

"I'm sorry you had gone through all of that but, it sounds like it was for the best. And you look good. I didn't notice before-your glasses are gone." She looked at me for a moment – her brow furrowed. As if she was really seeing my face for the first time. "You can be my date next spring for the awards banquet. Usually, I go solo to those things," she said in a joking tone.

A bell above the bar rang-loud. The even louder crowd became somewhat subdued. Usually, the bartenders rang the bell when they received tips. This time the host of the evening rang the bell and shouted out to the patrons of the restaurant with her pleasure and appreciation for their attendance. "Please take a moment to thank the staff for their service and friendliness to all of you. And my gratitude to our staff in making this evening possible."

I whistled as the group clapped their hands in thunderous applause. "Last call, everyone," the host continued "we only have about another half hour and then it will be time to end this shindig." And with that last notion, a huge surge of bodies flooded the bar area pushing me forward to the corner end of the old, oak bar. I

104

practically had to wrestle back to where I had once stood. Alex was gone.

I walked to the back of the restaurant looking for her and she was not there. I waved a hand to my friends and forced a smile as I turned toward the exit door. Outside, a gentle cool breeze had formed, typical of a late November evening. I felt a bit of a chill. The streetlamps lit the entire corner. There was still plenty of traffic. I played the evening over in my mind several times as I walked to my car in the far rear parking lot across the street. Getting out of the house certainly lifted my spirits. My hermit-like status had become my norm these past few months. I didn't realize how much I missed being out with people-who knew? And, to talk with Alex. That had been amazing! There was something to look forward to in the spring-the annual awards banquet.

Spring. By golly that was almost five months away.

I have not missed talking to her one day since that Wednesday evening. Our subsequent Friday dinner was the beginning of my new life. Saturday was movie night and Sunday-Hershey and a concert with the Eagles. We spent every weekend together. There was no more holding back; I spoke to her pointedly. I told her how I had thought about her so many times. My modus operandi was to connect with this woman and make sure she understood how much I cared for her and always wanted to be the man by her side.   I was dedicated to a life mission of possible.

105

CHAPTER 11 – JAN AND ROB

Alex and I were traveling to a familiar restaurant under far different circumstances than any of our previous car rides, mostly in silence. There had been a strain on our relationship since we returned home from our Aruban vacation. Weeks before our trip to Aruba we had agreed to dine with her friends–hence, the reason we were together this night. If the dinner had not been pre-planned, I am not so sure we would have been together this evening. Earlier in the week, over a brief telephone conversation, I reminded Alex about our dinner date with Rob and Jan. Alex had totally forgotten. I think the mere fact I remembered may have gained me a favorable light in my beauties eye. I understood the importance of her friendship with Jan. Unlike our first encounter at the networking event, we were not dining with strangers or associates from our business life. This was personal. All four of us had been to the restaurant before; just not together. I felt peaceful inside-just being by Alex's side. There were times–when I was alone-the mere thought of being in Alex's presence put a smile on my face. She had a way of making me feel wanted. And, much more than that her kindness and desire for happiness had an effect on me; that happiness enveloped my soul, too. Alas, I felt appreciated by someone other than my family.

I reached over and found her left hand and entangled our fingers-just enough to let her know how much I cared. Yes, I had somewhat lost her before. And I lost her a second time, too. But I was committed to doing anything humanly possible to keep Alex close to me now; even if it meant stepping outside of my introverted self. Even if it meant I had to meet people or participate in new experiences. My single most objective was to let her know how grateful I was to win her heart back for eternity. I had evolved these past months; I was a focused and determined man. By the end of the night, I would share our remarkable experience in Aruba with her friends. I would find a way to rekindle the fire with Alex-tonight. I could not let her just slip away. Fate had introduced us; my dreams, faith, and desires had managed to bring us together. My love was strong enough to bind us for life.

The restaurant was known for its good food and great service. I had been there a couple of times before with my family. The Cafe was located at the end of a small shopping center. The red brick facade gave the center a traditional yet classic look of elegance. Colorful floral baskets hung from the black, wrought iron streetlamp posts. I looked around the parking lot of The Cafe as we drove past the entrance. There were several nice eateries and shops neighboring it. The lot was relatively full for a summer Saturday evening. I found ample parking in the back row.

"Do you recognize Rob and Jan's car?" I asked. Looking about, Alex shook her head from side-to-side in response-she didn't. "We may as well park the car and wait inside," I said. The van was almost nine years old and had a few repair and maintenance issues. I could count the number of times I changed the oil on one hand. There were occasions when the air conditioning just wouldn't work. The air conditioning had released just a bit of cool air during our ride; thank goodness. We decided to wait inside the restaurant-it was humid and ninety degrees feeling more like one hundred.

I got out and walked around the car to open Alex's door. My mother brought this man up well. From an early age I found using gentlemanly manners, particularly with females, went unnoticed by few. Manners may be confused with manipulation at times. My efforts were nothing short of sincere. I couldn't help but smile as I opened Alex's passenger door. Alex always appreciated the small things I did for her. Her large blue eyes captured mine. Through them-an instant look-many years were spoken. I was further encouraged by her beautiful smile as it slowly radiated. It made me feel so good when she appreciated the small things. In my previous relationships I received little or no recognition for anything let alone the small meaningful things. With Alex it was different. She understood me and she wanted to please me. Yes, it had been a long time since I felt the true pleasures from a woman.

In just a couple of months Alex and I had bonded strongly together. We enjoyed sharing our past lives during the last months, not just about our relationships or sad times. We caught up and exchanged so many stories; we became more than friends. We did a variety of things during those months; the Eagles concert in Hershey-meeting each other's families and friends. And dancing–I finally had someone to dance with, hold closely, or jump up and down and do some head banging. We had rekindled a special relationship-not driven by money or materialism. Money could not buy what I had right now. I would regain Alex's unconditional love.

Ironically, the restaurant was owned by Jan's daughter and son-in-law. They were proud owners of the successful little restaurant in the suburban sprawling area of Baltimore County. Her son-in-law was the chef. Like a spider's web there are so many delicate strands that connect all of us to one another. Strands from our past, our lives, and our loves surrounded the two of us. Hand-in-hand, we walked toward the restaurant entrance when Alex observed Rob and Jan's car pulling in. We stopped to wait on the sidewalk. I seized the moment to squeeze Alex's hand as Jan and Rob strolled toward us. Jan was dressed in somewhat trendy, brightly colored clothing. Her blonde, whitish hair was parted a bit off center covering about a third of the right side of her face. She had what appeared to be a real zebra skin purse hanging from her right shoulder with matching 3 or 4 inch spiked heels. I couldn't help noticing her first.

"Hey, you must be Joe! I've heard a lot about you! You sure are handsome," Jan said as she gave me a really big hug and patted my shoulder. For such a small lady she had a firm, intense hug. I enjoyed receiving the compliment and never tired of hearing them. I bent over to meet her upturned cheek. At almost six foot, I towered over her small frame even with her spiked heels. She rubbed my shoulder blade in a circular fashion a time or two before stepping back.

"This is my husband, Rob," Jan added as she turned toward him. His white hair was offset by his rosy colored cheeks. Rob nodded in Alex's direction first, gave her a quick hug, and then shook my hand. His grip was firm. He was taller than I.

"Nice to meet the two of you", he replied with sincere gusto and a warm smile. Alex had told me she had met Jan at a business function- through the years they had become very good friends. This was her first encounter with Rob. The adage of first impressions generally holds true-to-form for me. I can tell right from the start whether I like someone. Jan and Alex teamed up and started their mutual chatter. Rob and I shrugged our shoulders and followed behind our women to the restaurant entrance. I sped up in front of the girls.

"Please do," I said as I held open the door for my sweetheart. Alex answered with a 'thanks, honey' and walked in first. I was getting good vibes so far. I let out a deep sigh of contentment. I couldn't quite tell if Alex was just being her happy self to be with her friend or if the wall of distance between us was starting to close. Rob walked up behind me and placed his arm behind my shoulder. Holding the glass door open, he nodded for me to go through. Little things. The ladies were so intense with their chatter-good golly they could do some fast talking. In all my years of being around the opposite sex, I don't think there was anything they couldn't talk about.

"Good evening and welcome to our dining room, Mr. and Mrs. B. Can I seat you at a table for four?" inquired the hostess with a broad smile upon our entry. You can always tell a higher end restaurant when they address frequent guests or those of prominence in a community using only the initial of the last name. The hostess gracefully walked from behind the tall, wooden podium. Her beaming face was reflective of the warm, sunny evening outside of the restaurant. She hugged Jan then Rob- carefully air kissing them on the right side of the cheek.

Taking the lead, I answered, "yes, it would be great if you could seat us at one of the booths over there." I pointed to an empty area where several dark burgundy, leather covered booths lined the far side of the restaurant. The high back of the bench gave you some

111

additional privacy from other patrons. Alex always preferred a booth over a table. I also noticed an entrance door behind the booths-opened to what appeared to be the bar area of the restaurant. I hadn't noticed the bar when I dined at the restaurant before. We followed the slender, younger woman to the side of the restaurant just off the main dining area of the café.

"I'm a lefty," I said out loud as I cut in between Alex and the table. She backed up a bit allowing me some room in front of her. Even though I am ambidextrous, I always eat with my left hand. It keeps me from banging my arm against the other person. I adjusted myself a bit to be more comfortable making room for Alex to spread out as well. Rob followed suit. Jan looked at Alex–not quite comprehending what I said–shrugged her shoulders and the girls sat down next to us. We uttered a unified 'thank you,' to the hostess as our bodies positioned themselves into the cushiony booth. My eyes roamed over the darkly stained, wood-trimmed surroundings and tables-noticing the stain and finish were beautifully crafted.

"Thank you so much Amy, Jan said as she grasped both the hostess's shoulder and gently rubbed the back of her shoulder."

"I will let chef know you are here," the hostess responded. "Your daughter won't be in this evening."

Our table displayed four place settings. The white cotton napkins were a nice touch. Four sparkling water glasses captured the light from outside and were strategically placed on the table. A grouping of pictures hung on the wall beside us. They were attractively arranged and in balance with one another. I admired the attention to detail by others. I appreciate straight lines, synchronism, and perfection. None of those traits I possessed mind you. My eyes toured other areas of the room. Artwork was on all the walls; lots of paintings.

I had acquired a bit of knowledge and drafting experience in college many years before. That class had given me the fundamentals to design the family room addition to my home with Gina. Sure, I had to have a contractor finalize the design but, the primary concept had been all my own. And, it had been an arduous task. The lines of the room, the placement of the windows, and the stone surrounding the massive fireplace-all me.

In response to my lingering observation, "Artwork from local Baltimore artists. Perhaps some of the 'starving artist' community in Baltimore," the hostess said as she interrupted my thoughts. She also offered brief information regarding each of the painting's origin. "Your waitress will be over in just a few minutes to take your cocktail order. Here are your menus," the hostess said as she gently handed us the burgundy, leather bound menus–first to the ladies and then to Rob and me. She placed the wine list on the center of the table which, boasted an extensive selection.

"I don't know if Alex told you or if you already knew Joe but, sometimes local football players stop in here for dinner," Jan said. Her face beamed of pride as she spoke. "Are you a football fan?"

"A typical fan of sorts I would say. Don't get to the games often and I thoroughly enjoy watching them on the tube. I'm not really one to fight the crowds."

"Rob and I are big football fans. Aren't we Rob?" Jan gently elbowed her husband.

Rob nodded in agreement with a broad grin. "Whenever we can, we have a house full of neighbors and friends on Sunday afternoons to watch the game."

Jan commented further as she leaned in toward the table, "I don't know about you two but, we have looked forward to dining at the restaurant with you *all week long*. Oh, my goodness-all month!" Her hand reached up to pull the few strands of hair from her face to the side. I noticed the large, emerald cut blue stone sitting off center of her ring finger. Her nails looked as though they were professionally manicured. She was a well-kept woman, well grounded, and full of happiness. No wonder Alex was so fond of her friend.

"I have, too," Alex replied. "I couldn't wait for the four of us to get together tonight. This is just great!" I knew Alex had completely forgotten the dinner. Work had become so stressful for Alex over the past couple of months. Her pay had been cut–her hours had increased–her bank account balances were lower. I also

114

knew how much she adored Jan and would never do anything intentional to disappoint her. Her secret was kept safe with me.

"I have seen several players from the football team when my mom and I had dinner here before," I said. "In the nice weather, she likes to bring her dog along and sit on the patio."

CHAPTER 12 – THE TALE BEGINS

The four of us were quiet for the first time. Everything sounded great on the menu to me. Generally speaking, I like fresh fish when I go out to eat. Most of the better restaurants around town offered several daily specials–at least one of them would be a locally caught fish.

The short lull in conversation ended. "I hear you had a really interesting vacation," Rob said. His comment was directed to me. His grayed eyebrows arched; his smile clearly indicated some knowledge of our recent vacation to Aruba. "Sounds like you had some fun," he added. Jan and Alex exchanged a knowing smile of childish exaggeration. On the way down, Alex told me she had filled her in with some of the highlights of our ten-day visit to the desert Caribbean Island. She had met Jan for lunch just after our return from Aruba.

"You know," I began slowly, "I've never had a vacation quite like this one. It had to be the most messed up trip to Aruba I have ever had in my entire life!" Peering at Alex, her face was an exaggerated pout. In sudden response I quickly reacted. "I don't mean to say that in a bad way. It's just that everything that could go wrong on a vacation went wrong on our vacation. But, without a doubt, I had the greatest time of my life. I don't think I would trade our vacation to Aruba with anyone." I wanted some clarity so there

116

was no doubt of my sincerity and placed my hand on Alex's thigh–a bit of a rub and gentle squeeze followed. I wanted her to know I truly meant no harm and for further benefit to Jan and Rob, "I've been vacationing to Aruba most of my adult life–my family has owned several time shares there for over thirty years. As a matter of fact, I also own two time shares."

I had to boast a bit–I was proud of my time shares, and I was proud of my beloved Aruba. And I certainly owned the bragging rights for my beautiful home there. I had utilized my talents toward the design of that house as well. "After vacationing in the time shares and in the crowded hotels, my sister, her husband, and I decided to build this beautiful vacation home. It took us about three years to complete. I wanted to take Alex and her kids there to experience the island with me–mmmm; to show it off."

"Wow, that was rather brave of you. I mean about constructing a home so far away–not taking a woman and her three kids on vacation," Rob said with a quick chuckle. "It's tough enough to build a house right here in Maryland. I couldn't imagine building a house in another country. Jan and I would probably end up fighting about all the construction delays and decisions. My Jan loves to change her mind rather frequently. You should see what she's like in the morning-just getting dressed each day. I bet you've never seen so many clothes, shoes, and accessories. She doesn't

117

have a closet; she has three and a whole room for her stuff." Jan gave a gentle jab with her elbow to Rob's side.

"You are so right, Rob, there were a lot of decisions—and a multitude of construction delays—my God it about drove us batty. The process certainly had its drawbacks. I think Aruban workers have banker's hours down there—by two o'clock, they stop all construction. Even when it rains, the rains are seldom long, they pack up their tools and head home. Selecting a builder you can trust made all the difference in our comfort level—of that I can assure you. We got lucky and selected a very good builder—an islander. When I met him, Dimitri was the manager of the subdivision where we built the home." I took a moment collecting thoughts of the experience and added; "the gated golf community was where my brother-in-law and I played many times while in Aruba and that is how we came to know him. One of two golf courses on the island, I might add, only the other one is just nine holes."

"Wow, did you say golf course?" Rob asked.

"And a tough course to play on if you've never tried it before. We quickly learned if you tee off by eight in the morning, you can avoid the strong trade winds and play a decent game of golf. To this day, Dimitri keeps in touch with us. He and his brother, Salvatore, help us with anything I need. I oversee the rentals and maintenance projects for the house. Salvatore is the caretaker and provides great service and information to our renters. If there are any issues or problems, he takes care of them right away and if it's a bigger problem I can count on receiving a phone call."

A young man stopped by our table, filled our empty glasses with water with a gentlemanly nod, and walked away. I had noticed the staff polishing the glassware earlier. I had a feeling this was going to be a long dinner. I whet my whistle; after all, I had much to talk about our trip. I enjoyed talking about our Aruban vacation. Granted; it's not like other vacation stories. This one just didn't know when to stop. No one could have captured this on film. No one could have written this stuff. As a matter of fact, since we had returned home, I had relayed my story at least a hundred times to just about anyone who would listen. I had become quite the storyteller; people couldn't believe the things that happened in Aruba.

"Our vacation morning started early. I had been quite impressed with just how organized Alex and her kids were. On the other hand, my organizational skills are a bit of a different story. I'm always frantically running around at the last-minute pre-departure–afraid of losing or leaving something behind. I start packing the night before the trip-around 4 AM I am done with the process. These guys were in bed by eleven. I'm forever leaving a toothbrush, shaver, or some other item back home."

"Perhaps you would be better off preparing a list before you leave," Jan said.

"That is a good suggestion and may work for you Jan but, I never remember to get around to preparing a list. To take the time to put a pen to a piece of paper just eludes me. I have gone so far as pack some extra clothes and toiletries, set the suitcases by the front door, and have left them behind because we went out the garage door."

"At least you try," Jan replied with a chuckle. "You are a thinking man, Joe. I can tell. You've got to give yourself a little credit here; you just have more important things on your mind."

"That's my Jan," Rob said. "She is a born nurturer of mind and body, the quintessential mother. This woman can find something positive out of the most outrageous things and situations. She amazes me when I am sick. I have a lot of issues-I'm the grumpiest of men mind you. She will wake up all smiles when I can't get my head off my pillow, and even though she has to be at work, she will make sure I have everything right at my side. Before she leaves, she tells me she knows I will be back to good health when she returns. She never changes."

"I can appreciate that. People tend to drift toward the negative side of things," Alex added. "I know my mind does. Jan's focus is not on the problem but, on the solution."

Rob shook his head, 'and it's always a positive solution.'

Seizing the moment and in an effort to get back to my story; "well, that morning of our departure I needed to find a solution to get our heap of luggage out of the house and packed into my van. Everyone had thrown their luggage the night before at the front door. I mean that door was barely visible with all the luggage in front of it." I illustrated how high the luggage was piled at the door with my hands and added; "black and red luggage was at least five or six feet high. I think they got too carried away and didn't think of how we were going to get the front door open." With this last comment, and not realizing what I was doing, I slammed my hands down on the table with a loud thud.

"How did you open the door to get out?" Jan asked with a startled laugh.

The sound of my hands startled the poor woman. I'm surely not Italian but, when I speak, my hands automatically wave kind of spastic like. The pitch in my voice gets higher. What can I say about myself here? It's not that often I have an opportunity to tell a tale like this.

With a toothy grin I smiled back into Jan's green eyes. I hadn't fully noticed her sea green eye color-so intense-a dramatic complement to her light hair. The waitress made a rather timely return to our booth giving me another minute or two to collect my thoughts.

"May I take your drink order?" she asked as she patiently stood tableside.

While everyone contemplated what wine would be best with our entrees, I decided to take control of the situation. I knew a bit about pairing wines with dinner. Glancing through the wine list I noticed they had a relatively good selection to make my choice easy. I was on a roll tonight with this group. It was my time to be the alpha male; rather a 'jack-of-all-trades and a master of none.' Alex would see another one of my hidden talents. I was suddenly anxious to continue my story of our vacation. I responded to the waitress before anyone else could raise their eyes from the wine list. "How about a bottle of Santa Margherita?" Pinot Grigio would be a light choice before dinner. And if everyone liked the wine, we could order a second bottle with dinner. The wine was also one of my mom's personal favorites.

"Sounds good to me," Rob said as he outstretched his clenched fingers, entwining them, and then resting them on the table. "Shucks, I never really know what to order or what-goes-with-what anyways." Rob and Jan leaned forward against the table— their torsos firmly rested against it. They made a rather striking couple; both had greying hair as well as striking features. His mustache perfectly matched his hair color. I am not necessarily a person that can dissect and distinguish body language per se nor do I focus on details—blah, blah, blah—such a waste of time. But they certainly illustrated an undeniable and visibly physical sign of eagerness for me to continue. I had lured them into the world of

Aruba Joe. Their facial expressions displayed a bit of intrigue-I clearly had an audience.

I was inclined to talk endlessly about my beloved Aruba; and this most recent trip would be no exception. One thing had become clear to me as a result of telling the tale so many times over the past couple of weeks; I had refined the story about this vacation. I may have even embellished on some of the situations just a wee bit. I turned to look into Alex's eyes for a lingering moment. "In answer to you, Jan, I had to move every piece of luggage before we could open the door. At five thirty AM the alarms started going off in all four bedrooms of the house with five different signals from different cell phones. The house got quite lively. We each took ownership of our bags and travel items and packed the van; there was not one inch of space available for anything but our bodies."

"Outside, a pale, glimmer of sunlight peaked through the early morning clouds. The air temperature was a warm seventy degrees already. Traffic to the airport that morning was light-no school buses to back up traffic. Ninety minutes later we got to Dulles Airport in northern Virginia. I pulled up to the US Airways section of the airport terminal. I'm an expert at parallel parking my van between the cars, shuttles, and taxis–years of experience. Jade, Alex's younger daughter, calls it my 'mom van'."

"Not only that," Alex added with a giggle, "Jade also says the mom van Joe drives is an embarrassment. She thinks he needs to get rid of it before it emasculates him."

"Jade is the one that just started selling cars, Rob," Jan added. "She's only twenty. Alex says she's a motor head. Jade started working on detailing cars and going to car auctions when she was only twelve years old. Her son, Vincent, is a cutie pie. I just love him. I haven't met Crystal yet, though."

"They are good kids," I quickly added. "As I parked, everyone was full of energy and super excited-the flurry of bodies and luggage pieces emptied quickly. I double checked to make sure no one left anything behind. I know how it feels to leave something back home when you go on vacation. Alex and her kids hustled inside the airport doors while I parked in the long-term lot. It could only have taken about twenty minutes, but it sure seemed a long time before I got back to my sweetie."

"Yeah, everything went smoothly alright," Alex said with a snicker, "until Joe got back from parking the van and we started checking in our luggage. He came through the sliding airport doors and he sure was a sight wearing his tan suede, wide brimmed hat and his flowered, Hawaiian shirt. When Jade took one look at him, she gave him a new name and started calling him 'Aruba Joe'. She is always nick-naming people or poking fun at them. His infamous hat has a braided leather strip wrapped around the base held together

124

by a brass toggle. Aruba Joe was quite the dapper looking traveler that morning."

"Jade likes making fun of my hat and me as much as she likes making fun of my van. She may have thought I looked funny but, I was in Aruba mode. Yep; everything had been going just great until I walked up to the luggage check-in counter. I began loading each piece of luggage on the scale. I took great pains to make sure they each weighed less than fifty pounds. I'm too cheap to pay those airlines any more money than I must."

"I can't say that I blame your thinking. The airline only allows one bag per person now and a twenty-five-dollar fee if you're overweight." Rob added defiantly. Then with a bit of a grin and a wave of his forefinger he said, "clarification; if the *bag* is overweight."

"Holy Christmas! The stupid, fool of a woman behind the check-in counter wanted me to pay sixty dollars extra for one of our bags," I said in response. "I personally checked each one of those bags the night before. I knew they all weighed under fifty pounds. The woman was relentless, and she insisted I pay the extra fee."

"Oh God, Rob," Alex piped in. "Joe just wouldn't let this part of the vacation rest."

"When she asked for that sixty bucks, she might as well have slapped me across the face with her hand. I ended up telling her; 'no friggin' way'. I didn't want to pay an additional sixty dollars for

125

anything; especially, for a piece of luggage." I could feel that strong surge; my blood boiled as I was retelling the tale. "The sheer audacity of the airlines to pick a poor man's pocket with such a ridiculous fee anyway. It's just plain ludicrous! I told her we'd carry the bag on with us and grabbed it. I was so ticked off with that woman. I have flown on that airline for years–I am a 'silver member' and never once did I have a problem checking in."

Jan chimed in with a wave of her manicured hand, "you know, Aruba Joe, the woman is just the corporate messenger. She was only relaying the company's policy."

Alex said, "Joe was really upset, Jan. I hadn't seen that side of him before. He had always been so calm and such a gentleman. He sure did make a scene with that poor lady. You should have seen the scared look on her face. At one point I thought she was going to call airport security. I was really embarrassed for her and for him to be like this in front of my children. He acted like a bit of a jerk."

"That's all you would have needed. Can you just envision the TSA dudes running through the airport?" Jan added. "I could see Joe pictured on Fox's evening broadcast–handcuffed–as they walked him through the terminal. A subscript reading; 'Aruba Joe–the reason the world thinks we are the ugly Americans.'"

Then Alex added, "his voice elevates to a higher pitch when he's excited. Can't you still hear it in his voice now–even five weeks after the fact? I just wanted all of us to get on board that

126

plane. I really didn't give a hoot about the sixty bucks and I most certainly didn't want the luggage issue overshadowing our journey."

"You've missed the principal of the thing here, Alex. The airlines just want to charge us more money. They think of every way possible to do it, too–as if they don't already get enough money for the plane ticket and their expensive snacks and drinks. Those airlines are money mongers. I just thanked that woman rather sarcastically and told her we'd carry on the extra pieces. And I hoped she seized the opportunity to take my valid complaint to her manager to take back to the corporate big wigs."

"While Joe was raising Kane with the woman at the check-in counter, Jade stood back from all of the commotion and had counted fifteen bags. I hadn't realized we had so many bags. The children and I began grabbing one or two of the extra bags to carry with us on the plane," Alex said. "One of mine was filled with my shoes."

"You can never pack too many pairs of shoes," Jan said with a wink and a nod in response-the two of them shared a spirited laugh.

This deviation from my story gave me a chance to compose myself. Perhaps Alex had a point-I was sounding a bit out-of-control. But, sometimes, I find it difficult to contain myself when someone is saying or doing something so stupid. Clearing my throat to remove any remaining malice in my tone I added, "you're allowed to take two bags of a certain size on the plane with you now." Leaning forward against the table I added in a lowered tone, "while Alex and her kids were busy getting their passports and bags organized, they didn't notice the entire conversation I had with the lady behind the counter. It wasn't all bad."

"Oh, yeah, he was busy alright," Alex added. "While the children and I were worried about sorting the luggage; opening every, single bag to redistribute our clothing and stuffing our carry-on bags with the excess weight-he was busy, too. I prodded the children to move quickly to avoid his out-bursting again. Joe, however, was making a major change with the seating arrangement. *His* seating re-arrangement, that is."

I wasn't going to even respond to the out-bursting comment. No need to go down that avenue-that could be trouble. "No, that is not quite true," I added as I moved my hand above the table; wagging my forefinger from right to left to make my next point clear. "I had told you several weeks before we left that our tickets might be upgraded to first class. Remember? Just after I made the reservations."

Perhaps my voice contained just a wee bit too much sarcasm but, I could not help adding, "*if* you may take a moment to remember, my sweet."

Alex rolled her eyes at me. Rob and Jan looked at me rather quizzically. "Now, hold on everyone. I have to set the record straight. I didn't know they were only going to upgrade *one* ticket.

128

That *one* ticket–mine-was upgraded to first class–all the rest of the tickets remained coach seats. I'm the one with the airline points and travel card so it makes sense I would get the upgrade." After all, I was the one that scheduled the trip, made the reservations in the first place, and I paid for all our tickets so why shouldn't I reap a benefit or two? This was not going as well as when I had told this Aruban tale so many times before. I realized my decision to upgrade my seat was not popular with this audience and just talking about it again tonight was still a bit of a sore spot with Alex. Her face spoke for her as she shifted her weight slightly away from me. But I felt the same then as I did now. Honestly, I truly had prepped her about the possible upgrade to first class way before we left for the trip. I remembered distinct details of our conversation and told her that we *may* be able to get the tickets upgraded to first class. We experienced one of those '*Venus and Mars*' moments, like the book. Surely, anyone in any heterosexual relationship has experienced those conflicts between the sexes. I do not stand alone in this phenomenon.

"Hey, someone had to take advantage of the ticket. Remember," I fully turned my body to face Alex to further my defensive position, "you turned the upgrade down. I gave you the opportunity to take the first-class ticket. I offered it to all four of you but, each of you declined. There was no way I was going to let an opportunity to fly first class bypass me."

129

Rob and Jan giggled at our bantering with one another. They could also tell the topic did not sit well with Alex. Occasionally, I admit, I push things a bit far. Perhaps my defensive strategy came from twenty plus years of the argumentative and mental warfare with Gina. I had been in constant defense with the female gender since my youth-surrounded by hormonally imbalanced females. Alex makes herself a good target for my twisted humor and antics. I guess it boils down to one simple fact; Alex and I don't share the same sense of logical and deductive reasoning. There are just some characteristic traits you must learn and accept about one another; this was one she would have to accept. I hoped.

"But Joe left out one simple fact; the probability of only one ticket upgrade," Alex retorted looking deeply into my eyes. She just couldn't let the subject end either. "His frequent flyer miles-or some such special reward airlines gives to their faithful passengers-was only good for one ticket per trip. He knew it. On the other hand-I'm a 'good for the group' type of person. We go together and we leave together-whatever we do, whatever the outcome, we do it together. C'mon; especially when you are traveling out of the country to some place you've never been before with your children. He waved that ticket like it was a golden trophy of sorts. Like he had just won the lottery or received some special accolade-knighted for his good deed. Or the Willy Wonka golden ticket. Obviously, Joe's a bit more of the selfish type."

"Ouch! Those words can hurt a guy, Alex. I don't know that I quite agree with you," Rob said. "I may have seriously considered doing the exact same thing."

"Oh yeah, Rob," Jan said jeeringly back toward her husband. "And, you would have walked home from that airport when we got back from vacation. Keep that in mind for any future considerations you may have my dear."

"See," I said looking at Rob. "These women just don't have the capability to engage in our sense of logic or humor. They jump to the wrong conclusion thinking we are selfish natured. I am a faithful, kind, and caring guy to my sweetheart and will always put her first." Rob put his arm around Jan giving her an exaggerated squeeze. Rob and I shared a fleeting chuckle. Rob knew what I was talking about. Yep; it was clearly an inter-planetary moment.

"Well," Alex added with a quirky smile as she looked at Jan, "You two have been together for thirty years, Jan. I cannot imagine what that would be like. I'm sure you've had quite a few of these situations. I've been single far too long and perhaps I need to change my way of thinking a bit. I sometimes feel I'm playing catch up with the rest of the world. I couldn't even own a house for over fourteen years because of my divorce. I didn't trust myself or even think I could ever own a home again. Being in a relationship again sure has been quite an adjustment for me."

For a moment I sat listening to Alex and looked at her with absolute amazement and appreciation. She had been single for a long time–it kinda hit me in the face as she spoke. Her primary focus had been her children and work–in that distinct order of priority. I admired her for that. I was confident her sense of humor would return–like how she used to be those many years ago-I would help her. Relationships–how the years together can give one such pleasure or such trepidation with another person. The crude aspects of her divorce had stripped her of many things–including fun and humor. Did she experience true joy? While we were on our trip, I had noticed a seriousness in her demeanor that had not been there before. In our younger days, Alex would laugh all the time–I wanted to make Alex laugh again.

I reflected on our conversation about the airline tickets. It was rather obvious Alex really didn't give any attention to the itinerary printouts. I had shown them to her prior to our departure. I was on one; her and her kids were on the other. For the first time, I may have begun to realize where Alex had been coming from. There was a few moments of silence between the four of us. Each of us lost unto private thought. As if someone hit a light switch, our waitress appeared at the table to pour some more wine jostling us back to our dining experience. As we clinked our partially filled glasses together, I got back to the subject matter. "I, on the other hand, was ecstatic about the upgrade.

132

"Oh, m-y G-o-d," Jan added with a giggle. "You are too much."

"I don't know what Rob or you would have done, Jan, but I chose to pick up my bags and told Alex and the kids we needed to get on board. I could have argued with her all day-trust me; I have lots of experience in that arena."

"All I can say," Rob said, "you are a very brave man, Joe. I don't think I would have been able to think that quickly and pull it off as well as you did. From my viewpoint, you gave her a valuable lesson."

"We are still learning about one another each and every day we're together," Alex said as she leaned toward me kissing me gently on my cheek. "You are a good man. After all, you planned a vacation with me and my three children. I don't know of very many men that would do something like that."

Good golly I was glad to hear her say that. Her words were soothing to me. Frankly, I had been feeling a bit off kilter the last few minutes. I knew Alex had thought I behaved rudely at the airport. Truth be told; upsetting Alex, in any way, pained me deeply. She had been through a tough time over those long years after her divorce. I felt compelled to make life better for her. After all, I wanted to be with Alex for the rest of my life.

In Alex's world, everyone sticks together and stands up for one another. I admire her strength and fortitude for this commendable facet of her personality. She is truly more of a team player than I am-and I had played in a lot of sports; I should know. From my perspective, I veer more to a sense of alpha male. In my world, it's 'let the big dog eat'. I think the difference between our diverse views is due to my playing sports when I was younger. I was smaller than most players on my team but, that never stopped me from competing. I had to try harder and practice longer than my teammates. I guess you could say my teammates and I competed with one another throughout our lives. We were in most school classes together. I was always trying to catch up or pass the other guys. And in the classroom, I struggled and competed just as much as I did out on the field; academically speaking. Sometimes I think it was because I grew up in a family of strong-minded females driven by mega doses of estrogen. Regardless of its genesis I had evolved with a competitive mindset.

I looked up from our table and noticed more patrons were filling the tables around us. It was mostly couples. The popular Saturday date night still existed–just like when we were teenagers. The sun was not as intense as it had been upon our arrival. It was beginning to go down as long, muted strands of light streamed through the large maple tree branches. Returning my attention back to my companions I began once again.

"Anyway, we started moving fast 'because just around the corner of the baggage area, I could see the long line at the security check point. The line had grown considerably longer in those few minutes as we stood at the baggage check in. The darned security system in the airport has surely made air travel somewhat less palatable than in the old days."

"I don't know about you, but I always like to get on board as soon as possible. I prefer to be one of the first flyers to board and store my computer bag." I saw a rather quizzical look on Rob's face and I began to explain. "You see, if you don't get to your seat early enough, there's not very much space in the overhead luggage area for your carry-on luggage. If it gets too full, the staff will put it down below. Then, you have to wait in the baggage area when you land. The last thing I want is to delay my arrival to my Aruban getaway."

"That's my competitive Joe; racing to get in front of everyone. He had his little passport necklace on and was determined to board before all of us. He didn't even look over his shoulder to see where the rest of us were," Alex said. "He darted past us before I could even wink an eye. He got through security before all of us. My handsome Joe was standing at the end of the conveyor belt watching us with his back straight-his feet were positioned shoulder width apart. His look on his face spoke of impatience for the rest of us as we managed through the unfamiliar airport formalities at the security checkpoint."

I quietly listened to Alex's rendition of the beginning of our flight to Aruba. I was rather amused by her wide-eyed expressions. I enjoyed looking at her blue tipped lashes; the setting sunlight filtering through the restaurant windows brought out the periwinkle-colored hue on them. Her eyes had an intense blue-green color with a fleck of light sparkling as she spoke.

"It's a braided nylon cord that has a pocket in it to hold my passport and a pen. It's rather convenient and functional in design. It has a clear plastic window on either side and keeps me from misplacing my passport. And, I always have it handy when I'm traveling. I couldn't find my passport one time and it cost me a flight delay. I never wanted to go through that strain ever again. My years of traveling taught me to become efficient where it counts the most."

"So," Alex continued, "you know how elementary school teachers put name tags with yarn around students when they go on field trips. Yep; hold that image of Joe in your mind for a moment. Joe was all finished going through the security checkpoint. Meanwhile, my three children were struggling with the routine security check. We're all over the place; putting on our shoes, finding our bags–grabbing our computers and putting them back in the computer bags. And I still don't know why the rush was so important–we had to wait for luggage when we arrived anyway."

"I urged them to hurry up. They were going slow as molasses," I said.

"The children and I finally reached a cluster of chairs and put all our things down as we frantically tried to get everything back in order. My goodness I was half a wreck. It's one thing worrying about yourself but, I had three other people to coordinate," Alex said. "We had been to the airport to Florida once before and it was not the same as with Joe. It had been relaxed before—well; pleasurable and rather exciting."

"All of a sudden, Vincent starts patting his pants pockets and checking his carry-on bag. He started ripping all of his clothes out of the bag and the look on his face was not so good. He looked like he was going to be sick. I asked him what was wrong," I said. "Vincent told us he couldn't find his passport. Now, I don't know how he could have lost his passport in that short period of time. We had just gotten through security; we hadn't even made it toward the gate yet. The TSA supervisor walked over to us curious about what was going on. He was a big, heavy guy with a sorry looking suit and skinny tie. Vincent told him he couldn't find his passport."

"Oh, my goodness—a nightmare," Jan added shaking her head slowly from side-to-side.

"The supervisor told Vincent to pull everything out of his bag again," I continued. "It was quite apparent Alex was getting upset. The supervisor asked Vincent to retrace his steps. He walked by his side as they headed toward the walk through x ray machine and conveyor belt. Alex was only a few steps behind them; her head swept the area from side-to-side searching every inch. Taking on her maternal role of due diligence she peered under the conveyor belt and looked in the plastic security bins hoping to immediately find Vincent's navy-blue colored passport."

"Actually, I thought Vincent was going to burst into tears," Alex said. "When he walked away from us with the supervisor, I forced myself not to show him how upset I was."

"I knew what Vincent must have been thinking because I was thinking the very same thing," I continued. "I thought we would have to cancel our trip – that was my first thought."

"I became so worried. Vincent had traveled abroad before in high school, and he traveled to several countries in Europe. I started thinking someone had accidentally picked up his passport or it had slipped into the machinery of the conveyor belt," Alex added. "We would never have been allowed to leave the country without it–that much we all knew. Vincent knew that as well. My poor son. I knew he was dying a thousand deaths. He's only eighteen."

"When Alex walked back toward the rest of us I thought of a solution. We could've left on our trip and had someone pick up Vincent from the airport. Clearly, that thought was not a solution to our dilemma. I could tell Vincent was growing more anxious with every minute. Alex had looked at me and I saw a single tear escape

138

and flow down her cheek. I immediately knew we had to find that passport. Her eyes became glazed over with tears. I told her not to worry–we would find Vincent's passport."

"Vincent and the supervisor walked back over to us," Alex said. "You should have seen the look on my poor baby's face, Jan. He was so upset."

"I would have been, too," Jan said. "Just imagine how he must have felt. He had to have been thinking you were going to leave him there."

"The supervisor asked Vincent to go through his bag and his pockets once again," I said. "Vincent did exactly that for about the fifth time. He was more frantic as he laid all of the contents of the canvas bag on the gray vinyl chair. Jade and Crystal stood still as they watched him–everyone did. We hoped the blue book would instantly appear and at the same time we feared Vincent had lost it. Vincent threw the disheveled pile of clothes back into his bag once again. With a look of disgust, he walked back over to the TSA staff. Helplessly, we watched him as he explained what he had done–he pulled out the white cotton lining of his pockets in his shorts; displaying his outstretched hands to the small group surrounding him."

"One of the TSA women had been watching Vincent and the supervisor. She must have been a mother too and understood Vincent's upset and began flipping methodically through each of the gray plastic trays. She sifted through the stacked pile we had checked through earlier," I said.

"Waves of worry swept over me as I watched my son in his frantic search. Suddenly, Vincent grabbed her and gave the woman a huge hug. The big bellied supervisor turned to Vincent, grasped his right hand and shook it, as he patted Vincent on the shoulder with his oversized left hand. Somehow, a bin with his passport had gotten placed in a different pile than the ones they previously searched. Vincent's face lit up like the morning sun over the horizon. Once again, we were happy travelers looking forward to our destination of 'one happy island'-Aruba!" Alex exclaimed.

Jan clapped her hands together and said, "my God that must have been horrible–right at the beginning of your trip! That poor boy-thinking you were all going to leave him alone at the airport. What a moment of dread and what a wonderful relief that must have been for all of you. You just don't think something like that can happen." With an almost breathless voice she leaned against the table and added most seriously, "especially, when you wait and prepare so long for a vacation like that."

"You know, Jan, I wasn't quite sure what in the world I was going to do if we hadn't found that passport. The possibility of any one of us not being able to go on the vacation–for whatever reason– never dawned on me. And that is unusual as I am normally a very good planner. Raising three children teaches one many things. I grew used to formulating alternative possibilities and scenarios for every situation. Generally speaking, I have multiple back-ups for everything I do as a precautionary method. I've learned that from my past. But losing a passport was not a thought that once entered my mind. I felt so helpless for my son at the time."

I spoke up. "Again; logic. I knew the passport had to be found. Our gate was the farthest from the terminal entrance. It was a brisk walk-run to get to the gate to board the plane on time. I kept looking over my shoulder making sure Alex and the kids weren't too far behind. The airport was getting busy and crowded. The last thing I wanted was for one of them to miss the plane."

Alex added, "I could barely see his head as he weaved through the crowd. At least we got to our gate just in time for our departure without any waiting. The staff boarded the handicapped people first. Then Joe in his first-class seat; then coach passengers—ahem—meaning my children and me. I felt like the steerage-third class-voyagers on the Titanic."

CHAPTER 13 – HERE COMES TROUBLE

"Good gracious those people sure were talking loud that morning. I put away my computer bag and took a seat–thinking I would look through the Sky Mall–the magazine the airlines carry. The overhead compartment doors slammed shut as people hoisted their luggage overhead. It was like a circus parading past me. Alex and the kids eventually boarded. As Alex walked by, she gave me a sideways glance. She had her right hand held in the shape of the letter 'L' on her forehead."

"That is so funny," Jan said. "She called you a loser."

"Not only that. I think she thoroughly enjoyed having my back to her as she walked to her seat halfway back on the plane so I couldn't see her. She probably made faces at me," I added with a grin.

"Truthfully, I was hoping some nasty, crying child would have sat next to you or some really chatty person," Alex said. "But, the person that ended up next to you didn't compare to my wildest imagination."

I completely discounted her sarcasm–it was not received as an insult by any means. With pleasure I responded with a chuckle "you just don't understand, woman. The important thing was simply this; all of us were finally seated on the plane and on our way to my desert paradise. I was more focused on other things–like my anxiety just before takeoff. The pilot announced the plane was at capacity but, the seat next to me was still empty and we were only five minutes away from departure time. I had begun to think I could stretch across the two seats and take a morning nap. This shadow engulfs me. I looked up from Sky Mall and this big, heavy woman wrestles herself into the seat next to me. She wore tight black stretch knit pants–I couldn't believe her seams didn't explode. She had a bright purple colored t-shirt with all kinds of sequins and rhinestones on it in the shape of a pink flamingo with scattered sea shells at the hem. She looked like a huge, purple Popsicle with two black sticks hanging from it. This woman was so big, her fleshy parts hung at least six inches from her upper arms right over my daggone armrest. I could barely open my magazine to read it."

"True; so true. I watched the whole thing from my seat. You got what you deserved. When I looked up front and saw the big lady sit down next to you, I got a good chuckle," Alex said with a slight downward tipping of her head.

They all smiled. Rob's mouth had formed the letter 'O' as he chuckled at our playful bantering. I knew some people didn't understand my line of thinking on the healthy body issue. And I would just never understand how people let themselves get so out of control with their weight. I don't feel bad about my way of thinking either.

"And, that woman was all sweaty," I said as I continued. "Her face was red from carrying all her stuff. I'm not talking about the bags she carried in her chubby fingers. I'm talking about the excess baggage she wore on her skeletal frame. I was thinking Alex put a hex on me or something. I knew the first part of the flight was only about an hour until our layover. I figured I could deal with Ms. Flamingo for that length of time, albeit in silent protest. I always have to pee several times when I fly; nerves, I guess. I got up and looked back toward Alex and the kids. They didn't see me. I had really wanted to smile at her. I was looking forward to the hour and a half layover in Charlotte before boarding the next plane to Aruba and making up to her in Charlotte."

The Cafe's waitress made her way back to our table. She stood with her slender frame poised-her shoulders down; her hands clasped behind her back. She wore a crisp, white button-down shirt underneath a black polyester vest with a silver paisley design on it. Her dark hair neatly pinned on the top of her head in a bun. "Are you ready to order?" she asked.

"No," I said in an apologetic tone. "Unfortunately, we hadn't been focusing on our menus at all."

The waitress responded, "may I make a suggestion?" All of us looked up at her and nodded. "Why don't you just order from the specials this evening? Chef has made some fabulous specialties for our guests tonight."

144

We nodded in unison to her, and she elaborately described a variety of the evenings' specials. She offered fresh grouper with a delicate dill and sour cream sauce, a pan seared center cut T-bone steak with caramelized onions, zesty shrimp marinara over angel hair pasta, and lamb chops with mint jelly. I was starved and hearing her describe the specials for the evening made my stomach growl in response. "They all sound so good," I said to the waitress as I looked at Alex, Rob, and Jan; delighted to finally order-I was getting a bit hangry. We each chose a different entree; to sample the array of chef's creations. Amazingly, the waitress didn't write one order down even though Jan must have changed her mind at least 3 or 4 times. Her red colored lips were slightly parted as she stood smiling toward each of us as we made our selection. I could barely remember two things at one time and used a pad and pen whenever I could: quite impressive. My mind is like a sieve; my short-term memory is poor at best. However, in my own defense, I possess a great memory for other things like history. I remembered the historic dates of the Civil War or the great battle at Gettysburg. And, politics-although I sometimes get myself in big trouble with that topic-depending on the crowd I'm with.

"Thank you," the waitress uttered softly. She bowed ever so slightly toward us then silently retreated around the corner.

As if reading my thoughts, Jan spoke up. "I don't know how they end up getting the order right; especially, after all the changes

145

we made. I couldn't remember half of that stuff. What am I saying here–I'm not sure I even remember what I ordered." She laughed out loud to herself shaking her head. She gently repositioned a few locks of her blonde hair from her eyes. Alex nodded in agreement. Rob shook his head and smiled. He was a good man not to take the opportunity and jab fun at his wife. I think Jan made him smile a lot–that 'blonde thing' again.

Satisfied dinner was ordered I quickly returned to my story. "Just as a bit of personal vacation history for you and Rob. Alex has only taken three vacations in twenty-five years. Two of those vacations were spent with her kids. Her most recent vacation was to a resort in the Dominican Republic to one of those all-inclusive vacations-Punte Cana. So, when I discovered Alex had not been traveling I wanted *my* vacation with her to be perfect."

Alex looked over to me with her head slightly tilted. Something was behind that look. She had always been a bit unreadable.

"And, during those twenty-five years I was focused on a home, raising my three children, and keeping a roof over our head," Alex explained. "Vacations are for people that can afford them. I could barely afford to pay our bills while they were growing up. Although, the four of us were saving spare change to go to Las Vegas when Vincent turned twenty-one. We had three more years of saving to go."

Not feeling the need to comment or lose momentum again, I chose to continue my story. There was no sense allowing her to rehash the tough job of raising three kids alone–not tonight. "Yes sir-ree-our trip would be a very special event. That morning, the flight crew started buzzing around again and before we knew it, the pilot announced the stop in Charlotte was in a few minutes. By that time, the big lady was heaving a little bit less. I guess it took that long for her body to calm down after she had been moving through the airport and plane. I was hoping 'birdy lady' wasn't going on to Aruba."

"Joe may have had an unwelcome visitor in the seat next to him," Alex injected, 'but, I did not. Vincent sat next to me. He was singing and acting up during half the flight to Charlotte. You know; I think he was a bit nervous. Jade and Crystal were across the aisle from us. The girls slept most of the flight." Alex averted her look toward the front door of the restaurant. I followed her gaze across the dining room as she said, "hey, isn't that one of those Ravens football players that just walked in?" Rob and Jan turned in their seat to look. Everyone within earshot of our table heard Alex. All eyes focused on the muscular frame entering the restaurant; the large man casually strode across the restaurant to a nearby table to join other diners.

Interestingly enough-although recognizable-none of the diners advanced toward him and we all immediately got back to our individual conversations. It was nice to see the man could dine in peace. A waitress quickly went to the table to assist him. I turned my thoughts back to Aruba and my story. "I was glad to land in Charlotte. I was cramped against the window the entire flight and thankful to stand up and stretch my legs. My lower back just kills me from sitting in those seats too long." I arched my back for a moment as the sheer memory made my body respond.

"Yeah," Rob added with a laugh toward me, "sitting in first class in those over-sized seats is just unbearably uncomfortable and rather painful for us taller people."

"Yep, first class is the only way for air travel–every chance I get."

"Joe was so wrapped up in his first class. I couldn't wait to get back on the plane," Alex said. "I wanted to get to Aruba. I would have ordered direct-flight tickets as opposed to a layover. He was trying to pinch pennies when he ordered the tickets to save fifty bucks."

"A total savings of two hundred fifty bucks might I add. That is a huge savings to me–more money to keep in my pocket." Jan stared at me. I wasn't sure she agreed with my line of logic. "The kids didn't care for the layover either and were bored and busy texting on their cell phones. I was excited to board the plane again."

"You know, I hate layovers and flight delays, too," Jan added as she tapped her pink tipped, manicured nails on the table.

148

"But I'm sure Rob would have done the same thing Joe did to save money. Quite frankly, I feel layovers are just another opportunity for the airline to lose your luggage. It happened to us twice before. We just love the beach and prefer to drive to the coast for vacation. I feel like a little girl all over again to wiggle my toes in the warm sand and soak up the sun's rays."

"Ditto Jan," Alex said as the girls high fived one another from across the table. Folding her arms across her chest, Alex turned her head toward me and added in a higher pitched voice, "oh, and don't forget to tell them about the stewardess, Aruba Joe."

All eyes stared toward me now and not just from the three of them-from the surrounding tables. I briefly wondered how long these people had been listening to our conversation. Alex must have captivated their attention and curiosity. I fought to keep my voice as normal as possible even though I was feeling a little uncomfortable talking at that point. "I wasn't sure you would want me to tell them about that part." I cleared my throat. "First class boards before coach. The stewardess's start taking drink and snack orders as soon as you board–way before they start serving in the coach seats. I always like to order plenty of tomato juice and extra vodka. Alex and the kids were seated a little closer to the first-class section this time. It was time to take off and....."

Alex interrupted me. "Rob and Jan, I will set the scene for you. On take-off, the stewardess's sit in front of the plane just behind the pilot's cabin; facing the first-class passengers. One of the stewardess's was sitting off to the left of the cabin door. There was Joe–facing the stewardess. He was looking up the skirt of one of the freakin' stewardesses. Let me tell you; she noticed it too. She had her legs spread apart as wide as the Grand Canyon. I was watching the whole thing–I am sure others were, too. I was so pissed. Not only was my man living large in first class without us; that was the first insult of the day but, here sits this harlot in front of him displaying her who-ha for him to gawk at and, of course, stare he did. The airline sure knows how to entertain their first-class passengers."

Alex had gotten a wee bit louder with her comment about the stewardess. Must have been the wine. I knew it was time to do a quick change up from the stewardess and move on. "Anyway, just four hours and twenty minutes after the crotch shot, our plane was descending on Aruba. I'll say-the airline does an exceptional job." Alex stated her piece of mind-I stated mine. Must have come from growing up with too many females.

"I just love looking out the window of the plane, looking at the blue green waters and small whitecaps in the Caribbean. I never tire of looking for that island–or seeing the airport–as we descend. I felt the gear go down and our landing went smooth as glass. The captain barely flipped the fasten seatbelt light off. The entire plane broke out in applause and laughter. People began crowding the aisle

150

and the luggage compartment doors flew open. I was the first one off the plane and waited for my baby to join me inside the terminal. Alex and the kids were smiling as they met up with me. Those smiles were a good sign. I gave her a quick kiss and led the way to the baggage claim area-glad our group was reunited once again."

"I guided everyone through the Aruban customs. A large picture of Queen Beatrix of the Netherlands hangs on the wall in the airport. The kids showed their passports to the customs agent like world travelers. By the time we reached the baggage claim area, the conveyor belt had already begun unloading the plane's luggage. We were right on time. There was nothing but sun and blue sky greeting us. Our much-awaited destination–just under 1,900 miles from home-was now our reality. I added: "you may not know this but, Aruba is in the same time zone as the east coast. During our daylight savings time in the fall, you must be cognizant of the hour time difference. I didn't want to waste too much time. I wanted to take advantage of the daylight and show them some of the island's sights."

"I can't recall how many times I have been in that airport over the years. It has changed dramatically from my first visit to Aruba. The airport has transformed from a shack to a more commercialized airport including shops and restaurants. I had rented a Jeep Sahara with a rag top for this trip."

"Doesn't your oldest daughter, Crystal, have a Jeep?" Jan asked Alex.

"Crystal has a Wrangler. A canary yellow one with a black top she named 'Felix'. She had told Joe she wanted to do some off-roading while we were in Aruba. Joe; always trying to please everyone. Joe had told Crystal some parts of the beach were perfect for off-road trips. We all looked forward to seeing the sights from the Jeep."

I was the son of a dentist. Even though Alex never wore braces, her teeth were as straight as if she had worn them. "Customs was a breeze. Since we were one of the first passengers to arrive, we got through the short line in no time flat. I guided the group quickly to the front of the airport. Just across the street there is a row of shops housing all the major rental car companies. The company I rent from is a minute or two drive from the airport entrance. As always-the white van sat along the curb. I have used the same company for fifteen years and the same guy picks me up. They had never let me down; always on time."

"The driver greeted us with a loud 'bon tardes'; extending his right hand toward me and grabbed one of our bags with the other. Always courteous those Arubans. The Arubans are a friendly people, too. They speak a form of Spanish called 'Papiamento'. It's a blend of several languages–the native tongue if you will-even though the official language is Dutch since Aruba is a Dutch owned island. The air temperature had to have been over 95 degrees at four o'clock in the afternoon. The air-conditioned van felt heavenly."

"Most of the time, the Aruban crosswinds hail at fifteen to twenty miles an hour. The winds start before noontime. The weather is very much like it is here in the summertime; without the humidity for the most part."

"I was worried about the trade winds," Alex added. "I can't breathe very well when it's windy. Crystal has the same issue. Must be genetic. I had heard about them and was a bit wary but, it's different there."

"We got out of the van and the driver unloaded our luggage on the curb. Crystal accompanied me while Alex, Vincent, and Jade waited in the parking lot with the luggage. There really wasn't much room inside of that small office. Otherwise, I would have suggested that everyone join us. The white, cinder block building was moderately air conditioned. Here in the States, air conditioning is cranked up in the summertime forcing people to wear light jackets and sweaters in public buildings."

"Like the shopping malls," Jan said raising her palms upward toward the ceiling in a rather dramatic fashion. "I always have to take a sweater when I shop in the summertime. I even brought a sweater with me tonight because I never know if the restaurant will have their air conditioning turned down."

"I agree, Jan. It was hot standing outside. We were so thirsty," Alex said. "Thankfully, we didn't have too long of a wait. Crystal came out first holding a set of keys and shaking them at us. Her hair is shorter than the last time you saw her. It's now shoulder length and her blonde hair was blowing in the warm breeze. She looked tropical-like in her short denim skirt and white sunglasses. We were ready to explore Aruba. Joe was kind enough to let her drive-with him as co-pilot, of course."

"Alex got a kick out of the license tag. The tags are a canary yellow color and have '*One Happy Island*' printed on them in black lettering. That's my Aruba-one happy island for sure. First, I wanted to pick up some groceries. There is a big super store near the airport–like our big retail stores. The local Aruban's shop there. I have a membership card. We got inside and walked toward the center of the store. I asked Alex what she wanted and didn't hear anything. I looked behind me and she was gone. I had no idea where everyone went so quickly. I picked up some essentials; milk, coffee, a bundt cake, and some bananas. I even remembered to pick up whipped cream; Alex loves whipped cream in her morning coffee."

"I went searching for them. As I turned around the last aisle, the sound of metal and glass clanging together was loud as we literally collided our carts. Luckily, nothing broke. I couldn't believe all the alcohol they piled into their cart. Oh my word! Their focus was not on staples. They had loaded up their cart with wines, tequila, and fruity alcoholic drinks. Crystal picked up some beer. She said she '…liked the cute little green bottles.' Vincent found the high caffeine drinks and Jaeggermeiffster."

"What's wrong with that?" Alex asked. "After all Joe, I don't know what you expected. We were on vacation to party in Aruba. I really had to laugh when we hit Joe's cart. Here's Joe with his milk and bundt cake and can of whipping cream in his while ours overflowed with alcohol."

"Yep. It was a good thing you got the basics, Joe. It kept all of you from looking like complete alcoholics," Rob said jokingly.

A flash-back in time occurred through my mind. Thirty years ago, when I met Alex, I had been the straight and narrow one of my friends. I was the serious one. Alex was the party girl. "You know the nuts don't fall far from the tree. Alex's offspring are so much like their mother. Oh, I knew we were in for a rather interesting week. The drinking and gambling age is eighteen in Aruba–it certainly wasn't my place to say anything-the kids were of legal age there."

"It was blatantly apparent the children and I had different expectations for the week ahead. Well, at least we had something to eat for the next morning to sober up–little did I realize but, we were going to need it on our trip," Alex added. "Joe said he only kept a minimum of supplies for the renters and his family in the kitchen cabinets. We continued at warp speed through the store until we hit the checkout. I wanted a quick exit from the store–we were in the home stretch. The lines were five to ten people long at every register. We waited for more than a half hour just to get to the conveyor belt. Then, the daggone card reader wouldn't accept Joe's credit card. The girl at the register pushed a button on the side of the machine–a red, flashing light rotated at the top on the metal pole overhead. The people in Aruba only know one form of movement–slow."

"Another fifteen minutes later and we were mobile once again. The sun was high in the sky and all I wanted to do was get to my house. The parking lot was crowded–packed with people and cars. Alex and the kids piled all the alcohol on top of the luggage–then stacked the rest of the alcohol in the back seat and on every available space on the floor and their laps. You know, I think there was more alcohol than luggage in that Jeep. Nothing mattered other than I was in my beloved Aruba. I adapt well when I vacation there. I wake up when the sun shines in my bedroom window and go to bed when I feel tired."

"My family has a long-standing tradition every evening. We sit on the balcony or by the pool sampling wines and eating fruits and cheeses-watching the sunset until the afterglow lingers over the ocean. The sunset is so beautiful in Aruba. It's different than the sunsets here–they don't have the air pollution particles to offset the colors. The sky is more subtle; not as red and orange as it is here.

157

Yes, sir; we had plenty of good times ahead of us. We were there for ten wonderful days of relaxation and sun. Pulling out of the parking lot of the grocery store we headed north along the coastline. I love the familiar smell of the Caribbean Ocean. It was cleaner-much different than Ocean City. I wanted to show them the homes on the way to the house—where the Aruban people lived. By the design of the houses, they could see we were far away from our native, rural country surroundings."

"Actually," Alex began, "I admit I had mixed feelings about going to Aruba with the girls. You know," she added in a bit of a low tone; the Holloway murder. When Joe first came up with the idea for the vacation, I was a bit nervous to take the girls there. Ironically, I had long thought about Aruba as this beautiful island tucked away near the equator and had fantasized about going to vacation-way before I even met Joe."

"You know, I had the same thoughts about the murder when you told me you were going there with the kids. I didn't want to make you worried. You were so excited about going to Aruba," Jan responded. 'And, you know, I always worry."

"If I may continue, ladies." Women: they were always drifting off to another topic and manage to do it so quickly. "We had a thirty-minute ride to Tierra Del Sol. That's where my house is. It's a gated, golf course community. I don't know if you've ever heard of it-a fantastic place. It has its own clubhouse, spa and fitness

158

center, and restaurant. I enjoy the baked red snapper there. It has got to be the best I've ever tasted." As an after-thought I added, "the clubhouse offers the fish dinner like nowhere else on the island. For that matter, nowhere else I've ever dined."

"As we drove closer to the house, we had an opportunity to view the local housing. Alex and her kids couldn't get over the colorful homes, which are typical in the Caribbean. The homes are a rainbow of painted tropical colored concrete in hues of yellow, green, and red. The islanders paint their homes like the vibrant colored tropical fish in the local waters. As we rode through the city streets of Oranjestad, one neighborhood was filled with wild dogs–slowly walking alongside the road.

"Wait a minute," Jan said, "I think I've heard of that city before. Isn't Oranjestad the capital of Aruba? "

"You know your geography, Jan. Very good. The island is about twenty miles long and six miles wide; about the size of Washington, D.C. Alex and her kids were in awe of the sights as we traveled through the side streets-Aruba Joe commandeered the Jeep for them. The residential homes are close together. The high-rise hotels line the mid-western part of the island. Evenings on the island are just as beautiful as the daytime scenery. At the very north end-the California Lighthouse and huge sonar-are functional. They are a part of my back yard view. At night, the stars appear so bright against the black, darkened back drop. And they feel so close to you."

"You have to drive carefully in Aruba. They have highway signs; just like here. The roads are shared with people on four-wheelers and bicycles. Tourists and residents ride around the island on everything imaginable; lots of alternatives to cars. My God, there are people on Segways on the streets. I bet the inventor of those Segways made a bundle from those machines. I think he is a Brit. The gas isn't cheap there either. Electricity and water costs about three times as much as it does in the US. The water process is done by reverse osmosis-right from the ocean. Everything must be imported to Aruba so even gas is twice the amount you pay here."

"Another word about those dogs; there are a lot of dogs alongside the road. I thought the dogs were like Australian dingos except the island dogs don't seem to have as long of a coat. They are just as restless and aloof, and some appear quite content lying in the dirt around the houses in neighborhoods. Those dogs were everywhere-no collars–scruffy, short-haired mongrels," Alex said. "I almost felt a bit intimidated when I saw them in packs traveling in the streets-they didn't bother anybody. When we came to a four-way intersection a little rinky-dink police station was on the corner. They built a large painted black and white sign to display the auto deaths for the past year versus the current year. Judging from the

160

dents on most of the cars down there I don't think people drive very well in Aruba."

"Sounds like a clever way to advertise a problem. Post it on a sign for the entire world to see. Sounds like a lot of drinking going on down there in the Caribbean, huh Joe?" Rob said jokingly.

"Some of the hotels are 'all-inclusives.' They offer food, drinks, and hotel accommodations for one price-very cheap. Now, I can assure you some of those people get 'overserved' while they are in Aruba. We typically drink our fair share of wine in the evenings and at dinner. But I wouldn't categorize myself as a really big drinker, even while on vacation. I go to Aruba to relax, do some gardening, and read a novel by the pool."

"I figured we would bypass the high-rise hotels and condos. Local businesses and multi-colored shopping centers decorate the streets. There are plenty of jewelry and clothing stores and small retail shopping centers–just like in the states-if you like that sort of thing. Plenty of 'tourist traps' I call them. Once we reached the northern end of the island, the remainder of the trip was along the coastline. The view of the ocean is breathtaking; the side of the island that faces Venezuela. Venezuela's about nineteen miles south of Aruba from that point. There is not much of a surf on that side. It is a pretty beach with fine, white sand. The ocean water is a monochromatic spectrum of contrasting green hues. There is something about breathing in the warm, salty air in Aruba that exhilarates me. I never tire of that smell no dead crustacean smells. The cooler early evening temperatures provide some respite from the heat of the summer day." As I spoke, I mentally envisioned the ride in the Jeep. Alex had been in awe of the landscape and waters– I was in awe of her presence. "We watched the evening sail boats as we drove past a picturesque view to all that ventured nearby. There is every kind of water sport you can imagine; sailing, snorkeling, diving, fishing, and swimming, of course."

"It sounds beautiful," Rob said. He had his head rested on the palm of his right hand. He was experiencing our vacation vicariously through my tale. Yep; I was a pretty good story teller. "On our vacations we can't quite depend on the weather but, we just love the beach."

"Maybe we'll have to change our plans one year, Rob and join Alex and Joe in Aruba," Jan said.

"Oh, we would love that Joe, wouldn't we?" Alex exclaimed as she nudged my arm.

"Just let us know when you want to go, and we'll do it. I love taking people there. I took some of my realtor friends earlier in the spring and they had the time of their lives. We finally arrived at Tierra Del Sol. The attendants showed their usual smiling faces and waved to us as we drove through the front gate of the community. They have two entry attendants on duty all the time. The entrance is a palm tree-lined street with a little hut and a security gate. They keep it open during the daytime. At night, a striped red and white colored bar is lowered across the roadway on both sides of the hut. No one can get in or out without checking with the attendants."

"Vincent was the first to notice the iguanas resting on the tops of the high, cinder-blocked walls along the entrance. It's hard to get close to them; they scurry away from you so fast. The iguanas have carte blanche and can be found all over the island and the golf course. The first time I played golf there, I was amazed by how many of the green iguanas sunned on the stone walls and golf course greens. Some of them are three and a half feet long."

"Yuck," Jan said. "I would not want lizards squirming around me. It just gives me goose bumps thinking about wild, slimy lizards running all over the place."

"You watch too many movies, Jan. They don't bother anyone," Alex responded reacting to Jan's screwed up expression. "They are quite content to stay away from people just as you want to stay away from them. And, slimy-they certainly are not. They are scaly–yes–but, dry to the touch."

"Well, just the same-I will not get close to any lizards or even snakes for that matter," Jan said.

"Tierra Del Sol is one of Aruba's golf resorts. It's located on the 'norde' or north side of the island. It is a highly acclaimed and has a unique cluster of multi-million-dollar homes. The properties are owned by people from various parts of the world. Some of the local wealthy Arubans live there a nice blend of rentals, vacation homes, and condos. A significant amount of the homes are owned by US citizens. There is another nine-hole golf course on the island, too."

"Wow," Rob responded. "I didn't know Aruba was that popular with Americans. I always considered Aruba to be more of a European destination."

"Surely there is a large number of European travelers, too," I responded. "Aruba is second only to Hawaii as the most sought-after travel destination in the world. The island's location is westward enough to avoid hurricane activity in the Caribbean. I think that makes all the difference to most travelers when they are making vacation plans-you *never* and I mean *NEVER* have to worry about bad weather in Aruba. Well, at least I used to think that about Aruba-more about that later."

"As a matter of fact, there is still a lot of construction going on in the community. A new phase is being built right behind my house. And one can only work in Aruba if you are either a citizen or from Holland. Terra cotta roofs, concrete, and cinder block construction dominate the landscape of the sprawling multi-acre community resort."

"It's a lot different from where we live-it's a wonder anything can grow down there," Jan said, "I mean since it's a desert."

"The entire island grows desert cactus. The island's unique and infamous natural Divi trees are scattered throughout the island. The Divi trees plumage of branches and trunks are bent horizontal and downward. The horizontal growth is due to the constant trade winds traveling across the island. These trees are living monuments. The Arubans use wood or metal poles to hold up heavy branches that would otherwise break off-they have a respect for their native trees. Tropical plants and palm trees are professionally planted and landscaped. Otherwise, they would not survive. Most people have rock gardens for both their beauty and easy care. Aloe is grown on the island. You can visit the manufacturer of aloe products and buy them."

"I guess they don't have much grass," Rob said. "I love cutting the grass and keeping it green."

"Natural growth of any vegetation is relatively sparse. The island averages seventeen to twenty inches of annual rainfall as well as an 85-degree temperature. The constant trade winds keep the insect population down, too. The winds are a welcome relief from the tropical temperatures. I'm thinking they were a good fifteen to twenty miles per hour with temperatures hovering in the high nineties during our visit. It is no wonder the warm, year-round weather combined with its tropical location of the island is a primary vacation spot. We reached our destination-pulling the Jeep into the red brick driveway, I announced–'bon bini.' That means 'welcome' in Aruba. Before I could say anything more, before I had put the car in park, the kids got out of that Jeep faster than Grant going through Richmond. I left the luggage in the Jeep and unlocked the front door. Crystal took a quick tour of every single room in that house. She had the layout of the house down in minutes. She knew where each bathroom, bedroom, and doorway led. Before I could get any of the bags out of the car and into our bedroom, Alex and the kids went out back admiring the view, the pool, and the ocean."

"It all sounds so wonderful. I'd love to be able to view the ocean from the back of our house," Jan said.

"Jan and Rob, every time I go to the house, the smells of the ocean, the salt air and the overall smell of the house just makes me feel so good. It just feels like home to me. While they got acclimated to the house, I carried the rest of the baggage into the house; not to mention the ton of alcohol. They had a lot to take in. The sun was just beginning to go down. Sunset in Aruba is around 6:30 year-round since the island's proximity is closer to the equator."

"The house is magnificent. Palm trees grow in the rock gardens on either side of the back of the house. Birds of Paradise grow along the outside back wall of our bedroom. Joe even has a metal fountain in the shape of five dolphins riding a crested wave at one end of the pool," Alex added. "They named their home 'Desert Dolphin' after the metal fountain. Joe has all the amenities of an upscale home-comfortable, too. The kitchen has a gorgeous black granite countertop with sparkling flecks of gold. Ceramic tile is throughout the whole house. He's decorated it with nice, comfortable furniture. He did well with the color scheme; shades of teal, brown, and a touch of rust."

"All of the homes in the Caribbean have tiled flooring. Different woods from all over the world are used in the construction of the houses and they are primarily constructed from concrete block. The view from the back yard is comprised of some clay and multi-colored dirt hills leading to the lighthouse and the sonar tower. Part of the community golf course is just before the hill. Much of the hills are sporadically covered with dense, thorny bushes and cactus. Dingos and iguanas are not the only creatures roaming the island. Herds of wild goats graze on the hills. You can see them as you golf. It sure was a great feeling to be back in Aruba-peaceful. Every time I go there, I am in my second home; my second country. Not a vacation home if you know what I mean. I'm comfortable there. Instead of slipping into my bedroom slippers back home, I step into a pair of canvas sandals. Nice; really nice."

"And, you were down there for the Fourth of July," Jan said. "That must've felt a bit strange–not seeing any fireworks."

"Quite the contrary, my dear. We were especially excited about spending Independence Day in Aruba. Since there are so many Americans visiting, they set off a huge display of fireworks downtown. You can see them from all over the island."

"Wait a minute," Jan said. "Didn't you say Vincent just traveled to Europe for a couple of weeks?"

"Yes," Alex responded. "He went with his German class to Germany, Switzerland, and Austria. He sure has gotten a taste of the world this year. Not to mention, he just graduated and turned eighteen in June. Talk about exciting; that young man has had an interesting life lately."

"All of us had an exciting time," I said. "The Caribbean Island is a lot less crowded in July and most of the summer–it is known as the off-season, you know."

"Overlooking the ocean every day is so relaxing, isn't it?" Rob said. "Jan and I enjoy going to the beach, too. One week each year it's our little bit of heaven on earth. Aruba sounds like my kind of place. Yes, I think we're going to have to visit Aruba, honey." He looked at Jan and she nodded in agreement. "We haven't been on that kind of vacation since our honeymoon!"

"Oh Rob," Jan said with a sigh as she rested her chin in her palmed hands. "Go on Joe. Tell your story. I like hearing you talk. You certainly can tell Aruba was the perfect place for you to take Alex and the kids. It's so special to share a favorite place with ones you enjoy being with. You know, Rob, Alex celebrated her birthday in Aruba. She turned fifty-two while they were there."

Jan had this knowing, animated look on her face. You could tell Alex had previously given her some of the details about her birthday in Aruba. She was anxious to hear more and there sure was a lot more to say. "I'll get to her birthday, in due time, you two. That was a night we will never forget. Rob, we must keep these girls focused."

Rob grinned at me and shook his head. "Not a chance, Joe, not a chance."

"Sssshhh," Alex responded as she looked toward Jan. "Joe's right. He'll get to that part-oh my God. Oh, what a day and night that was. He has a lot to tell you, don't you Aruba Joe?"

Alex was learning. I didn't need much encouragement to return to the spotlight. I was beginning to feel quite at ease–the wine was having its usual mellowing effect on me–and I *was* anxious to continue. "Our first night in Aruba was absolute Caribbean bliss. We had a great dinner on the patio. The girls made penne pasta with shrimp. I corked a bottle of red wine; I think it was a Venezuelan Syrah. Venezuela has wonderful wines much like South America. The evening was perfect. We sat under a couple of ceiling fans on the back patio–they keep the air circulating and the bugs away. The Aruban sunset was the backdrop to our scenic view. There are a variety of wild birds that help keep the bug population to a minimum. The lizards do a fine job of that, too. Three beautiful green parrots pass right over the house throughout the day. Alex loved their synchronized, high-pitched chatter as they flew over the back of the house. I never understood why they fly as a trio but, they have done that since we first moved into the house."

"My God, Joe," Rob said. "I think you've just described paradise."

"It certainly is paradise, but some of us added a bit of reckless excitement while we were there," Alex said with a sideways glance toward me.

"I have a decent view of the ocean and Alex's kids thoroughly enjoyed taking a late evening swim in the pool after dinner. We went to bed early that first night–a bit tired from being up so late packing the night before and getting up early the next morning. Not to mention all the excitement from that stewardess in first class." I peeked over at Alex–she pretended like she didn't hear me.

"Our first morning in Aruba was fabulous. For whatever reason and no matter who I vacation with, I am always the first one up. I let Alex rest while I did some gardening. The Bird of Paradise underneath my bedroom window sure needed a lot of attention and pruning. The bushes were so dry. One-by-one, everyone gradually started waking up and came out on the patio. I had been up a whole two hours before Alex came out with her morning coffee; whipped cream on top. Alex has told me its 'little things' that hold true value in her heart."

Alex said softly as she looked at me and said, "Joe, you have a piece of my heart."

Now, that was nice to hear. I had begun to think I had lost everything; everything I had wanted most of my adult life. I had worried all week; was this dinner the last meal we would share?

Alex continued, "Jade came out with a Smirnoff Ice in her hand and a big smile on her face and said, 'whoa, we are in Aruba! Mom, I just took the longest poop. Kinda scared me–it wrapped around the inside of the toilet like a foot and a half long snake.' I took that to mean she was relaxing-in Jades' way and was happy girl. You don't have the stress level on the island that you do back home or maybe it's the proximity to the equator. I know I felt different inside. Her digestive tract was calm–Jade has a serious problem with constipation. Perhaps that is a bit of T – M – I – too much information about my daughter's digestive problems. Crystal wasn't far behind Jade. She came out in one of her wildly printed string bikinis and jumped right into the pool. The girls were delighted to be able to swim in the morning. That was something they hadn't been able to do in years. When the children were younger, we had a pool in the back yard. Sometimes, they were in it before breakfast and even as late as two o'clock in the morning."

"I never had a pool," Jan said somewhat sadly. "My mother was afraid we'd drown."

171

"You are so much like your mother, Jan,' Rob said with a kind face toward his beloved. "Such a worrier about all things and all people."

"I can understand that. Moms are always looking out for their children. I can't say I wasn't worried when they were younger. I laid out strict rules for friends and times they could swim. Especially, while I was at work in the summer. Personally, I enjoyed lying by the poolside in Aruba with my book and my coffee. Every chance I could I took off my bathing suit top–wanting to get as much of an all-over tan as I could. Joe just shook his head at me. Our first full day in Aruba, and where was Joe? Inside–totally engaged in his computer and the internet functions. That man cannot leave his electronic gadgets alone. You'd think they were one of his appendages. He's so excited to answer the phone, play games on it, or check his e-mails. At home, he holds on to the remote the whole time he watches tv and his cell phone is not far away from the other hand. I spent the rest of the day listening to one of the local radio stations. The children went somewhere in the car."

"Remember, my sweet, I had already been outside doing yard work a couple of hours by the time you all woke up. I needed relief from the sun. Let me clarify something here." I didn't want these people to come to any more wrong conclusions about me–as if they hadn't already after listening to some of Alex's comments. "I had purchased a camera security system on my last trip in the spring and installed it at each entranceway. At some point, it had just stopped transmitting. I had the system set up so every time someone walked through one of the exterior doors, the images were sent directly to my computer. When I had a break-in after the house was built, they had damaged the teakwood front door. I never could get the door fixed right after that. They stole every television in the house. That morning, I eventually found my transmission problem; the IP addresses in the Caribbean constantly changed. That's why my transmissions back home had been out-of-whack."

"Are there problems with break-ins down there? I hope they don't have the type of crime issues we have here in the States," Rob said. Then he added, "I thought you said it was 'one happy island'?"

"Initially, we did have a problem during the construction with some break-ins in the community. Whoever did the break-ins just took televisions and computers but, that was a couple of years ago. Now, the community has a lot more people living and staying there regularly. The neighboring homeowners are quite good at keeping a watch out for one another. Plus, they have the security gate at the entrance to the community. Staffing it was no problem. Getting the management staff to properly vet the security people is a work-in-progress. I haven't had any more problems, thank goodness. I just thought the security system was a good idea. An ounce of intervention if you will. I finished working on the problems with the computer. Never could get the daggone camera apparatus to work right.   I tried everything from every angle possible. Rather than allow the computer to get the best of me, I finally decided it was time to take a break."

"Hmmm," Jan mused as she gently swept the hanging light-colored hair off her forehead. "I think the saying is 'an ounce of prevention', Joe."

"I think you are right, but in this particular case it was 'intervention'. The Aruban polis want Americans to visit. They will do everything they can to get involved when crime is on the island and find a quick resolution. The last thing they want is bad, international press. They've had ample bad press you know. They depend on tourism. At first, I thought my main issue was with the wireless connection but, the salt air down there had corroded the outside cable box and the wires just crumbled in my fingers. Another thing to put on my to-do list down there. Seems we must replace the box cover every year or two. Oh, the complexities of home ownership; always a new lesson to learn about a house and its quirky particulars."

"I remember Alex talking about family time-shares in Aruba," Jan said.

"My family has owned time shares in Aruba for decades. My mother found a time share in Aruba with a friend and simply fell in love with the island. It was very different then. It had really strong trade winds, had only a few high-rise hotels, and a lot less vacationers on the island."

"That's odd," Jan said. "What made the winds change?"

"Ahhhh, the trade winds are now bumping into the high rises and buildings that were added over the years. They act like a buffer if you will. I remember my mom telling us a story when she returned from her very first trip. It was in November. It was cold here when she left. As she and her friend were getting ready to go out to dinner, they could hear the winds whipping against the outside of the mid-rise hotel they stayed in. They decided to put on their winter jackets. They went down the elevator-the Riu was only a couple of floors then-walked into the lobby and began walking across it. Well...they realized everyone was in shorts and dresses and short-sleeved shirts. It was ARUBA! Boy, did they get a laugh."

"Too funny," Jan said.

"But this was the first house my family owned on the island. Owning a vacation home has a lot more responsibility than a time-share. The interior care is minimal as opposed to the exterior care although some maintenance can be costly. Painting and scraping are required annually. Once I got the computer cable issue resolved I was back on-line and functioning. I checked my real estate calls, answered my emails, and got back outside. The kids were taking turns and emailing their friends. They were just as anxious as I was to connect to the rest of the world. Alex, on the other hand, could do without the computer. She's on the phone and computer constantly at work. My baby needed a break."

Rob said, "I can appreciate that. Computers have taken over my workday as well. I cannot wait to disconnect at the end of the day. I never take my computer when we go on vacation. I don't want a job that depends on me that way. Heck; I've given them plenty of my time. As far as anyone calling me, they can wait until I get back to work."

"I know what you are saying there, Rob. Service on your cell phone is always an issue down there. The phone kept dropping our calls. The roaming fees are outrageous, and I found it's wise to keep your phone in airplane mode at all times and make sure your location is turned off. Trust me; I found that out last week when I received my first phone bill," Alex added.

"We have a phone signal tower just behind the house. I never could understand why she kept dropping her calls. I wasn't having any problems at all. I guess it was just one of those carrier issues or maybe her type of phone."

"I just had to come to the realization, the trip to Aruba had some unique inconveniences and caveats to it; like first-class tickets for the privileged, low-life stewardesses, and dropped calls," Alex said.

CHAPTER 15 – ARUBA DAYS

"Everyone fell into their own daily routine while we were there," I said. "We did our thing. After sleeping in til noon, Vincent went to the clubhouse gym for his workout. Crystal and Jade laid out on the upper deck; sipping coffee with a healthy splash of Amaretto or some other liquor added to it. They had no problem adjusting. That is a vacation."

"Girls just want to have fun!" Jan added. "Can't blame them for that. Hell, when we were their age, we were doing the same thing."

We all laughed a bit as our own private thoughts flashed through our minds. "Since the computer and camera were uncooperative, I decided it was time for me to use my efforts elsewhere. I went outside through the garage door. The house has an oversized two car garage. I figured I might as well remove the Jeep's soft top-do something more productive than fooling with the security system. Well, let me tell you something about taking a soft-top off of a Jeep. I've watched Crystal take off her soft top on her Jeep many a time. However, my experience with our rented vehicle proved to be another ordeal. I pulled and tugged on that thing, and it just did not want to cooperate. Admittedly, I've never removed the canvas top from a Jeep-I didn't think it could be too challenging. Crystal is just a little bitty girl and she doesn't have any problems.

She climbs all around the Jeep like a little monkey pulling the clamps and folding up the top. I figured if it took her twenty minutes, I certainly could get the job done in half the time."

"I had decided to get out of the sun for a bit," Alex said. "I began washing the breakfast dishes in the kitchen and looked out the window. That was a sight to behold. Joe was extremely aggravated–I could hear the expletives one after another. He'd shake his head, stand with his arms folded, and return-pulling on the canvas top of the Sahara–he was so dramatic! When he gets mad, everyone better look out. At one point, he had his hands on his hips- just standing there looking at the Jeep–looking defeated. Joe was not having a very good morning. He should have stuck with gardening. He does such a wonderful job making the yard look picturesque. I went upstairs to get Crystal and told her Joe needed help. Crystal rolled her eyes, shook her head, and went to help Joe."

"Crystal came out and offered her help-she shook her blonde locks and got right to it. We struggled with the black soft canvas top of the Sahara. Crystal told me Alex had been watching me from the window and that it appeared the jeep was winning the battle."

"Crystal stands about a foot shorter than Joe. She buzzed around Joe in her yellow, Bill-a-Bong bikini like a little bumble bee. I had given her a screwdriver to prod the clamps apart–they were a bit corroded. Crystal pried off the clamps and removed the canvas top; didn't miss one," Alex added.

"Yeah," I said, "and every time she opened one of the clamps, the darned plastic supports broke into pieces. The roof literally came apart in our hands. Vincent and Jade joined in to help us. By the time we were finished, we had a plastic and canvas pile of rubble lying in the driveway. The intense sun does a lot of damage to rubber and plastic. The salty, dry air wears everything out-not just cable wires. I had absolutely no clue how we were going to put the roof top back together. I figured we would worry about it later. After all, we had more than a week to figure it out. We moved the remnants of the top into the garage. Not that rain is an issue. Even if it rained, the Jeep interior is water resistant and doesn't get damaged. While the kids finished carrying the fragmented pieces of the rooftop into the garage, something in me decided I needed to start the Jeep. I hopped in and turned the key. The Jeep wouldn't start. I tell you, that Jeep was getting on my last nerve. I tried multiple times. There was no sound—the engine wasn't turning over—not even a click. I thought the battery was dead. While I was sitting in the drivers' seat, Jade leaned in, pulled the hood latch, and looked under the hood. She bent over the front end of the Jeep, checking all the wiring and the cables. She checked the battery and hoses. Then, Jade came over to the driver side again and told me to get out. I gladly got out of the Jeep, partly because of all the frustration I had over the past hour and partly because I didn't know what else to do to make the dang thing start. Besides, I figured a

179

twenty-year-old needed to learn a valuable lesson. I don't know why she thought she could get the Jeep to start when I couldn't. We had a second set of keys–Alex had given them to her. Jade started the Jeep right up. She looked at me and started laughing. At that point in time, I had just about enough of that stupid Sahara and threw the screwdriver down. It bounced all over the driveway resting in the rock bed."

"Now, there was some consolation to the whole fiasco. We may have ended up with this pile of rubbish inside the garage but, the jeep was fully topless. That's what you had wanted and that's how it ended up. By golly, no task is unattainable for Aruba Joe," Alex said as she patted my shoulder. "You went off to the back of the house sulking. I thought of it as a bonding experience between you and my children. The children and I were excited and couldn't wait to tour the island in the Sahara."

"I was fed up with experiences. Besides, I had a couple of errands to run. I wanted to pick up some light bulbs and a few other things at the hardware store." Turning to Rob and Jan I added, "they wanted to swim and sunbathe by the pool before we did any sight-seeing. It was at least noon, and the temperature was about 95 degrees with trade winds of fifteen miles an hour - another great day in Aruba."

"How far is the beach from your house?" Rob asked. "It couldn't be too far if you could see the ocean from your patio. What am I saying; the beach can't be too far from anywhere on that little island."

"It's about fifteen minutes from the house if you walk to the beach. We usually like to drive to the high-rises though and lay out on the beaches there. It's just a few minutes' drive. There are some nice beach areas in front of the hotels. My mom still owns a time share at one of them. At one time, it was a quaint gorgeous low-rise Caribbean hotel. They did extensive renovations, and it now is one of the largest hotels on the beach. Over the years, we accumulated a magnitude of wrist bands from the hotel so we're able to park our car in the garage and visit the pool area. You can't get on the property and use any of their facilities without them. There is also a pier on the far-right side of the hotel with a nice bar that serves halfway decent food. It's called the Boogalu. You can't miss it. A divi stump under a huge wooden iguana appears as mascot to the entrance of the bar-greeting visitors. I had promised Alex I would be back in an hour and to be ready to go to the rough side of the island for some off-roading in the Jeep. I gave her a kiss and drove toward Oranjestad. I shop at a little hardware store about twenty minutes from the house. After my succession of challenges at the house, I was beginning to feel back in control of myself."

"What do you mean, 'the rough side'?" Jan asked as she cocked her head to the side. You could tell by her expression; she thought I meant it was a dangerous area and was quite sure she was referring to the incident of Natalie Halloway. The college girl had disappeared after a night in a local bar; she was also considered murdered by a local resident. Aruba sure had its share of negative media attention from all over the world after that incident. The media pummeled the island daily with negative press-demanding the police to locate and release the perpetrator. Like a large cat on the hunt, the press was thirsty for blood and a carcass. It was certainly a traumatic situation for the family, the US, and for everyone in Aruba. The island is dependent on tourism-the people of the island need their jobs. Not just the US, other countries had also changed their travel plans going to other destinations. Aruba felt the rapid decline in their purse strings.

"No, it's not what you are thinking," I said. "The rough side is the Atlantic side of the island. The waves are about five to six foot high and crash onto the coral and lava rocks-unlike the side facing Venezuela-the hotel and time share side-where the waves are more like that of rippling water along the shoreline of a big lake. I wanted everyone to see the California lighthouse, too; another island landmark even though it is quite visible from the back of my house. History tells the tale of how the lighthouse was named after a ship known as the S.S. California. The ship had gone down off the coast in September of 1891-passengers were busy partying as the ship met its demise. Much of the ships luggage and trunks were consumed by the rough waters-their contents to be salvaged by the island locals

182

and thought to have been sold in Oranjestad. A huge sonar sits atop a metal structure to the east of the lighthouse to detect any foreign boats coming toward shore. The islanders tell me drug runners and the illegal transport of prostitutes have been known to enter the island from that area. It is quite a scenic location for vacationers during the day. The lighthouse radiates its bright beacon of light by night. Visitors and locals drive there each night to take in the nightscape of the island-over miles of darkness-tiny sparkling lights dot the view. It can be a bit of a spooky view on moonless nights as car headlights drift through the darkness until they reach their destination. You can see them both-the lighthouse and the sonar tower from my back yard."

"Amazing stuff," Rob said. "Vacationing can be so enlightening. I bet there is much to learn there–I mean how those people lived and survive on such a small piece of land."

"So, it's getting late in the afternoon and no sign of Joe. We waited and had coolers and towels ready to go. Joe got back around three o'clock," Alex said with exaggerated distress. "By that time, we had been swimming and drinking wine coolers to keep cool. The sun got so intense, and it was about 100 degrees. July was hot. It was like being back home."

"I lost track of time. I just got caught up trying to find these energy efficient light bulbs. There's a certain light bulb that I like to buy that lasts eight to nine months at a time. I make sure the house has ample lighting. The last thing I need is to pay Salvatore to change light bulbs for God's sake. He gets paid enough to take care of the place and schlep the renters from and to the airport."

"You have a caretaker?" Rob inquired.

"Oh yes; Salvatore. He's lived on the island all his life. His brother, Dimitri, built the place for me. I spoke of them earlier I believe. Even though they are brothers, they do not share the same political views nor do they even look alike. Salvatore is my right-hand man in Aruba. He is the greatest. I don't know what I would do without him."

"Salvatore and Joe have their unique ways of communicating, whether it's broken Papiamento or email," Alex explained. "Joe doesn't seem to be able to understand Salvatore's voice over the phone. He tells Salvatore what needs to be done. Salvatore takes care of the maintenance as cheaply as possible-he is frugal as most islanders tend to be and he is one handy person. He also knows Joe takes his good old time to get around to doing things and he makes sure it gets done. The house stays looking beautiful based on what I could see."

Alex nodded toward me with a slight smile. An acknowledgement. Did I mention how much I really liked making Alex smile? She was learning to understand me. She knew I was not the greatest organizer and wasn't the best at following things through. I am more like the procrastinating type. I forget appointments and am late to arrive when I do remember them, and she forgives me when I'm not on schedule–most of the time. Salvatore became accustomed to my traits, too. Somehow, he managed to work around them with no rebuke.

"Yes, Salvatore is a great asset," I said. I was secretly hoping Alex was not going to bring up the issue about the pool pump. I tried to remember to call the pool company; really I did. I just kept forgetting.

"Like the pool pump," Alex began. "Salvatore told me he had emailed and called Joe for months about the pump for the dolphin fountain. It kept shutting off. It became quite dysfunctional after one of the renter's kids had managed to turn the main water faucet in the wrong direction-emptying the pool. Salvatore had made sure the fountain was fully operational for our visit." After taking a small sip of the pinot, Alex continued. "Salvatore likes everything perfect for Joe. Joe never did get around to calling the pool company even though Salvatore had given him the part number as well as the telephone number-several times. Salvatore confided in me-he paid for it himself. Now, that is coming from a man that lives on meager means-different from the grandiose homes he takes care of."

"Well, it got fixed–didn't it?" I remarked. "I was proud of the fact I finally had gotten the pump installed when we arrived. Surely, it had been on my mind before we left on the trip. I finished replacing all the light bulbs throughout the house and felt another profound sense of accomplishment. Kinda like you, Alex–I believe the little things can do so much for one's sense of both appreciation and pride. By the time I put away the ladder and screwdrivers, it was time for sunset. The kids wanted to go to the casino. Quite honestly-I had wanted to go out for a nice dinner."

"Obviously, you got a bit side-tracked there, Joe. I am sure you had plenty of time to go to one of your favorite restaurants. You have probably been to every restaurant on the island. It sounds like the trip to the rough beach was out of the question, too. Isn't that where you were all supposed to be going after you came back from the store?" Rob looked first at Alex; then at me.

"The day had started out with some frustration," I said admittedly. "Besides, I paid for the trip and at some point, I should be able to do what I wanted to do. Even though they did not say anything when I came back from the store, I knew I had messed up plans to go to the rough side of the island. No, Rob, we did not make it to the beach that day. And, yes, over the years I have visited about every restaurant in Aruba. I know where to go and what their menus are. I enjoy the better restaurants; the island is full of them. Fine dining is one of my greatest pleasures."

Alex looked at me first, then toward Rob and Jan. She hesitated, shrugged her shoulders and said, "*everything*, was all about Joe on that trip and *everywhere* we went was because he wanted to go. We went to dinner where he wanted, we went to the beach when he wanted, and the children and I were at his mercy down there for the entire ten days. Joe and his family have this thing about going to the priciest restaurants on the island. I, on the other hand, could care less about going out to eat at some restaurant. I've been to enough restaurants in my life and just wanted to relax and see more of the island– different restaurants-where the islanders like to go and taste local foods. The children and I wanted to see things other than a dinner menu. My idea of sitting at a table in uncomfortable chairs and waiting twenty minutes for just a glass of water is not my idea of pleasant dining. I think Joe had experienced a bit of culture shock. Our group dynamic was far different from his past experiences with his family." Alex tapped my leg with her hand to make sure I understood her point of view.

"I do not mind doing anything new. I enjoy showing people around the island; not just dining in restaurants. Many of my friends enjoyed my personal tour guides. Anyway, by that time, the kids were anxious to go to a casino. We ended up watching the sunset and ate some fruit and cheeses for dinner by the pool. I will never grow tired of witnessing a sunset in Aruba–it makes me happy."

"The children were getting restless and wanted to get out of the house. It was a perfect night. We climbed into the topless Jeep for an evening drive to the high-rises. The Jeep started at the very first turn of the key." Alex said.

"The Sahara finally knew Aruba Joe was now back in control," I said. "We pulled away from the driveway in the afterglow of the Aruban sunset without any hesitation from the Jeep. The kids envisioned a prosperous evening at the Holiday Inn Casino."

"Joe drove along the water," Alex said. "What a spectacular view of the Caribbean from the coastal road. I loved watching the water roll onto the white beach. Sailboats glide along the calm ocean waters. Pleasant as it is scenic. The houses along the beach road are beautifully landscaped with tropical plants and huge palm trees. The night air is so warm. The trade winds calm down in the evening and a light breeze crosses the island."

"Hey, I'm taking this all in," Rob said. "I can picture it. I loved when I had vacationed in the Caribbean."

I said. "Speaking from my experiences to Aruba–there has been many changes. Some good; some not so good."

"We didn't have anything to compare it to," Alex said. "It is just beautiful."

"By the time we arrived, the high-rise parking lots and garages were completely full," I said. "The sidewalks were crowded with people. It was Friday night in Aruba. Open parking spaces close to the hotels are usually few and far between. Luckily, I found this really close parking space along the street near the Holiday Inn

188

and figured their casino would be perfect for first time gamblers. Expert that I am at parallel parking."

"He parked the Jeep halfway on top of the curb and the sidewalk– some parallel parking job," Alex said.

She knew how to add in all sorts of little mindless details. Details, quite frankly, I had forgotten. Women were quite good at remembering details.

"All three of the kids were ready for some casino action. Their father was a professional blackjack and roulette player. They had gone with him to Atlantic City before he had passed in June the year before. Although they had never been allowed into the casinos, they walked through the outskirts of the casinos to the elevators-the players and slot machines visible to them-I think it's in their blood-especially, Jade."

"So," Jan said, "naturally they were excited.

"You should have seen them, Jan," Alex said. "They scanned the casino and located the slot machines. Side-by-side the three of them sat on stools in the front of the penny slot machines. They each slid a twenty-dollar bill in their machine as if they had done it a thousand times before. Their eyeballs linked to the bright screens. They were looking to win some money. I think they each had visions-massive amounts of dollar bills and bright lights and bells ringing in their heads. They had heard it many times before and now they were part of the action."

"How exciting was that?" Jan exclaimed. "They must have felt all grown up."

CHAPTER 16 – VOODOO

"Just after they pulled the handle on the machines the lights went out–I mean in the entire casino. It was as though they turned off the lights in the casino with the simultaneous pull of the levers. I started thinking since they pulled the handle at the same time they must have blown a fuse," I said. "There was no music playing anymore or any bells ringing. It was silent and dark. I quickly turned and looked around the rest of the casino. Behind us, the blackjack and roulette tables were dark. The emergency lights started flashing on and off a couple of times; then lit up. The whole casino floor changed looking more like a night club-waiting for the performer to enter. We watched as the hotel staff quickly darted throughout the casino. I told the kids to sit tight while Alex and I walked around the casino to find out what the dickens was going on. I thought about the Great Brink's Robbery of 1950. We went to the bar on the opposite side of the casino. We couldn't even get a drink. I reflected on the day-a precursor for the evening."

"Uh oh," Rob said with a sparkling twinkle in his eye.

"Oh, Rob–shisssh-you haven't heard anything yet," Jan said in response as she softly elbowed her husband.

"From the bar, we could see a couple of people standing at the side of the casino entrance. Alex and I decided to walk over. We hadn't noticed it before because of all the noise in the casino-we could hear the wind howling outside as we got a little closer to the front door. When we had arrived just minutes earlier there were only a few clouds in the sky and plenty of sunshine; certainly not enough clouds to give warning for what we saw next. The rain was pelting down sideways in torrential sheets and bounced like little silver bullets off the pavement. The wind blew the double glass doors inward and startled both of us. The rain splashed on the red foyer carpets-leaving puddles. Water was filling the entranceway–it looked like a flood–like someone had just turned on a huge hose. We are at sea level for the most part. It was totally dark outside-the lamp posts were dark as well. In just a few minutes, the sky had turned from a beautiful sunset vista to dark and tumultuous as if the sun disappeared. Visibility was minimal from our view by the glass doors and all you could see was grey rain. Alex and I walked back to the slot machines. The kids were still sitting in front of their machines claiming ownership and protecting their investments. The security staff strode through the casino–making another round. You could tell who oversaw the casino. The well-dressed man in a tuxedo, red bow tie, and white button down shirt slipped quickly from each table on the gaming floor. He spoke briefly to the staff in Papiamento as he circled the room. There was little noise except for a low hum of the voices of the patrons. It appeared everything was under control but, eerily the same. Alex and I told the kids we were going to find out what was going on and headed toward the hotel lobby on the opposite side of the casino."

"The corridor of the lobby floor was well lit," Alex said. "People were wandering all around the hallways. Some had their hair in curlers–some were in robes–they had been getting ready to go out for the evening. Others gathered around in small groups discussing the power outage and storm. People were seated on a tan, circular leather sofa. About a dozen people ran into the lobby from the driving rain–their hair and clothes soaking wet."

"Alex and I decided to walk across the lobby; the tan ceramic tiles were covered with water and rather slippery. We finally found the rear entrance of the hotel facing the beach. The pool at the Inn is located out back. Lounge chairs had flipped on their sides in disarray. Palm branches and debris were scattered on the patio and in the pool–the pool boy would have to spend a lot of time getting the stuff out of the pool. Wet towels, cups, and God knows what else were everywhere. It looked like a hurricane had whipped through the courtyard dumping trash cans of the days rubbish everywhere. Aruba didn't have hurricanes. We joined several people standing under the protection of the covered porch area. Looking behind us, toward the inside of the hotel, it had become more crowded with hotel guests exchanging their experiences. No one knew what to do at first. Looking toward the southern end of the island, the only visible lighting was created by the emergency lights in the stairwells of neighboring hotels. During the intermittent lightning, we had limited visibility of the casinos and hotels and shops across the street. They, too, were in total darkness. The rain continued to pummel earth bound in liquid walls at a forty-five-degree angle. The palm trees in the rock garden around the pool were bending southward. The pool water was dancing with the rain as it hit. Thunder was loud and frequent."

"Vincent came outside to check in with us," Alex said. "He reported the slots were not working and the casino was still dark."

"A skinny young man stood next to Alex and started hopping around-his flip flops flew off his feet and were carried away by the winds into the darkness. His body flailed against the small crowd as he screamed like a banshee-'there's an iguana on my foot!' We had formed a dense group. Not sure of what was going on, Alex moved closer to me almost knocking me over. Like a domino effect our bodies knocked into one another and ended up supported by this big lady against the stucco exterior wall. Everyone looked down toward the tiled patio."

"Oh, my word," Jan exclaimed. "I would not want to be in the dark with an iguana running around my feet."

"There wasn't an iguana out there. It was a frightened, little white dove hobbling around. The fool of a man. Some kind of scared he was. What a laugh we had. I think the laughter was more of an expression of relief; relief to see a bird rather than an out-of-

194

control reptile running loose. The bird kept making attempts to fly away. Each time he tried the wind just blew him into the crowd. The bird chirped and flapped its wings. People moved all over the place–some back inside-tripping over one another to get out of its way. I think they thought there might really be an iguana roaming around in the darkness of the garden. I managed to pick up the little bird. I could feel its small heart pounding against my fingers. The dove's chest was heaving. I felt sorry for the poor thing. Once the bird realized it wasn't going anywhere, it sat quietly in my hand. It perched itself right on my finger–both sets of claws were wrapped tightly around my index and middle fingers."

"Yeah, birdman of Aruba. Aruba Joe was holding this silly little bird. It pooped on his hand. The only light was the occasional lightning streak across the sky-jerky scenes like a strobe light produces," Alex said. "I couldn't help it but, every once in a while, I looked down at my feet as well."

"You know, I've never seen so much rain in Aruba before. It rained only once in the thirty years I've been going down there. Aruba has about twenty inches of rain a year. I bet they must have gotten seven or eight inches of rain that night. The months of June, July, and August are considered the rainy season in Aruba. We got some serious rain-oh what a night."

"I think you meant—what a day and night in Aruba," Jan laughed. So much happening. But, I will let you finish telling the story, Joe."

Alex had told me Jan worked for a local radio station-one of those oldie music stations-owned by some Hollywood celebrity. I could see other people in the restaurant had turned their heads to listen to us. Some were even leaning back in their chairs. "By that time, the kids were getting a little bored. They kept walking from the casino-just checking on the rain and the status of the lights-for a periodic update. We must have stood outside for another hour or more."

"The rain was outrageous," Alex added. "It was like the skies throwing water buckets at us. The weird thing about the night in Aruba was the transformation from such a gorgeous day—blue sky—to gale force winds and heavy rain. We had absolutely no warning. What a strange weather experience. The last time I experienced anything like it was when Hurricane Agnes hit us in the early seventies. I had been out that night, too, watching the storm. I was sixteen. I sat in the parking lot of our favorite sub shop. We didn't have an alternative other than sit there. The water rose so high-so quickly."

"Alex and I finally decided it was time to leave the casino. I sat the little dove under one of the shrubs; just barely able to see it hop under a larger bush for protection. We went back through the casino gathering the kids from their slots. We felt sorry for them—they clearly did not want to leave. There was no denying-their first time in the casino would be a memorable one."

"Probably a sign," Rob chuckled. "They shouldn't have been gambling in the first place–the storm saved them from losing more of their hard, earned money."

"True, true. Even still, it was a huge let down for them. We stood in the foyer watching the hurricane-like rains coming down for a few minutes. I didn't feel waiting any longer was going to change anything. The hotel manager told us the entire island was without power. He also told us no one knew how long the electricity would be off. The rain hit the road surface so hard and bounced off the pavement a couple of inches. From what we could see, the parking lot had formed mini lakes."

"The intensity of the rainfall gives me a bit of appreciation of what Noah went through while hording those animals onto the Ark. Good thing you only had four two-legged animals to herd Aruba Joe," Jan said.

The woman had a bit of good humor-I liked her quick quip. "There are times when one just must make an executive decision–for the good of the group-I suggested we run for the Jeep rather than stay at the Inn. I tightened my neck toggle on my hat. Together, the five of us pushed the double glass doors open and bolted. We ran through the rain. The water was above our ankles. We couldn't hear one another the thunder was deafening. I just ran in the direction of the Jeep and hoped they were behind me. Jade must have run in a different direction. She wasn't with us when we got to the Sahara. Alex was on the verge of hysteria. We sat in the Jeep for a few minutes–frozen in the driving Caribbean storm–waiting for Jade to emerge from the darkness. I had totally forgotten we had left the top off- there was six inches of water on the floor. We were like drowned rats. My leather hat was stuck to my head."

"The thunder grew more intense, and the lightning bolts seemed to strike from one area to the next-it was hard to hear-like having natural fireworks display overhead. Joe turned the ignition key time and again. I could not tell whether the engine was on or not–the noise from above was that loud. I looked at the dashboard-nothing was lit," Alex said. "My head was spinning with worry over Jade. My thoughts were like any other mother when it comes to the safety of her children. I could not bear to lose her. I kept thinking; 'where had she gotten to and how afraid she must be.' Other scary thoughts kept popping up and I just shut them down."

"Initially, I was not worried about Jade, she is a different sort of girl–quite self-sufficient; resourceful. She could not have gone too far–we were parked directly out in front of the casino. When the Jeep didn't start, I glanced over at Alex. Little waterfalls poured down the back and over the sides of the rim of my hat. At least the rain wasn't on my face, and I could see. I knew, rather than saw,

Alex had shed a few tears about losing her daughter. It was a small island. We would find her."

"Oh–my–God!" Jan exclaimed. "Alex, when you first told me what had happened, I didn't feel the impact of losing your daughter. I almost half-thought you were kidding. The pain and anguish you must have felt from being beside one person one minute and then without them in the next. That must have been absolutely horrifying."

"Thank you, Jan," Alex said "for being such a good friend. I've lost a dog and I have lost a friend. At one time, I even lost Jade in the middle of a very crowded mall when she was about five years old. When I found her, she was standing next to the water fountain looking at the lights. I felt hopeless then and in Aruba I felt so much more. It was a sense of fear that penetrated my entire body. I never want to feel anything like that ever again. I just kept looking for her and I could not even see, Jan–I couldn't see."

My heart sank as I felt the pain from Alex's words. Her eyes glimmered with tears-still remembering and she would never forget. She took the blame. It wasn't her fault. "I'll tell you what I did. I began spewing a lot of inappropriate expletives–enough to make the entire S.S. California's sailors blush-as I tried to get the Jeep's engine to turn over. I normally do not swear –especially, in mixed company. We needed to start physically looking for Jade and were constrained by nature's forces. I wanted to be mobile. Headlights of other cars broke through the darkness and provided some visibility. None of the streetlamps were working. An occasional car horn could be heard faintly through the whistling sounds of the wind. Jade was alone in the dark in a place she had never been. Her mother's mind just went straight to the worst fears. I wanted to find her as soon as I could. I may have flooded the car or something– I couldn't tell. I felt useless-the car would not start and we were stuck without any cover, *and* we had lost Alex's daughter. Our first night on the town was a literal vacation nightmare."

"Traffic was at a standstill. Everywhere we looked, cars were just sitting idle in the roadway in a maze-like pattern. People had no sense of where to go. If we would have sat there much longer, we would have ended up deaf. I knew how that little bird felt–scared and confused. The greyish headlights from the other cars gave us some sense of dimension and distance. I couldn't tell how deep the puddles were or even see the curb. Intermittent bolts of lightning provided our primary means of visibility."

"Vincent and Crystal were in the backseat. I could hear them yelling but, I had no idea what they were saying–whether or not they were even talking to me-and I was not in a mood to hear what anyone had to say about the car not starting."

"Vincent jumped out of the Jeep and headed toward the Inn. We couldn't do anything other than wait for him. We sat staring toward the Inn; our heads turning constantly looking for Jade.

People were still running from cars into the adjacent buildings or toward the Inn. He was gone for an hour or even longer-it was hard to keep track of time-before returning. No Jade. Anywhere.

Alex said. "I just wished we hadn't taken the canvas top off that morning–that was a huge mistake. I wanted to see my daughter appear. I didn't care about being wet."

"What in the world did you end up doing and how did you ever find Jade?" Jan asked. "My God, you had to have been too far from your house to walk home."

"Vincent saw the cab before any of us could even think of what to do. It came out of nowhere-right beside us."

"I didn't really recall whose idea it was." Alex added, "But, we got out of the Jeep and ended up slithering like wet, slippery fish into the front and back seat of some car with a lit 'taxi' sign on top."

"It was a station wagon–it was too dark to see the color."

"The cab driver, a middle-aged woman, looked a bit startled when we jumped in her car," Alex said. "Once she collected herself to the realization we were a harmless family, she told us traffic was really bad and asked us where we were headed. Her English was a bit difficult to understand but, she spoke English better than I spoke Papiamento-which is nil. I pointed toward the Jeep behind us and told her we had problems starting the thing. She told us cars were parked all over the road. People had abandoned them."

201

"I apologized to the woman for our intrusion. Hell, I think we startled the pants off her when we jumped into her car. You couldn't see her face like I did, Alex. When I jumped into the back seat, I saw part of her initial expression in the rear-view mirror–her eyes were as big as saucers."

"And, once we told her where we were staying, she became more at ease. She must've deduced we were some rich Americans-staying in the wealthiest part of the island–safe for her to take us home." Alex injected. "Oddly enough, I just started crying to her about Jade. I told her we just lost my daughter when we were running through the street, and I was afraid I would never see my baby again. The woman shook her finger at me. She spoke with a strong accent-not to worry– 'Luci' would ride with us or without us– all night if she had to–and she would find my daughter. Luci also told us to 'remember her name-like the rich red hair lady in America-L – U – C – I.' Remember that Joe?"

"All Americans are rich compared to the native Arubans," I said. "One thing the Arubans have-that some of us Americans have lost-is family value. They are a close people-time with family means everything to them–more valuable than money. On Sunday nights after church and dinner, the Arubans head to the beach–the entire family. That woman was there to help us-help *our* family. Funny thing too…. I didn't notice any other cabs out that night. Yep; the only cabbie. It was as though she was an angel sent to help

202

us find Jade-a native that knew the streets well. I had lost my sense of direction that night. I give the driver a lot of credit. She pulled out expertly into the darkness–zipping through the deserted vehicles-their headlights had been left on and provided sporadic light along the streets. The intensity of the rain was so great her headlights barely guided us. You couldn't even make out the buildings. She maneuvered her station wagon to avoid the deeper puddles. Mind you; there were still no traffic lights working either. She went up and down every street within a half mile radius. She drove up to doorways. She drove us back to the entrance of the Inn–I went inside the lobby asking everyone if they had seen her-no Jade. She drove around to the side at the casino entrance. I ran inside and searched everywhere asking anyone I saw if they noticed a young girl. The cab driver eased the car onto the main road traveling at a snail's pace. I looked out the driver's rear window side while Alex looked out the other side."

"Crystal told us she had her purse with her. I could only hope Jade had put her cell phone in it and it would be dry enough to call us," Alex said. "I kept looking at people in cars-expecting to see Jade–I couldn't make out their faces. You know, it's funny–I couldn't even remember the color of her shirt. I worried that we had just unknowingly missed my daughter with each passing car. Perhaps she had jumped into a strange vehicle. We spent a couple of hours just riding through the same streets until I knew it was no use. We figured Jade must have walked toward home-or so we hoped. I didn't know what else to do or think. My mind was soaked with worry and frustration."

"The main reason I fell in love with Aruba is the dependable good weather. Unlike other islands there are no extreme changes in temperatures or rainfall. Never say 'never' right? It took us at least forty-five minutes to drive the usual eight minutes home. We traveled at an island pace of slow. Only one car drove past us from the opposite direction and it just barely missed hitting our taxi as it hydroplaned across the road surface. Aruban drivers are not the best by far. You can tell that by looking at all the dents or missing bumpers on the cars down there. Seldom do you see a car without any damage."

"I don't know about that," Rob piped in. "We have some pretty bad drivers in Maryland. Good grief! It can be sunny and not a drop of rain in sight and people still manage to flip their cars upside-down around the Baltimore and D.C. beltways. Maryland residents would benefit if our legislators designed some sort of idiot tax for those people who caused accidents on a perfect, sunny day. I say charge them a thousand-dollar idiot tax—in cash—that might stop them from being so reckless. Yep, hit them in their wallet." Turning toward Alex he added, "Sorry. I went off on that tangent. I'm assuming you found your daughter."

"Eventually. But it was a long night. Since the local radio stations were down, the woman driver had been playing one of Celine Dion's greatest concerts on her DVD player in her car," Alex said. "It was apparent she enjoyed our North American culture and the Canadian vocalist. At that point in time, we didn't care what she was watching. We were anxious to get back home and see if Jade found her way there. And, I wanted to get into dry clothes. Every street was flooded–not just along the coast. Water was a good foot deep. There aren't any grates for water run-off or drainage along the roadways."

I added, "most of the entire island is at sea level-Tierra Del Sol is surrounded by hills. When we turned into the resort, there wasn't one light visible in the entire neighborhood-not even at the clubhouse. The taxi driver crept up the road. Water streams flowed downhill on either side of us. I could barely make out the familiar left turn at the top of the hill. My beautiful paradise neighborhood was in the dark. Luci tried the radio occasionally but couldn't get any news in the car. She told us she had driven from the downtown area earlier. Lights were out all over the island; except, for emergency lights at the hospital and hotels. The entire island, for Pete's sake, was in absolute darkness."

"When Luci pulled up to the front of the house, I yelled a 'thank you' to her," Alex said. "We raced to the front door and Joe let everyone in. That's when I realized we didn't pay Luci and back out in the torrential rain I went. Her car was gone. I didn't see her drive past the house and there is only one way back to the entrance-the way we came in."

"I think Vincent paid for the ride–he was the last one to get out while the rest of us high-tailed it into the house."

"No, he didn't," Alex slowly answered. "I asked him and Crystal the next day."

"You know; it is uncanny the way everyone remembers something a little different from the same situation. Anyway, Crystal ran through the house screaming for her sister and went out on the patio. Jade was not home. The house was still cool from the air conditioning. We changed into some dry clothes and sat out back on the covered porch to watch the wind and the rain; and wait." I looked at Alex as she nodded in agreement. "It was still early mind you. None of us were tired after all the excitement; our adrenaline was pumping. I grabbed a bottle of wine and a couple of glasses. Alex and the kids found some candles. We sat by candlelight; sipping on some South African red wine; the candles blew out and we just sat and waited in the dark."

"You know, Joe," Alex said as she patted my leg, "at another time, it would have been a rather romantic finish to an unforgettable evening in Aruba. The house phone didn't work, and I kept my cell phone right in front of me. We tried calling the police station-there was no answer. I felt helpless and kept wondering where she was

206

and how she got lost from us in the first place. I played the evening over and over in my mind like a broken record. I kept picturing her shivering somewhere-all alone."

"I cannot imagine," Jan said. Her eyes cast a moist layer of tears as she spoke directly to Alex.

"I'd walk to the front door and look out and kept it unlocked," Alex answered. "I kept looking around the corner of the patio at the driveway. We couldn't see the sonar and the lighthouse-they were always lit. I felt the rest of humanity had left and we were the only living survivors on the island. Jade is a strong girl-I knew that. I wanted my baby to come home. Joe convinced me to lay down."

"I ended up lying awake most of that night when finally, the lights in the kitchen came on; I saw the light from under our bedroom door. I got out of bed and turned the lights off in the living room and wandered upstairs checking all the bedrooms. No Jade. I opened the doors and repeated the earlier search. I went back to the kitchen. It was four in the morning. Alex, on the other hand, had finally drifted off to sleep. She sounds like a mother bear scolding her cubs when she gets into a deep sleep. She doesn't breathe well through her nostrils."

"Alex snores?" Rob asked. "In my household, I'm the one that snores. Honestly Joe, I hope this vacation gets better for you. It sounds like the first day was a bit eventful; to say the very least. Not exactly the way you had planned it at all, I'm sure."

Rob could have a good laugh. It wouldn't be his last laugh at our vacation antics.

"The front door slammed. I was on high alert and the sound was like a nuclear explosion; there stood Jade. I instantly noticed she wasn't wet-the rain had slowed. Hugging her, I told her how worried we had been and to go wake her mother. By that time, Crystal and Vincent came running down the steps and the three of them followed single file into our bedroom. I started brewing a pot of coffee."

"Where was she all that time," Jan asked. "My God I would have been such a wreck-such a *wreck*. Wouldn't I have been, Rob?"

"Jan, my dear, you are a wreck when one of the girls call you and tells you they have a cold. I can't imagine what you would do if you lost one of them for a couple of hours."

"Jan," Alex began, "I was the only one that didn't hear the front door slam-and that door is a very, heavy wooden set of doors. Jade told us she had yelled to us when we were running across the parking lot toward the Jeep. She had left her purse in the casino and when she came back out, we were gone. Since she had no idea how to get back to the house, she went into the restaurant and waited for us. She said she tried calling dozens of times and none of us answered. She said she was a little scared but, there were so many

208

people to talk to and everyone was doing the same thing. Interestingly she remembered our family rule. In our anxiety-we forgot. I had always told my children-if one of us gets lost, always go back to the place we last saw one another and wait. She did-in the dining area."

"Jade is a strong young woman-not easily frightened-she has 'grit'," I said. "But, the weird thing about her coming home was this-and I swear to God-from her lips to our ears. Jade told us a little dark lady walked into the dining area and sat across from her. At first, Jade said, the lady just smiled and was quiet. But, Jade said some of the other people just sat quietly, too. At first, she didn't think anything was odd. Then, the lady asked Jade if she needed a ride home. Jade said she told her she didn't know where she was staying and her family was on vacation. She said she told the lady she was just going to wait for us to pick her up."

"Who was the lady," Jan asked. "Did she take her home?"

"Jan," Alex said in a quiet voice with tears stinging her eyes, "it was Luci. Luci brought Jade home."

"Nooooo... Goose bumps are going up and down my body," Jan said. "How in the world did that woman find Jade? That woman must have a gift I tell you. First, she appears and disappears with all of you and then she finds Jade? That is too much."

"Exactly," I said. "I am not a believer in ghosts or anything of that nature. But there is no way you can convince me this woman didn't have some special talents. I was in the kitchen turning off the lights when Jade came home. I didn't notice any headlights and it was still plenty dark outside-just barely raining. Jade said the woman told her she would take her home. Jade said she couldn't even tell where they were going. The woman knew where she was staying."

A rather plump, dark-haired woman at the adjacent table spoke up, "I bet she was one of those voodoo people-like in New Orleans. I've heard of them in the islands." We looked over at her. "I believe there are people with those powers, Aruba Joe, even if you are a bit skeptical."

"Not that I am a skeptic," I began answering the woman slowly, "but, I personally had never experienced anything like that before. And, Jade was so calm when she came home. That was another peculiar thing."

"Let me add a couple of other interesting details. Jade told us she could not see too well when they were driving to the house and that it seemed like hours before they arrived," Alex said. "She told us the woman played Celine Dion on a screen in the car and the song to the Titanic never stopped playing. She said the woman told her all about the island and talked to Jade about different people that lived there and that she spoke particularly good English. Jade said she never felt afraid. Luci drove her to the front of the house and

Jade ran to the front door. When Jade turned to wave to Luci the woman and the car were gone."

"What did I just say," the plump lady added. "Some of those dark women have powers."

I couldn't help but sit there for a few moments thinking about what the lady had said. Could it be true? Did we have one of those 'experiences' that night? I hadn't given much thought to the timing and coincidences until now. I hadn't really discussed the vacation in Alex's presence before since we hadn't seen each other until tonight. I forgot some of the details.

"Well," Jan began "you can ponder away at what happened that night and you will just never know. All ended well and everyone was safe. There was no scandal, and no one got killed for God's sake. At least your family didn't end up in the papers."

Alex and I gave one another a knowing glance with a smile. In due time.

CHAPTER 17 – OCEAN VS POOL

"My vacations to Aruba have always been sun, sand, and sea," I said to Rob. "I was determined this trip would be the greatest. I wasn't about to let a Jeep, iguanas, or a black out on the entire island ruin our trip. We only rested a few hours that night-more like a few minutes but, awoke to a morning as spectacular as all the others I've had in Aruba. Jade made us a nice breakfast-she *never* cooks at home. I don't recall her making anything other than a sandwich."

"Actually," Alex added, "you are right Joe. Jade is not a 'good cooker' as she has said many times. I was as surprised as you were when she made breakfast. I didn't know my daughter could even cook let alone turn on a gas stove."

"Even though I didn't get much sleep from the events of the night before, I felt rested and in absolute control that morning. I was determined our day was going to be a fabulous one. No sir. I was not looking back. I went out front to check on some of the hoses of the sprinkler system and there was the most amazing thing sitting in front of the house-the Jeep!" I exclaimed. "Now, if that wasn't the surprise; I had both sets of keys in the house. I checked the inside-it was dry as a bone. I looked around for a note or something that would have given me some insight as to how it got there and I didn't find a thing. Just to satisfy my curiosity, I called the rental car company and asked them if they had found the Jeep in town and dropped it off. The guy started laughing at me and called me a 'silly American.' I know other people had told me the rental car companies have towed their vehicle after it ran out of gas and they abandoned it. I just hung the phone up with his annoying laughter dimming in my ear. I figured since we missed the opportunity to off-road to the rough side of the island the day before we needed to get an early start. The morning sun was already intense. Alex packed a picnic basket full of wine coolers, beer, and water. We didn't' need anything else.

"Bone dry," Alex said a bit wistfully as she looked off toward the bar door.

"Oh, no; that Jeep did not drive itself home. Someone brought it there. It had to have been Luci," Jan said with a smile tapping her index finger on the tabletop. "You should have turned it in for another one anyway. I think I would have at that point."

"Well, the day almost started out all right. The Jeep did act up again," I said in response to Jan. "Interestingly enough, the Jeep was still warm. So, someone had dropped it off that morning but, it wouldn't start. Jade did her magic under the hood again and got it started on the first turn of the key. I felt a bit ridiculous that she could start it right up every time; the girl is so handy with cars."

"You know Joe, I'm beginning to think that Jeep didn't like you from the start; no pun intended," Jan said with a giggle.

"I think that daggone thing was hormonal. It certainly acted like a contrary teenage, female at that time-of-the-month. Anyway, we headed out to tour the back of the island. There's an old historic church I wanted everyone to visit. The Alto Vista Church was built in 1952–at the same location where the first Catholic church of Aruba was built in the mid 1700's. Lots of visitors go there; by tour buses or four wheelers. We only stopped for a few minutes because our crew was eager to get to the beach."

"Vincent sat next to me; the sun was high in the sky. The three girls were standing up in the back holding on to the roll bar and just enjoying life. Vincent had the radio on loud and the girls waved to all the passing four wheelers and other Jeeps. There were quite a few others off-roading. The view of the rough water was beautiful–high waves smash against the surf along the lava rock walls. The color of the ocean on that side of the island is much darker than the other side and much deeper along the shoreline."

"The view from any point on the island is spectacular," Alex added in a wistful-like voice.

"On the rough side, the blue-green waters, rocks, and the desert landscaping are truly breathtaking. All of us enjoyed taking in the sights. It had been quite a few years since I had gone there. It was a life experience you never forget. One of the poor bastards in a Jeep had a flat tire and another Jeep driver was helping him. We rode past all of them to a more isolated area. It felt as though we had

214

the whole island to ourselves; a sensation of freedom and a real connection to the arid island."

"I was amazed by the stone formations consisting of six each–large and small stones–along the ocean and hillside. Joe told us the islanders believed the formations ward off evil spirits and bring them good luck. Crystal loved this notion. When Joe stopped the Jeep for us to get out and look at them, she had to build her own stack of rocks," Alex said.

"Riding around in an open Jeep in Aruba is the ideal way to travel and see the island. There are a few structures along the water where you can get a bit of shade. People horseback ride and use them to tie up the horses to take a swim. I've done that before. Alex said she wanted to go horseback riding on her birthday. We drove past some impressive large rock and lava formations and decided to pull over. There were two enormous natural rock formations that jutted into the ocean on either side of the beach–kind of like two natural jettys–mostly formed of volcanic rock. They were about a football field apart from one another. I parked close to the shoreline. I certainly did not want to get stuck in the sand or surf. It was low tide. The last thing I wanted to do was spend time waiting for a tow truck to pull us out. It felt great to take off our t-shirts and walk the small beach. The girls looked for seashells. They found a chunk of brain coral and were elated. Some of the largest brain coral found are nine hundred years old. Alex couldn't wait to get into the water.

She was carefully hopping around trying to get her feet onto some solid sand in the surf. It's full of lava rock and coral and is uneven along the beach-a bit tricky navigating past the rocks to the sandy part. Once you make it past the rocks the waves are great for body surfing."

"Before we left home, one of the first and last questions I asked Joe, was whether we needed shoes for the water. Of course, he forgot about how rough the beach was. His family primarily ventures into the calmer waters on the other side of the island. All I had taken were sandals and dress shoes," Alex said.

"He probably just wanted to test your adventurous side," Jan said with an upturned brow.

"I just forgot about how rough it really was. While the girls picked up pieces of coral and shells–Vincent and I focused on body surfing–starting just beyond the waves. The water felt great. There is such a great surge of energy when catching a half-way decent wave into shore. The waves were coming in consistent. We would ride a wave in toward shore, dive under the next couple of waves, and catch the next one in. Vincent and I must have ridden a dozen waves together. And, I quickly found out I wasn't as young as I used to be. They wore me out."

"I love to do that, too, Joe," Rob said. "I usually go out with a couple guys in Ocean City. It does wear your butt out. The best time to go body surfing is just before a storm comes in–when the waves are a good three to four feet high."

"I used to do that myself when our family had a summer home there. Good golly; the next thing Vincent and I knew a huge wave came in. I mean to tell you; it was without a doubt the tallest wave I've seen in Aruba. It came out of nowhere. Following that first big wave was a couple more in rapid succession. I took a quick inventory to locate everyone and make sure they were okay. The next thing I heard was Alex letting out this loud 'oh, shit!' as she locked eyes with me. I immediately knew something was wrong. I wasn't sure what had happened to her; the first thing I thought was a sea creature had stung her. Quickly, I realized she was in trouble. The high waves were knocking Alex under the water. I took off toward her in an instant. She didn't appear to be moving with the waves. She was standing in the same place. With each stroke I swam straight toward where she was. I wondered what was going on–why she didn't move. Those waves were strong-even closer to the shoreline. As I got in closer, I could see her blue eyes were as big as saucers."

"Your squinty, little eyes would have gotten big, too if what happened to me had happened to you," Alex said. "Jan and Rob; I truly thought I was going to drown that day."

"Alex's cussing up a storm. The girls ran up the beach toward their mother. They stood directly behind her but dared not venture into the water. None of us knew what had her. Alex was only about thirty feet from shore. The huge waves continued to thrash her body around in the water. Her body moved spastic like—whipping against each wave. The whole time I swam toward her I felt I wouldn't get to her quick enough. In between the incoming waves, Alex would bend over frantically pulling on her leg. The girls jumped up and down and were screaming from the beach. Every so often I had to stop for a moment to catch my breath. I was getting tired, my strokes less effective, and my head was starting to pound. I was determined to gain ground though. I glanced over my shoulder for Vincent. Vincent was doing his best to swim to his mother. He was in some kind of undertow and had more of a struggle than I did to get in toward shore. He was also a lot less experienced. The last thing I needed was for Vincent to get into trouble too. I couldn't help Alex and Vincent at the same time. There was too much distance between them. I did the best thing I could do under the circumstances. I yelled toward Vincent to get on his back and float for a while to save his strength."

"That is precisely how people drown. They get so tired fighting against the current. Vincent must have been so afraid out there all by himself," Jan said with a sincere, worried look on her face.

"There was no use fighting that ocean current, Jan, not as strong as it is on the rough side in Aruba. Vincent's a smart, strong young man. He understood what I had to do as well as what he needed to do. When I recognized he was calm, when he no longer appeared frantic, I turned my focus on getting to his mother. By that time, the tide was starting to work with me and made it easier for me to get into shore. I knew Vincent was just as concerned as I was about his mother. It was going to take him a bit more time to get to shore than it did for me. He had been out farther than I had been. Since I was now within earshot, I could hear Alex scream out-'my foot!' I kept my eyes focused right on her. When I finally reached Alex, she was holding the top of her leg. I figured she had her foot lodged in some coral. I grabbed her arm to help stabilize her–my feet spread apart to gain stability. Like this," I said as I stood up showing everyone how I rescued Alex. "She started screaming and told me not to pull. I didn't know what to do at first. Looking down into the water I couldn't see clearly to figure out what the actual problem was. She was waist deep in the water and the waves were coming in up to her chin. I let go of her arm. Vincent was just about a hundred yards away from us by that time. Jade was jumping up and down yelling at me to get her mother-I found out she becomes emotional so quickly. Alex was yelling at me to be careful. I must admit; I was feeling a bit helpless."

"You should have felt something-like it was safer to stay at home. My God, Joe, chaos was lurking all around you on that vacation," Rob said.

"What happened? Did she break her leg?" Jan asked with a real concern in her eyes.

I just want to note something here; Jan is a natural blonde. I think it may be possible Jan is the reason why all those 'blonde jokes' originated. And, if you would ask her today, Jan would laugh and nod her head in agreement.

I looked over at Jan as she giggled. "Of course, she didn't break her leg; she would have it in a cast right now. That was a silly thing for me to say."

"No, thankfully she did not but, my presence allowed her to relax a bit. When Alex calmed down and stopped pulling on her leg, she managed to get her foot loose. Vincent came up to us. He was out of breath but, managed to put his own discomfort to the side to help his mother. Vincent and I supported Alex on either side and lifted her toward the beach. We still weren't sure what had happened to her. I looked down through the green water at her ankle and didn't see any blood in the water; thank God! The force of the waves pushed us the rest of the way into the shore. Jade was in tears. She never stopped yelling at us to get her mother out of the water-her voice had become hoarse. She started coughing. Crystal stood patiently by her sister; both her hands were cupped over her mouth as she watched the three of us making our way out of the surf. Alex was tired and a bit limp from fighting the pummeling waves. I could tell she was hurt although she wasn't saying much. Vincent and I sat her down on some larger rocks close by and just caught our breath. We were exhausted."

"I was never so relieved to get out of the ocean," Alex said. "Those waves banged against me like they wanted to just tear me apart."

I said, "I was glad to get Alex out of the water safely. Crystal got some ice from the cooler and held it on her mother's foot."

"I was quiet because I was so mad at you," Alex added. Turning to Rob and Jan she added, "before we left the house I had specifically asked if there was anything else we needed. You should have warned us about the rough, bottom in the surf."

I shrugged. "She told me it was my fault she had gotten hurt— maybe I hadn't prepared her ahead of time for the roughness of the surf." I thought for a second and continued. "Honey, I had been calling it the 'rough side.' I guess you didn't understand. When you travel outdoors sometimes people get hurt. Not that that was my intention. In all honesty, I had completely forgotten about the rocky bottom in the surf."

"I'm beginning to think you forget a lot of stuff, Joseph," Alex said snidely.

"Whoa," Rob said. "The guy had just rescued you."

"Now, Rob," Jan interrupted, "we weren't there. Alex was scared."

"It had been a while since I had gone swimming on that side of the island. Regardless, I don't ever think I'll forget that detail in the future though."

"Joe, from a man's point of view, it sounded like you just couldn't catch a break," Rob said.

"You know, Rob, that very thought must have entered my mind dozens of times on our vacation." I wasn't kidding. I thought at any moment Alex would surely fly off the handle, pack her bags, and go home. She got plenty mad a couple of times at me. That is for sure.

"There were a bunch of lava rocks-all sizes and shapes. A small pool of salty water fed between them from the ocean. The girls sat by Alex's side to comfort their mother. It was a perfect place for all of us to sit down. Alex kept her feet in the water. We all saw how badly bruised her foot was–it was a deep purple color from just under the arch and covered over half her foot."

"I could have spit nails at Joe. The fact he didn't say anything to me about the rocky part of the surf still baffles me. How in the world didn't he think it was important is beyond anything I can comprehend," Alex added. "Furthermore, to have my children along to experience his craziness really upset me. I felt like he screwed up things on purpose. Then, Jade kept saying she wanted to go home. She thought her mother was going to drown. To hear Joe talk, it was just another day. We'd get some relaxation and start

222

enjoying ourselves and–BAM! –something else went hay-wire. I should have known something was going to go wrong when we passed those guys with the flat tire-it was a sign-like the rock formations warning off evil. It must have been an hour before I felt confident enough to walk to the Jeep. I knew I had broken a few bones or severely twisted something. The skin was scraped off my big toe and was raw; half my nail was scraped off."

"Her big toe was the darkest black and purple color I had ever witnessed on a human, and it had swelled at least two sizes. It looked broken." I turned to look into those beautiful blue eyes, "it's not like I intentionally tried to mess up our vacation, Alex. Stuff just happened. Not to mention, you did get some sun and were able to enjoy the island views like no other. Most people never have that opportunity."

"*Just* describing the way her foot looked to us makes me lightheaded," Jan said. "Seriously, Alex-I don't think Joe wanted to make your vacation a nightmare, sweetie. He seems like such a nice, handsome man."

Rob added, "some vacation you took them on, Joe. You and ole 'broken-purple-toe' meets Aruba! This story sounds like a dichotomy between a tragedy and a comedy. Man!"

Rob's voice boomed over the conversations of the diners close to us. I looked around the restaurant. A dozen people were looking over at our booth again. I smiled at the people at the table to the right of us and nodded. I noticed one of the other diners was a football player. I nodded and smiled to the group at his table; they were easily within earshot of our conversation. The big guy shook his head from side to side–a toothy grin on his face. I took a long drink of the glass of water in front of me; then took a sip of the pinot grigio.

"Jade gets very emotional. I always tell her she is 'my emo child'," Alex explained. "I think the neural receptors in her brain receive information and internalize situations as a '911' call. She has always been that way. On the other hand, her sister thinks first and long into things. Crystal is more like '*The Thinker*' Rodin sculpted. She is a serious young lady and always deep in thought. When she was just a little girl, my brother once said, 'I talk to Crystal and can see she is thinking hard–her eyes are so intense.' She is the same to this day."

"My two girls are the same way, Alex," Jan added. "They are just like night and day."

"And I'd like to point out another positive aspect from that afternoon. Once the kids relaxed, they began talking about what they wanted to do that night. Going to the casino was the main destination. They were looking forward to winning some money. Their resiliency and ability to calm down so quickly was a pleasant relief. When Mamma Bear is okay, her cubs are okay. Just a few minutes before everyone had been so emotional. Quite frankly, I was

224

worried Jade would convince Alex to go home," I said. "Truth-be-told, I felt a little bad at that point and was sure glad to hear they were making plans to have some fun. The last thing I wanted was to let them down."

"You gave us an interesting vacation, Joe," Alex said to me. "We have no regrets–only laughs and great memories of some really messed up situations." Turning toward Jan and Rob she added, "I don't know if I would ever go back with him though. To Aruba I mean. The trip was like having a baby-sheer joy when you look back on it but, you knew it had been hell getting through it."

"Okay. So I take that as a good thing." What else could I do? The baby analogy was a bit of an unsettling thought. I wasn't fond of babies.

"After that day, I was glad to hear the children wanted to go back to the casino. I wanted to try some slots myself." Alex added to Rob and Jan. "Their father gambled a lot. He lost a lot more than he won. I think Jade has a bit of his gaming blood coursing through her veins. And talk about a lucky streak–she surely possesses that."

"They even talked about going back to the Inn. I wouldn't have given that place another thought! Not that I held them responsible in any way but, why go back to the place where the nightmare began? They had wanted Alex and me to join them. Even though Alex said she was fine, I wanted her to elevate her leg and reduce the swelling. She was able to move it around fairly well. So, I didn't think it was broken."

"The drive back to the house from the beach was a bit somber. We weren't singing to music on the return trip as we had earlier while anticipating some island off-roading. We still enjoyed viewing the coastline but just weren't quite as enthusiastic."

"No wonder. After that experience," Rob said, "I think you were all a bit played out."

"The kids began taking showers. Good thing we have three showers in that house. Alex took a couple of Aleve and sat by the edge of the pool with her foot in the water for a while. I helped her to a lounge chair and propped her sore foot up on a pillow and wrapped an ice bag on it."

Alex said, "the wild, green parrots soared above us–their chirping was loud and cheerful. It was as if they were telling us Aruba was still the same wonderful place as they chirped– 'welcome home-nothing has changed.'"

"You took very good care of me-you did a great job Aruba Joe," Alex said. "It was just that," and then she hesitated. During that slight hesitation I was worried what she would say next. It was a critical moment-and I could sense some tension before she added, "so many things just kept happening down there. Each day I felt like we were on a series of emotional roller coasters. Like the Wild

226

Mouse at Hershey Park. Whipping us around corners, slow upward climbs, and heart racing downward vertical slopes."

Before the conversation could generate any negativity or toss the situation into a path I was not interested in following, I quickly piped in. "I was right by your side throughout the thrill ride of my lifetime. I had been through such hard times with Gina and never want to have them with you. I understand it was tough on you, though. If I would have been with anyone else, I *never* would have attempted those things. You brought out something within me. Maybe you are still a bit mad at me, Alex. Gina would have slain me if anything would have gone different from what she had planned on vacation. It was always pool or beach or shopping."

A deep, male voice from another table spoke. "Quite a romantic sort of fellow, aren't you Aruba Joe?" We turned to see a big, dark-skinned man smiling at me. Several of the other patrons let out a little snicker as well.

"Just admitting the truth to my beautiful woman," I responded with a wink in his direction.

Alex started talking to Rob and Jan again. "We sat around the pool overlooking the back yard-just in time for the sun to start setting. I figured Joe and I had plenty of time before we had to decide to go out. Besides, he needed to unwind from fighting those daggone waves. We were both exhausted. At that same time I was struggling internally with the vacation. I felt like maybe it had been a mistake–

maybe I should not have committed my children to the vacation. We had only been dating and seeing each other on weekends for about six months. For years, the children and I had stayed home every year-saving for Vincent's twenty-first birthday-saving for a vacation. We had planned to go to Vegas since he was fourteen."

"You all needed that vacation. Since the day we met, I could not wait to take you to see my great vacation home. From the time we got to the airport and Vincent lost his passport, everything kept going wrong." I turned looking into those amazing eyes of Alex's and told her what I had been wanting to do for decades-the truth. "My greatest fear after finding you again was making you mad at me and losing you all over again."

"Nothing horrible happened-like someone dying at least," Alex responded. She stared away from us-her eyes fixed upward. "We will laugh about memories that will last a lifetime-won't we, Aruba Joe? After all, the swelling in my foot went down after we propped it up with the ice. Hey, some Aleve and lots of red wine helped me get through the soreness for a few days."

Our appetizers had not yet arrived, and I wanted to tell more about our vacation before the waitress came back to our table. "Since Alex was a bit incapacitated, I prepared the usual snacks for sunset; some fruit and cheeses and a couple bottles of pinot grigio. Let's say; she may have felt pain that day but, she felt no pain that night. The kids joined us on the patio chairs-viewing the ocean sunset together. It was almost eight thirty by the time we finished drinking our wine."

"It was the Fourth of July," Alex added, "and the Arubans had huge fireworks display scheduled downtown. Joe moved everything to the second-floor balcony. I hobbled up the steps. Our seats gave us the perfect view of the city; no crowd to deal with either."

"I really didn't know they celebrated our holiday in Aruba," Rob said.

"The Arubans are all about celebration–even our holidays. Keep in mind-a significant amount of island vacationers are American. I'd say the Dutch and Europeans dominate much of the rest of the visitors. We felt a little melancholy–we enjoyed our patriotic tradition as we watched the brilliant colors in the darkness. The grand finale of lights filled the downtown sky. My family normally listens to the Baltimore Symphony Orchestra in Hunt Valley for the Fourth. After the sky is completely dark, the fireworks and symphony play in harmony. It's become a tradition. I think they missed me being there with them."

"Hey-I would pick watching the fireworks in Aruba as often as I could if I had a house like yours," Rob said. "Family tradition or not!"

"My mother always gets our family together for that event. It's just one of her family holiday rituals."

"Well, after drinking a bottle of wine, I did feel a bit better," Alex said with a little giggle-cupping her hand around her mouth. In a lowered voice she added, "kind of like I feel right now. I have a very low tolerance to alcohol."

"There's not a whole lot you can do about a bruised foot and Alex and I decided to stay at the house. The kids agreed the Inn wouldn't be a lucky place to re-visit. I suggested they choose one of the larger casinos. Crystal wanted to drive and the Jeep started without any ignition complications. I'm not sure anyone else realized it at the time, but I made a mental note of it. The trip was an easy one; three rights and a left along the oceanside road. The grounds around the high-rise hotels are beautifully landscaped with tropical plants with vibrant colored flowers of red, orange, and brilliant whites accompanied by gigantic palm trees. Some of the blooms resemble our azaleas and oleanders. At night, the hotels and grounds are lit up with accent lights and are gorgeous. They even have caged parrots and tropical birds along garden walkways. The caged birds are as beautiful as they are talkative, and they speak Spanish-Papiamento blend. Alex liked talking to them and got a kick out of their responses in Spanish."

Alex must have thought I was leaving out some of the details because she jumped right in. "The open-air bars have several different types of seating. You can sit at the bar, at high top tables, or individual wide canvas covered, chaise lounge seats-depending on where you go, of course. There were even canopied beds to lie on. The beds I saw had thin, white sheers hanging around the sides for a truly romantic experience. One of the restaurants has a patio overlooking a pond with a pair of black swans swimming around. A waterfall trickles down a couple of stories of rocks from the casino and lobby above."

"Just listening to Joe describe the plant life takes me right back to Aruba," Alex said with a sigh. "At night, the stars were so brilliant and brighter than any I have viewed before. They seemed so close I felt like I could reach up in the sky and touch them. The night air was warm–not too humid. I have not experienced such beauty in the night sky since I visited Oahu with my mom back in 1982. Diamond Head was equally as impressive at night with its calcite crystals visible in the darkness."

"Sometimes, I feel chilly at night down at the beach," Jan said. "I take a sweater even in the summer-just in case I may need it."

"You're always cold," Rob responded.

"I had been feeling like the hero of the day. I felt I had finally redeemed myself. My sweetheart was happy, and the vacation was on the right path. The kids got to go to the casino-their family vision of a vacation has become reality.   Alex enjoyed the ambiance of the evening and running her fingers through my hair. She likes to tease me about the touch of gray in my hair. Romance lived under those stars in Aruba. We sure did share a lovely evening together."

"You speak like a poet," Jan commented. "Alex, you never told me about that side of Joe. I mean– 'Aruba Joe'."

Smiling at Jan's comment I responded, "I know; I'm guilty as charged.   I have been called a true romantic more than once before."   I looked over at Alex. Perhaps my interpretation of her body language may be different than logical Alex would like to admit but, I thought her eyes spoke sensual, silent words to me. Did she still remember those same details of that evening-just as much as I did?   Were they so significant she would come to the belief in us?

232

Allowing myself a moment to reminisce-I decided those memories could wait to savor yet another time-I turned back to my story. "I must admit; I was feeling mighty grand that evening. We sang some Eagles songs in the darkness. I think we did a good job of harmonizing, too."

"The Eagles–wasn't that your first date together?" Jan asked.

"It was our 'first' *official* date," Alex quickly answered.

One thing I noticed, all kidding aside, Jan did seem to have a good memory on certain details. Alex and I really did not agree on our first date–whether it was the night of the networking event, a dinner two days later, or the concert two days after the dinner. Really, it didn't matter. What mattered was this dinner together-tonight. What mattered was she didn't back out on me–my greatest fear earlier in the week.

"Now, I bet that was a wonderful sight," Jan said with her chin resting in her hand. "Alex hobbling along with her bruised toes-singing. And, you probably didn't feel any pain did you?" She giggled as only women do when they share an intimate secret or situation with one another.

"I like to sing-although the ears around me may not particularly appreciate the key in which I sing. I'd say I'm one of those rather out-of-time and off-key people. We were on vacation, and we really didn't care one bit. We enjoyed paradise just like everyone else. We hadn't eaten much after we got back from the beach–except for a bit of some fruit and cheese and, perhaps a few peanut M&M's. I learned something else about Alex that I never knew. She liked to keep fruit and chocolate in bowls while we were away. She does the same at her home. The sun and the rough surf had taken away our appetite earlier and the wine totally mellowed the two of us."

"We ended up sitting around the pool until late. I enjoy a couple laps in the pool under the stars over Aruba. Alex is right about the stars. They appear so incredibly close to earth."

"I have to agree," Alex added, "it was a peaceful and wonderful evening. Joe and I turned in somewhat early. I was so daggone tired. It had been one heck of a long-assed-day."

"Well, it was quiet up to the time the kids got back in the house. Alex and I were in a dead sleep. Sun and wine do that to you. We were sleeping like babies-buck naked babies. The next thing I heard was a crash at our door. Jade came in and jumped on our bed. I was trying to cover up and Alex was, too. She was somewhat tipsy and laughing."

"Oh–my–God," Jan stated with just the slightest hesitation between each word and a bit of a higher pitch on 'God'.

"Crystal and Vincent were right behind her-jumping up and down. Jade had won twenty-five hundred dollars on the penny slot machine," Alex said. "That girl-she has some kind of luck."

"I wasn't feeling so lucky," I added. "Grabbing her robe, Alex shooed them out of our bedroom and into the living room. I was in shock from what they could have seen."

"Oh, Aruba Joe," Alex added, "it was probably so dark. I bet they didn't see anything at all."

"I don't think so, woman. Didn't you notice the way the girls came out to breakfast the next day and giggled when they looked at me? They sure saw something."

"Well," Rob added, "nothing different than any other household. Sounds like it all happened fast though. A little added drama to your vacation-who would have thought?"

"You're right, Rob," Alex said. "But I would have probably felt the same way in that situation if it were me."

"I couldn't look those girls in the eye at all next day. I took the opportunity to pull some weeds and trim a few of the bushes. I just went about the day doing my thing. Thank goodness we purposely hadn't made plans. We had all agreed to plan each day as a team—I think that was Alex's idea. I knew I had wanted to get some gardening done while I was in Aruba. They like sitting by the side of the pool. It didn't matter to me what we did. Around eleven am, the sun starts getting hotter and the trade winds pick up. I decided to do a couple of house projects. Those exterior light fixtures get corroded quickly and were begging to be scraped and painted."

"Aruba Joe just couldn't seem to sit still," Alex added. "He flits around the house doing one project or another. And he leaves stuff all over the place. I can't tell you how many times he asked us if we had seen a tool he misplaced."

"Yeah. Maybe I forget to put things away but, I eventually get things done and done right. That's from working around the house with my father and the farm with my grandfather. Although, my father had a unique way to keep his tools. He outlined them in white chalk on a peg board. He could tell instantly if one was missing. I was usually the culprit. Anyway, the night before I noticed the lamps on the upstairs balcony looked a bit rough so I figured I would take care of them. A good scrape and paint job made them look new. Alex and Vincent were reading a book–enjoying the sun and water. I had a bit of a shocker at the top of the stairs though. The girls, on the other hand, were up on the second floor practically tanning in the nude. They had put bottle caps on their nipples. Those girls have no sense of discretion. I tell you; they just do it like they feel it."

"You know, Joe," piped in Rob, "there is one thing I have learned about children and their parents."

"Oh yeah, just *one* thing?" I asked.

"Well; the nut doesn't fall from the proverbial tree." Rob said as he turned his head slightly toward Alex.

Alex smiled in return as she raised her well maintained eyebrows. You would have thought she had just had them waxed, every hair in line and perfect. Her dimples on either side of her mouth were fully displayed. I like seeing those dimples.

There was no denying it. Alex could not take a defensive stance to Rob's analogy; they were also partiers like their mother had been. Quite frankly, the free spirit in Alex is far from my conservative ways. But strange as it may seem, it's the facet of her personality which initially lured me toward her. After all; opposites do attract.

"The kids were intrigued by all the lizards running around the house. I once discovered a toad that was as big as a cantaloupe," I showed them using my outstretched cupped hands to illustrate the size. "The toad sat under the palm trees out back. Every time I visit my house there is some new and exotic creature taking up residency in the yard or the house."

"If that toad was as big as you say, I would not like having him hop around me while I was sun tanning," Jan said.

"They don't do anything to you. I tend to enjoy reading by the pool too and joined Alex. The only sound was from the water spewing from the mouths of the metal dolphins into the pool. An occasional cluster of parrots or Oriole bird chirped overhead. I got a couple of chapters read and could feel the heat. It was a good thing I had my SPF 50 on."

"A blood curdling scream came from inside the house. Taking no time to put on our flip flops and sandals, Alex and I leapt across the patio and reached the back glass doors simultaneously. Alex pushed past me to get inside. Both girls were standing at the door of the downstairs bathroom; the door was wide open. Jade screamed again and pointed toward the floor behind the toilet base. Crystal had both hands covering her mouth; her feet were dancing around. A scorpion–its tail curled in that defensive attack position was scurrying across the ceramic tile."

"Scorpions! Oh my God! Those things are poisonous. You have scorpions in your house?" Jan exclaimed. "There are scorpions in Aruba?"

"I had never seen a scorpion before. Not once in the twenty years of visits to Aruba had I even heard of a scorpion citing. Never even saw a snake. Truth be told, the scorpion was about an inch and a half long. Crystal and Jade were just overreacting. They must have seen something on television about them. I don't think they have ever seen one either. I told Crystal to get the broom and dustpan. I figured I'd sweep his venomous self to the rear of the back yard where he belonged. Instead, she came back with one of my running shoes."

"The left or right shoe?" asked Rob chuckling with a snort. "Go on, I was just trying to be funny."

"Vincent came in and saw the girls running around and screaming. He arrived just in time to see Jade grab the shoe out of Crystal's hand. Jade pummeled the creature to a pulp. Her wrist flew up and down-the sharp slap of the shoe on tile filled the air. She must have whacked it a dozen times. Vincent didn't get a chance to see the critter in its normal state. He said he was used to his sister's loud out-bursting and didn't take her screaming seriously at first. I'm telling you she was so loud the dead would have woken up for goodness' sake. Jade explained the situation to her brother-her voice full of emotion. She told him a poisonous scorpion had tried to bite her when she was in the bathroom. Jade showed Vincent the remains of the 'poisonous scorpion'. The heel of my shoe had what remained a few scorpions body parts, and a creamy, gooey substance was wedged in the crevices."

"Vincent shrugged his shoulders and went out the back door. I think he mumbled something about his sisters being too emotional over everything," Alex added.

"Sounds like a normal brother's response to his sisters' dilemma to me," Jan quipped. "Men always try to bring logical sense to a situation and just throw out the emotion. I don't get it. The poor girl was trying to take a pee and this, this creature wanted to poison her."

"That's Aruba; always finding new creatures, plants, and birds. I had an agenda-there were plenty of other sites to see in

Aruba besides scorpions in the bathroom. Since they really didn't know much about the island I suggested going down to the Natural Pool for the afternoon and dinner at the Clubhouse afterwards. Aruba Joe made an executive decision for the good of the group, you see. Before we left, I made reservations for the restaurant. I can practically taste that crusted red snapper. It's one of the best meals on the island. Alex and her kids were always willing to do and try anything I suggested." The latter statement and meaningful glance were sincere. "I've never traveled with a group before where everyone was always so upbeat and copasetic."

Alex grinned back at me and said slowly with deliberation, "I don't know that I always had a cool head. But, for some silly reason we kept going along with you so *we* must be a bit strange to have kept following your lead."

"The Natural Pool known as *"conchi"* by the islanders is one of the main attractions on the island. It was formed by volcanic rock right on the beach. The pool fills with ocean water as it breaks against the exterior lava rocks and runs down the interior rock walls. It's a rather remote area on the beach and quite difficult to find. Most vacationers and even some islanders have been known to hire a guide. I knew if I kept driving southbound toward the center of the island and then traveled eastward some sort of land marker would jostle my memory and I would find the pool."

240

"I have to give him credit," Alex added. "He maneuvered that Jeep through every, single dusty back road and hill. At least we got to see more of the island than just hotels and downtown. Vegetation on that area of the island is sparse. It's a lot rockier and desert-like and not uncommon to see a couple of goats, donkeys, or chickens grazing in the typical Aruban family yard. The houses are quaint and simple on that side of the island and is less inhabited than anywhere else we had been. I don't think some of those people have electric and running water."

"I wasn't watching the scenery so much. It was a good day. I just focused on finding our destination. I finally recognized one of the road signs and parked the Jeep. The trade winds carried the brown dust from the tires in the air–a clear announcement of our arrival for anyone within a mile of us."

"I hate to interrupt you Aruba Joe but, at this point I must. The parking lot was more like an open patch of hard dirt with deep ruts. A huge hill slanted upward at a twenty-five-degree incline. A couple of small shacks were scattered on the property. We were in the middle of 'nowhere'. The only cars around the shacks were broken and rusted with most of them on cinder blocks since the tires were missing. The way Joe described it to us earlier that morning was somewhat different than what we experienced. He had described it as an area cordoned off by this wonderful swimming area; a romantic and scenic place inside of a naturally formed rock

241

wall along the ocean. I had envisioned an oasis. Go ahead with your story, Aruba Joe."

"Uh, oh," Rob said. "Maybe the back yard pool is safer when you go to Aruba. Let's see if I can remember the details correctly. Oh yeah-Vincent almost drowned in an undertow, his mother had almost broken her foot and nearly drowned, and his sister almost had a nervous breakdown. You sure have a weird concept of a 'good day'. I wonder what your definition of a bad vacation day would be."

Someone from the next table overheard Rob's summation and started to snicker. We looked over and laughed along with them-if you can't beat 'em-join 'em'- right? Alex laughed the least. I made a quick mental note to work on that part of her. The woman's humor had simply vanished. One of the football players, the one with the deepest laugh, said, 'go, Aruba Joe.' I readily accepted those few simple words as sheer encouragement. Even the diners beside *them* joined in the laughter. No one has ever laughed at me like that before; well, except my sisters. I think those other diners laughed because I am just such a funny storyteller.

"I have not modified anything," I said. "Especially, not about this vacation. And I'll tell the tale each and every time as it was. Hands down-Aruba is a wonderful place to visit and explore. In all honesty, the last time I had gone to the natural pool was on horseback about ten years before and we had a tour guide, so I was

242

a bit off track. You are correct, my sweet, in saying the area was a bit rustic. One of the shacks was a retail store with a canopied, small structure behind it. The canopy looked like someone had loosely stitched some old, torn umbrella canvases together and tied them with hemp cord to four wooden poles. A cinder block wall was on one side of the canopy. We had been driving over an hour and I stopped to get directions to the pool. The place was typical Aruban housing on that side of the island. A couple of geese, some chickens, and a goat grazed on dried grasses out back. A rather friendly short-haired gray colored cat sat on one of the old wooden chairs seated under the canopy. Some late modeled rusty junk cars and car parts were strewn around the yard."

"It sounded like the shack had a lot of character," Jan said. "When I think of a place like that here in the states it is 'ghetto' in the city or junk yard in the county. In the Caribbean it's homey-a reflection of the owners' personality."

"And a 'homey', short Aruban woman came out of the shack. Her dark-skinned face exposed white irregular teeth as she smiled and waved to us. Her dark hair was pulled back from her chubby face with a large, red rubber band. She wore a long, colorful cotton skirt and yellow tank top. She welcomed us with the island's traditional 'bon bini.' I told her we were looking for the Natural Pool and asked her for directions."

"She responded to us in broken Papiamento and English stating it was too far to walk and way too hot. Looking at our car for a moment she told us her daughter was over at the cruise ships and would drive right over if we wanted a ride to the pool," Alex said.

"We agreed to wait for her daughter and sat under the colorful canopy. At least there was something to sit on. There were several partially broken wooden chairs-fit right in with the shack's decor. I checked my watch a couple of times-unsure of when we had arrived–like it really mattered. We had to have been there for a good hour watching the goat and a few geese wandering around the junky back yard. At one point, we even started walking up the hill to get a look. I wasn't sure of the distance from the rocky dirt road to the ocean. My bearings were off. When we reached the top of the hill, we couldn't even see the water. Sweat was pouring out of my eyeballs."

"The road leading toward the ocean was just as pitted with deep, rocky ruts from years of four wheelers and jeeps navigating the hillside. We would never have been able to maneuver the Sahara through the ruts without risking damage to the Jeep. We had forgotten to bring water and the sun was intense. Waiting for the woman's daughter was clearly our only option at the time," Alex said.

"We had an opportunity to view the old cars and trucks strewn in a cluttered mess over the field behind the shack. We didn't notice when we pulled up how many there were. Tires and car parts sat up against the rusty, sun-bleached vehicles. I wonder if those people just don't like to throw anything away."

"They probably sell the car parts to each other," Rob said. "We live in a throw-away society. Those people have learned to be quite resourceful."

"Or it's too expensive to transport junk and garbage off the island. Another car had pulled up. Three people got out and looked around. They spotted us sitting under the canopy and walked over. They were also on a journey to the Natural Pool. They were from Boston. They had never been to Aruba before and had visited several of the other historic sites earlier, including the lighthouse and the old church. Being the gentleman that I am, I offered my seat to them. They graciously declined and the threesome propped themselves on the wall. We watched as a three-foot iguana sauntered across the dirt covered driveway. He appeared to be in no rush and vanished into some dense brush behind the old cars."

"Another car pulled up. A couple got out; the woman slung a small knapsack over her shoulder. They looked like people from Holland; tall, slender, and blonde haired," Alex said. "They started walking up the hill. I figured they would be walking back any minute, but they kept walking. We never saw them again."

245

"I had truly hoped they had some water with them. They sure were going to need it. The animals at the shack appeared oblivious to the humans around them. A large goose started flapping its wings and chased some of the chickens milling around. The cat lazily watched from his post. For the first time, I noticed a black dog laying under one of the rusted cars. He hadn't moved until the goose made all that racket; barely lifted his head. At least we had some entertainment while we waited in the hot sun. A short little island woman wearing a big white, wide brimmed hat pulled up in a large Jeep. Her relationship to the woman in the shack was obvious. She shared similar facial characteristics. Other than her youth, the only other distinct difference was the younger woman's teeth were straight. Her smile spanned her mouth as she introduced herself; her name was Carmen. The Jeep was extremely different from any of the others I had seen on the island before. It looked like it could hold a dozen passengers. The tires were extremely large and showed signs of wear-gray in color than black. Carmen explained she had purchased the Jeep from some company in South America."

"Probably right out of the marijuana fields from one of the cartels," Rob quipped.

"You may be right, Rob," Jan added in response. "I think I saw those kinds of vehicles on the drug raids reported on the news."

"While I began negotiating a price for the ride, two other couples had joined us and wanted to ride along to the pool. Carmen agreed to take all of us down to the water for $80."

"Wow," Jan exclaimed, "that was some expensive ride to the beach."

"Perhaps you might think so but, it was truly our best alternative. Incidentally, the rental car companies in Aruba won't even allow you to take the rentals to the Natural Pool because of the dangerous hillside. Good thing we decided not to take the Jeep. In all the years I have rented cars in Aruba, I've never had any problem with any rental cars down there and had planned to keep it that way. I had a superior record of car rentals. The group piled into the Jeep like canned sardines. Our bodies were separated by clothing or sweat. Carmen began the drive with a loud grinding of the gears. There were no windows, just a windshield. An army green colored canvas canopy protected us from the sun's flesh burning rays. The temperature was in the high nineties and the air was remarkably still in between those hills."

"During the entire drive to the pool I don't recall having any breeze at all," Alex said. "It was the first time we didn't have a breeze in Aruba."

"Brown and deep rose-colored shrubs grow on that side of the island-no green foliage at all. The kids couldn't get over the herds of wild goats grazing along the hillside. It's interesting how the look of vegetation doesn't affect them and yet they get nutrients from eating that stuff. They appeared rather plump. There were no visible signs from the heavy rains a couple of nights before. Whatever rain fell on the island during the storm must've run off the hills into the ocean."

The waitress came back to the table with our dinners. "Here you go," she said as she expertly placed two of our meals in front of us without the slightest hesitation. A young man stood behind her with the other two plates and handed them to her. "Enjoy your meal. Is there anything else you need or that I can get for you?" She smiled pleasantly. Everything about the night was pleasant.

"Thank you," Jan responded to our waitress. "I think we are fine for now although you may want to bring another bottle of the wine in a few minutes."

"Very good," the waitress responded as the top half of her body bent slightly toward us. "I'll take care of that for you."

We sat in silence for a few minutes while we arranged our glasses and made room for our dinner plates. I tasted the first bite of my sushi grade, wild Alaskan salmon. "Very good-done to absolute perfection."

I figured I'd allow everyone a chance to eat for a few minutes before I returned to my story. I was hungry. I took another sip of my glass of pinot savoring its slightly chilled, crisp flavor.

"She shifted those gears–grinding them into position. Our bodies thrashed into one another-we couldn't avoid hitting each other. The vehicle wasn't equipped with seatbelts. We held onto whatever piece of metal or seating we could to limit slamming each other. Carmen tried to keep a steady pace without deviating too far from the dirt and rocky roadway. I could tell she was quite experienced with the drive to the beach. At some points, she was riding on a thirty-degree angle to avoid getting the tires trapped in two-foot ruts. She was great at answering our diverse inquiries about the island's natural inhabitants–snakes as well as the four-legged creatures. I learned something new about Aruba's wildlife. Our guide told us there were poisonous snakes on the island. Not once have I ever seen or heard anyone say anything about poisonous snakes before that day."

"Nor did you hear about scorpions," Alex added.

"I only saw wild goats and dogs roaming freely on the island And, of course, I saw plenty of iguanas. Iguanas and lizards are everywhere-you can't avoid them. I've seen some rather large iguanas on the golf course at the clubhouse or downtown at one of the marinas."

"I wouldn't be caught dead on a golf course with iguanas and lizards running around," Jan said with a squirm. "That gives me the creeps!"

"Good grief, Jan," Rob said, "you've watched too many movies. They don't attack you. Those creatures are more scared of you than you are of them."

"Rob is correct, Jan. They move out of your way fast. They do leave their tell-tale remnants of their presence though–iguana poop-lots of iguana poop."

"Do you mean they allow them to poop everywhere?" Jan asked with a sincere look on her face.

Jan was too much. How remarkably naïve she was of wildlife. "No, the grounds keepers at the golf course have never trained the iguanas to use the bathroom facilities!" There was that blonde thing again.

"Well, I don't know what they do. Just go on and tell your story, Joe," Jan sheepishly added.

"It took about forty-five minutes from that raggedy shack to get to the bottom of the hill. The next time I will remember to take water along. We only carried a camera that day. As you get to know me, you will notice my biggest flaw is my forgetfulness. That day I felt like a typical vacationer. Alex and Crystal clicked away at the sights with their cellphones. There is much beauty to capture. So many shades of brown with pops of colors like reds, orange, and yellow although the colors are like small dots compared to the vastness of the countryside."

"I still had a colorful purple foot which had started to turn a few other colors like yellow and green. My foot was a bit swollen, and I had worn rubber flip flops that day." Alex said. "I had pictured a large pool with a parking area next to it. Maybe, that was just me expecting something without asking."

"You'll be better prepared next time you go to Aruba, Alex," Jan said as she reached over and patted Alex's arm in a nurturing manner.

"Our first time to Aruba was a true learning experience, Jan," Alex said. "A beautiful island surrounded by the most beautiful ocean."

I slid my hand over Alex's under the table with a gentle squeeze. She had claimed to be limited in the area of romance. Alex's dreams and passions in her youth had been damaged through a series of bad relationships. During the past nine months she was gradually changing. It was moments we shared-like this-I treasured most. I got lost for a moment or two. I looked at Rob and Jan–they were staring at me. I also noticed everyone seated around us was listening to our conversation. I tried not to let their staring faces bother me and returned to my story. I had a lot more to say.

"Well, we finally got to the bottom of the last hill. There is a huge, flat area, full of hard brown compacted dirt. You know the saying 'old as dirt'? If ever there is a picture one can associate with that saying this spot would be it. There are large black and gray boulders. Some of them had to be thirty feet high. Several other Jeeps were already parked there. There was no sign of the Holland couple. My entire back was wet from sweat. Carmen ground the Jeep's gear into park and got out. We followed her as she led us to the top of a long, steep rustic wooden staircase. The steps were made from compacted dirt and rock. A group of big boulders-the size of dump trucks-were at the bottom of the staircase. I didn't have that view when I had gone there before since we were on horseback. Beyond that-as far as you could see-was the ocean. We watched the green ocean waters as they turned into white crested waves pummeling the white sand. A large, wooden sign posted next to the base of the man-made stairs had two short phrases in bold black lettering– 'Natural Pool' with another short blurb: 'no climbing on the rocks'. You certainly needed a good pair of knees to navigate those stairs. The steps were rather uneven–quite solidly placed–certainly not meant to be used by the handicapped. Alex did a pretty good job considering she had a bit of an injury. The kids, on the other hand, were full of energy and got down to the bottom first where a huge, massive cluster of black boulders curved around the beach. Our guide told us the best way to get to the pool was to walk along the small rocks around the side of the boulder formation. The kids took no time following her instructions and were climbing alongside the natural configuration. The rocks were a bit slippery, and you had to hold onto the small rocks jutting along the large

252

boulders for support; inserting our fingers into crevices in the boulders to stabilize ourselves. On the other side of the boulder are beautiful, black lava rocks forming the pool. The wet, black lava rock is what makes your footing a bit challenging to say the least, but everyone in our group managed rather well."

"I tell you two; it was rather challenging," Alex said to Jan and Rob. "If I was a goat or a mountain climber, I could have managed to get through that part of the island effectively. I'm no sissy but wearing flip flops is not what I would recommend for footwear if you ever ventured to Aruba's Natural Pool."

Alex finished up by saying to me, "it's a good thing you don't work as a tour guide in Aruba. Perhaps your chosen profession is what you excel in here at home because you wouldn't get very many referrals and tips. People need details. I needed more details."

"My word, woman. You got to see a lot of the island, didn't you? And, you have fabulous memories. It was a fantastic trip. The view of the ocean from the pool was spectacular. Alex perched herself on one of the lava rock ledges. She wanted to rest her swollen foot. The water, from the rushing surf, was pulling at her and she had a lot of difficulty holding on. She was determined to stay seated on those rocks though."

Alex said. "The cutest little yellow, black, and blue tropical fish swim in the pool. And I also remember those nasty little crabs scurrying around my fingers every time I put my hands on the rocks; curious little devils."

"You want details? I will talk about details. The pool water is about twenty feet deep and forty feet wide. It is a magnificent place for a swim. The surf crashes against the outside walls and cascades down the inner rocks into the pool. The constant surge of water over the rocks keeps the pool water refreshingly cool. It didn't get too crowded people of all ages shared the afternoon with us. Several little kids were having the time of their lives; they had no inhibitions whatsoever and jumped into the pool from the rocky ledges. They were just as intrigued by the tropical, saltwater fish in the pool-the fish sparkled in the green water. It was like swimming in a giant fishbowl. Something you would see in a travel guide. Breathtaking. The coastline spans for miles in either direction. There aren't any houses, roads, or traffic."

"Alex's kids got brave as they watched me diving into the water. I had taken the opportunity to show off a bit for Alex. I wanted them to know the pool was safe. It wasn't long before everyone, everyone but Alex that is, was swimming in the water with me."

"Now, wait a minute. I was content to sit on the ledge; until those little crabs started coming up to my fingers and touching me with their spindly, little legs. I did not like those crabs one bit. And, secondly, I did get in the water Aruba Joe. I didn't want my children thinking I was afraid–I don't have any fear-of anything. I was a bit leery of the black fishes, though," Alex said and in a softer voice and added, "they looked like mini piranhas."

"Hmmm…I will take note of that," Rob said. He held his left hand up and with his right, animated as though he were writing something down. "Alex is *leery* of tiny, black tropical fish. Yeah, I don't think there is anything more frightening when you are swimming in the Caribbean."

"Pirates," Jan added "they are something to be afraid of in the Caribbean. I hear they have been robbing people down there. You could have been robbed, Alex."

Jan sure did have a way with coming up with some stuff. From fish to pirates. What the heck. I was glad the conversation was going well and enjoyed Rob and Jan's company immensely.

"No pirates where we were but, there is a pirate ship on the other side of the island. A touristy kind of thing where you pay a fee and snorkel and sail around a sunken ship and coral. They have a rope swing off the side of one of the sailing vessels. We were swimming on the complete opposite side of the island-the east side. Some of the little kids had brought plastic rings, put them around their waists, and floated in the water. The constant current moved them around the pool water like a giant, gentle whirlpool tub. They had a blast. Several adults brought fins and goggles and ventured to the bottom. I feel so alive when I'm there." I wanted Alex to feel the same way. I sipped my wine.

"I was wading on the perimeter of the pool when I had this incredible urge to climb the lava rocks. Everyone was busy talking and swimming; no one even noticed what I was doing. I found out how sharp the lava rocks were. They looked a lot smoother from an upward view. I stood to admire the coastlines. Over time, the surf had formed a hollowed groove at the top of the rock formation. It's just wide enough to fit a body or two into."

Suddenly someone from the table next to the football player shouted in a mocked tone, "did you forget what the sign said, Aruba Joe? 'Do not climb on the rocks?'"

The diners surrounding our table laughed out loud in unison. I surveyed the people and saw one guy in particular-his face was beaming. I assumed he was the wise guy and spoke directly in his direction. "You know, sometimes you just must be defiant and break a rule-live a little. Quite frankly I'm just glad I didn't break a limb as a result. Could have been a different twist to this part of the story."

The small crowd of onlookers nodded in agreement. Most of the diners were in the forty-to fifty-year-old range. I am sure they could relate. Hell, I wasn't known as a deviant by anyone's stretch of the imagination.

"I looked up just as I saw Joe somewhat sliding down the rock. Hmmm, let me clarify that–tumbling spasmodic like and in the most awkward way. A huge wave enveloped his body like a bubbly water blanket. It must have literally knocked him down the front side of the rock. He squealed some wild, Tarzan-like chant as his arms and legs flailed down the rock and into the pool. It all happened so quickly. It was as if I was watching him on a fast speed frame of film," Alex said, "everyone at the pool watched as Joe's body plunged sideways into the pool."

"My God, Joe" Jan said in a reprimanding tone. "What in the world were you thinking? You could have been killed. I would not have been able to watch you. I would have been in hysterics. I would have been like Jade–hopping up and down and crying. Alex, what did you do? Did you scream at him?"

Jan was dead serious–she was not the adventurous type. Her body language spoke volumes during my story. She'd wince and move around when I spoke about things getting physical. I shook my head at her. "Alex didn't scream. But, I assure you, that yell she heard from me was from physical pain as I slid down the rocks. Those darn sharp rocks. I ended up with deep scratches on my left side, elbow, and underarm. I was a bit bloody–not enough for stitches or anything. The salt water helped with the stinging. Really, I've had far worse injuries. Besides, the view of the coastline from the top of those rocks was worth every second of pain. I felt great

257

doing something out of the norm. I'm just glad one of the kids didn't decide to replicate my act of adventure. Even the adults in the pool didn't try it. Perhaps they were smart to follow the 'no rock climbing' sign," I took a moment to nod at the man at the other table.

"It is people like *you* that show other people *why* a sign like that is necessary," Alex said.

I then added, "I think it was best said; 'God has put us on this earth to set examples for one another.'"

I liked when people appreciated my humor. They recognized I was a good storyteller, too. And I realized how good I was tonight. The smiles on Rob and Jan's eager faces were like a flashing green light for me– 'go, go, go'–they seemed to say.

"My grand entrance into the pool was radically different in my mind's eye than the actual event. I could tell by the sun's position in the sky it was nearing our departure time. I didn't want to miss my red snapper at the clubhouse. By the time we packed up our shoes and shirts my wounds had stopped bleeding. The saltwater had done a good job–curing my skin. As Alex got out of the water and slid on her flip flops, I noticed her purple foot looked a bit less swollen. The Natural Pool's water seemed to have some homeopathic medicinal healing powers. Like a herd of goats, Carmen led us around the boulders, across the dirt parking area, up the irregular stone steps, and back to the Jeep. Just as we were

258

leaving, the couple that had started out on foot drove up in the back seat of another four-wheeler. A good thing for them-a relief for us."

"Only a few minutes had passed but, we became extremely hot again. It was like the sun possessed some magnetic powers through invisible tentacles from the round, pale yellow ball. Our energy was pulled out of us. The ride back to the shack seemed longer than the ride to the beach," Alex said. "But this time I wasn't as cramped during the Jeep ride. Joe sat in the front seat next to the driver."

"Sounds like he was in first class again, eh Alex?" Rob asked.

"He is something. But this time I think he deserved a bit of special treatment. I watched him get into his seat," Alex answered. "Joe was sore."

"I didn't want to be thrashed into the side of the Jeep and start bleeding again. I was looking for a painless ride back to the shack. I needed those minutes of respite."

"During the ride back, we found out Carmen and her mother raised ten kids. Amazing. The people in Aruba are hard workers. They may be a bit slow by our standards but, they are hard working. When we finally arrived at our destination, I gave her an extra ten dollars. A couple of the other people did the same. She had been a great guide through the desert hills. We will have to remember to see her again," Alex said.

CHAPTER 19   SNAPPER SUPPER

"I took a different ride back to the house. I drove through downtown Oranjestad. The sidewalks were full of tourists from the cruise ships. The port provides an opportunity to shop at designer shops like Gucci, Ralph Lauren, the many jewelry shops, and various small shops. There are also locally owned businesses selling clothing and other trinkets out of kiosks and sheds."

"Wow!" Jan exclaimed. "Shopping in Aruba sounds like a wonderful experience to me. I love to visit the jewelry shops when Rob and I travel."

"Face it-you just like to shop and spend money anywhere Jan," Rob said to his wife with a good-natured smile. "You know what we do on the weekends? I drive her to different malls and stores where I sit in the car for an hour or two while she goes shopping."

The things we do for our women to keep them happy. I knew Rob was a good man not long after we met. Men are quite simple in that respect. "Keep the queen happy and everyone in the kingdom will be happy. Anyway, I wanted to end the day with another good memory and had every intention of finishing it with a fine meal. Everyone agreed with my choice of restaurant for that evening; especially, since I raved about the food and service. Vincent wanted to work out at the clubhouse before dinner. They have a universal fitness center complete with massage and salon if you are so inclined to partake in that luxury stuff. When Vincent returned, the girls were finishing getting dressed. I took a bit of a long shower–the water hitting the scratches on my back and side felt good. Alex gave me a personal massage with aloe body lotion. By the way–aloe lotion is another product of the island."

"I dropped everyone off at the restaurants' front doorstep and parked the Sahara. By the time I joined them Alex had selected a table on the veranda overlooking the ponds and gardens surrounding the clubhouse. We viewed the entire sunset from the restaurant."

"After a hot day like that I would've chosen the air conditioning," Jan said. "I love the beach, but afterwards I want to be nice and cool."

"I like dining outside as often as I can in Aruba. We listened to the soothing sounds of the water trickling over the rock gardens. I just enjoy being outside any time."

"Our waitress arrived at our table. She was pleasant, quite attractive, had shoulder length blonde hair and pale, blue eyes. She introduced herself as 'Trees'. Making conversation when she came over to fill the water glasses, Trees said her name stood for harvester. Her great, great, grandfather was a farmer as were all the males in her family. Hence, the reason for her name. She was on her college summer break from Holland. The Arubans can attend college in Holland for free. College is a great way for students to see the world. I should know. I went on a high school ski trip and ended up down the wrong side of a slope in Switzerland but, that's another story."

"I think we were more thirsty than hungry," Alex said.

"Everyone ordered a mixed drink concoction of some sort or another."

"You left out a rather significant detail about the short chairs, Joe. The clubhouse had these really low chairs—more like oversized lounge chairs you sit in around the pool. But, these chairs were around the dinner tables. When we sat down, our chin practically touched the top of the table. Your arms were up like this to your plate." She raised her arms upward to show Jan and Rob-a fork and knife in each hand. "It was practically impossible to cut your food. Joe was comfortable enough, of course; I was not. He was razor focused and, on a mission, and had just one thing on his mind-getting his red snapper."

"They were low, I agree, but that simple fact was not going to deter me from enjoying my dinner. Everyone ordered something different-much like we did tonight. Well-we waited. And we waited some more. The kids were getting tired—we had had a pretty long, hot day. No one was in the mood to linger around the dinner table."

262

"Trees came out and apologized for the long wait, poured some more water for us, and took off. I bet it was an hour before we saw her again," Alex said.

"By this time, the kids were getting contrary. There is no water left in our water glasses. The sunset turned into darkness. Conversation had hit a dead silence. The most activity on that patio came from the overhead ceiling fans. Alex was just trying to crack a smile to keep the kids from getting angrier–it wasn't working. Even, I was getting irritated–snapper or no snapper. It was bad. Although, I did my best not to show it. After all, it was my idea to go to the clubhouse for dinner. Now, don't get the wrong idea about the fine dining in Aruba, Rob and Jan. That evening was no comparison to the usual meals I've had there."

"Ms. Holland came back to the table and said something about the chef. Apparently, they were experiencing some '*issues*' in the kitchen," Alex said. "We found out from the neighboring diners the friggin' chef had not even shown up for the night or had walked out. We never did get the story straight. You would have thought they would have told us about that one-minute detail when we called for reservations–or at least when we arrived for dinner. I just wanted to go home at that point."

"Could you imagine Rob," Jan said, "if Angelo wasn't here at the restaurant to serve his guests? Or, if he didn't have some other chef here when he was away? Oh, my goodness. How absurd for the chef not to be there."

"I'm embarrassed to say, it didn't get any better at dinner that night. The kids were threatening to take off and walk home. I was tired, sunburned, and feeling a little sore–my side was achy. Alex was complaining loudly about the service and asked me to go into the kitchen and find out what was going on just as Trees came out with two plates in her hands-my dinner and Vincent's salad."

Crossing both her arms and moving her head from side to side, with a deep sigh Alex added, "And, Ms. Holland told us she would get the rest of the food. That's why the girls and I told you two to start eating. It sounded like she was on her way back to the kitchen to get our dinners. Well, that was wishful thinking."

I learned to understand those sighs. I discovered Alex used them to reduce anxiety–kind of a cleansing breath. She told me she had migraine headaches in her twenties that were so extreme she would lie in bed for days suffering, lethargic, and unable to go to work. She had learned biofeedback and meditation techniques during the height of her frequent episodes. I remembered her telling me about how she used cleansing breaths to reduce the pain of the migraines. Sighing had become a useful tool.

"I dug into the snapper and Vincent started eating his salad. He and I finished eating our meals and still no dinners for the girls. Dinner had been a truly bad experience."

"The girls and I were mad." Alex said. "HA!-'*the vacation of a lifetime*.'" She held up her hands on either side of her head moving her forefinger and middle fingers like quotation marks.

"All I know was this-I had to find a way to keep my attitude positive; for the good of the group in an effort to follow Alex's lead. And, yet I was absolutely dying inside to obtain a small nugget of redemption. The girls' food finally arrived to the table. It was cold, portions were small, and some of the things the girls had wanted were not on their plate. Trees quickly explained the kitchen was out of some of the vegetables we had ordered. Although, we did manage to get some more water from her. I can tell you the mood at the table was lower than the chairs we sat in. At that point we needed to get through dinner and just get the heck out of there."

"We even waited for our bill," Alex added. "Like salt to Aruba Joe's open wound-the bill came to three hundred and fifty dollars."

"The waitress refused to take anything off the check. I can't tell you how horrible I felt. There wasn't anyone in a supervisory capacity available to talk to–other than the bartender. Alex and I left exhausted and disappointed and yet relieved to be able to go home. The kids had already started walking home. It was just the two of us." With a nod and wink to Rob and Jan I added, "truth be told; the only person happy with the meal was me. When we returned to the house, I turned on the pool lights to change the mood.

265

Alex and I spent the rest of the evening sipping wine glasses filled with some African merlot she found. Yes sirree; I was back at the castle and King of my domain once again."

"It's a wonder I didn't bop you on the head after that day," Alex blurted with a tone of aggravation. "You kept making suggestions and taking us places and doing such stupid stuff. I'm still shaking my head about all that went on. All I wanted to do was lie by the pool or go to the beach. I wanted to get some rest. I wanted a suntan for goodness' sake. My days are so intense, Jan and Rob, and pressure is constantly on me to perform and face unrealistic demands and keep a happy face to my clients. It is exhausting! This was my second vacation in three years now. Something I was not accustomed to."

"I wouldn't say our first couple of days in Aruba weren't fun; they sure were. It had adventure and just the sun made my vacation. We had a few hiccups during the first few days; that's all. I will admit; it was quite emotional for some if not all of us at some point. I got a bit frustrated at times. But everyone left the island with a great tan and good memories. We drank a lot of wine and saw some remarkable sites." Turning toward Alex one adorable dimple seemed to wink at me. The woman captivated me with her smile.

CHAPTER 20 – PINEAPPLE PANTS

"Each morning, I made sure I lathered Alex with sunscreen. The kids took care of one another. I certainly didn't want anyone to suffer from sunburn. I knew of the sun's damaging rays from experience. Since the island is so close to the equator a burn down there from the intense rays would have put a huge damper on our trip."

"Didn't you have some friends come down and join you?" Jan asked.

"Mary Lib and John," Alex responded. "They are huge world travelers. When I told Mary Lib we were going to Aruba she practically invited herself. They came down the day after the Natural Pool."

"That day–what can I say," I added with outstretched hands, "was the start of another gorgeous day in Aruba. I left Alex in bed to get some rest–to sleep off the previous nights' liquid essence from the fruit of the vine. Vincent and I engaged in male-bonding and laughed about the dinner fiasco the night before. The girls were fixing breakfast. Crystal and Jade had found the Amaretto. They laced their coffee with its sweetness-claiming it was a great way to start the day. I think the Aruban weather had something to do with it." I paused as I sipped my wine. I need to whet my whistle.

"I first heard the loud engine noises while working in the front garden. When I walked around back, there were several huge, older 'beater' trucks in the lower part of my back yard-three trucks in all. They were rusted heaps of metal with huge cracks in their rubber wheels. Four people were running around-a woman and three men. They were dressed in jeans and long-sleeved shirts and floppy, straw hats-common work clothes in Aruba. I realized they were doing work for my neighbor. He owns one of the local shops on the island."

"What's a 'beater' truck?" Jan asked with a quirky smile on her face.

"I hear you, Jan," Alex responded. "Jade introduced us to the term. It's used for a vehicle; it's usually inexpensive to drive, older, and may not look all that nice."

"Oh," Jan said, "it figures Jade would have come up with that one."

"My Aruban neighbors built their homes after mine. My house was constructed before most of the ones on my street. The management company of Del Sol was rather strict with the exterior colors, overall size, and the positioning of the houses on the lots. Building and getting all the approvals is pretty much like any subdivision here. All the structures are somewhat uniform and still unique from one another. Their values are in excess of a million. My screwball of a neighbor ended up building his house way too far back from his original approved plans. His house is now blocking part of my ocean view." I could feel a bit of heat surface under my collar, and I knew my neck and face were turning red. "I still get so upset about my neighbor and what he had deliberately done to me. His actions toward me are quite contrary of your average Aruban. They want Americans to visit and live on their island. We brought them both jobs and prosperity of proportions they had never known. Apparently, my neighbor did not share the typical Aruban attitude."

"Needless-to-say; from that time forward that neighbor and I don't get along. I contested his construction site as soon as I saw the poured foundation. The ruthless son-of-a-gun started building his house twenty feet back from where he had been originally approved. He destroyed my view of the ocean, a large part of my decision for building on that particular lot.   I wanted to condemn his place but couldn't get anything done about it. Aruba's court process is so slow I hired a Dutch attorney–all the contracts are in Dutch. I even had to hire an interpreter. But the legal costs kept mounting and were too hefty for my purse strings to bare.   I could not continue to lose my hard-earned money. I withdrew my court documents and learned to suck-it-up."

"Wow," Rob said, "a million dollars. That is an expensive home by anyone's measurement device. That was messed up. But when you take on a project in a foreign country like that you're almost sure to get screwed. Sounds like some high stakes gambling to me."

"How can anyone gamble with real estate, Rob? Real estate is one of the best investments you can make. I'm a realtor-have been for thirty years. I walked down to the trucks in the back yard. Picture this; my back yard stretches about an acre and a half behind the house. It has these wonderful, native cactuses and grasses on it. The neighbor's contractor decided to come across my property with his big trucks. One of the trucks stalled and oil had leaked all over the place; it looked like the yard was a bubblin' crude. When I got down to the foursome, I asked who was in charge. The woman answered in broken English using the word 'supervisor' as she pointed to one of the three men. He looked a bit familiar although I just couldn't place him. I asked the contracting supervisor to move the truck; that he was on my property. The supervisor was a rather portly man–dark, weathered skin, and unshaven. I insisted he remove his vehicles from my property–he had absolutely no reason or right to be there. This fat bellied dude looked at me with his small, beady dark eyes like I had three heads. He told me he was waiting on another truck to tow his broken truck away to get it fixed. He told me he thought it was okay to pull across my property and *everyone* does it when I wasn't there. That made me mad. I was never aware of that going on in my absence. He also pointed out that I didn't have a wall around my property."

270

"A wall in Aruba designates property lines-much like our fences here in America. It speaks proudly to all– 'this is mine–my domain–my castle and stay out.' Most of the homes on the island have a brick or cinder block wall along the perimeter of their property. The homeowners paint them with bright colors-only in the islands I tell you. But, in Del Sol, that is not necessarily the case as the colors and designs are approved by the developer."

Rob spoke up, "I want to hear more about what *you* did to get this dude and his rusted junkers off your property. I can't imagine my neighbor's contractor pulling his trucks across my back yard. I wouldn't have wasted my time arguing with the man-I would've shot him. Bang!"

Nodding her head in testament Jan added, "he certainly would have shot him. Rob doesn't want anyone messing up his yard for God's sake. He's always out there laying down grass seed or adding fertilizer. Our lawn looks more like a green carpet than grass. I'm surprised he even lets me walk on it."

"Well, I ended up walking away. I was satisfied he was waiting on the other truck to tow him out. I wanted to get back to gardening. John and Mary Lib were flying in around 4:30 that afternoon. I wanted the place looking good for them. I got back to the house-the kids were still busy in the kitchen. Alex was in bed. I went around front and got back to pulling weeds. Much like here; those darn weeds grow no matter what down there. The front of the house is nothing but a huge rock garden. I have palm trees, some beautiful flowering shrubs, and a variety of cactus plants all over the yard. There is a low cement wall in the front and a wall on either side of the patio around the pool with a cement railing behind the pool. It has white cement posts so you can still see the view. It's beautiful. I use one of those timer-controlled sprinkler systems to go off in the early morning and later at night. Otherwise, absolutely nothing but weeds would grow."

"Amazing isn't it," Alex added "no matter where you go there are some things that are constant–like weeds in the garden on the island of paradise."

"Awhile later, I decided to go around back to get some water. I needed to refill my water mug too. The trucks were still parked in my back yard and the men were working on my neighbor's yard. I stood watching them for a few minutes. They were taking rocky loads of dirt from the neighbor's yard and piling the dirt, chunks of concrete, and old shrubs in my back yard. Within that few minutes I grew madder than a hornet. I went back down the hill behind the pool; taking long deep breaths every, single step of the way and fought to keep my cool. I am told I can be a bit of a hot head. I owe my manners to my mom and my temper to my dad. First, I asked the supervisor about the tow truck and he said they were on the way. And then the next thing I knew, the supervisor and I started arguing. I walked over to the boundary lines of the two properties and showed him where they were. I ordered him to get the piles of dirt off my property; he was on my land. In his broken Papiamento he kept saying 'everyone does it'."

"For clarity I asked; 'does what?' He told me everyone drove over my property when I wasn't there. The son-ova-bitch. Excuse me, ladies–got bolder. The supervisor started questioning me. He decided he was going to turn things around on me like the swamp alligator he was. He wanted me to show proof I *owned* the property. He said there weren't any walls. He turned to his workers and asked them if they saw any walls. He shrugged his shoulders and shook his head. I wanted to knock his head right off his fat shoulders. Sakes alive! This guy was too much. He told me he had been a contractor on the island for years. He rocked back on his heels, outstretched his hands, and said with a smile 'everyone has a wall around their house in Aruba'. Let me tell you all a little something about me," I hesitated for a moment and looked at Alex before I went further. I wanted her to know this but, also knew it might come out a bit too rough. "When I know what I am talking about I will argue it until someone dies on his last breath. That is my nature to argue. That is how I grew up; arguing with the women in my family mostly. It got rather heated. He knew enough about Del Sol and knows how the property lines run. I waved the three other workers to join us and showed them where my property lines were. I pointed toward the two houses, where there was a wall between the properties, and pointed down the property line through the two back yards. The wall extends to the back of my neighbor's house on that side-beyond the pool; not all the way through to the back property line. The contractor instructed one of the men to call whoever was on their way to tow the oil leaking, rusted, bucket-of-a-truck to get an update on their arrival. The bulky man promised he'd have the truck off my property in a half hour. I was still mad but walked away somewhat satisfied the tow truck was on its way. I returned to my gardening. The temperature was starting to rise, and the winds were picking up as I walked up the hill."

"The nerve of that contractor; telling you 'everyone does it' when you weren't there," Rob said. "Jan's right. I would have been mighty p.o.'d myself. I may have gone down the yard with my pistol. My good ole buddy, Mr. Glock, and I would have had a bit of a conversation with that man and a lot less talk."

"Didn't feel like I needed a gun. Aruba is just not that type of place." I wanted Rob and Jan to understand that. I realized some people still think of Aruba as a very dangerous place; because of the widely publicized murder. I get that. "In Aruba, my family and I have never felt threatened-even walking downtown at three am. Also, our community is gated with multi-million-dollar homes owned by people from all over the world. I took a quick peek at the back from the driveway about a half hour later. The trucks were still there, and they were still dumping dirt in piles in my yard. I was

274

livid with this game. I half ran back down the hill. My adrenaline was pumping by that time; I'm tired of this guy. I demanded he remove the trucks immediately or I was calling the police. He started yelling back at me. That was the wrong thing for him to do. The three workers walked over to us; it's four against one. This guy just would not reason. I told him he was an asshole and to move his friggin' truck right now. The next thing I knew-he hit me in the face. I was stunned, more than anything, that the guy had hit me. My body took his punch well. I stepped back a bit, but I walked right back up to him, and stood one inch away from his round face. I was going to show him I wasn't backing down with one lousy sucker punch. I was determined to get this situation resolved right then and there. Before I could say anything else, he hit me again; took me by surprise that he hit me a second time. That second punch knocked me down on the ground. He lunged toward me. His workers caught him in mid-air and grabbed his arms and started pulling him away from me before I could get back up."

"Now, slow down Aruba Joe," Alex said. "I must provide some sort of details on what was going on up at the house. First, I was awakened by loud voices. I wasn't quite certain where they were coming from. I started walking across the living room when I looked out the back door–I saw a man hit Joe and knock him down on the ground–shirtless–wearing nothing but his pineapple print swim shorts and canvas sandals. Just so you understand, Rob and

Jan, the entire first floor faces the pool and back yard with glass doors and windows. The children were all standing at the kitchen back door. Jade went into hysterics–her hands were covering her face. She screamed, 'I want to go home' and 'take me to the airport'. Crystal told me Joe was in a fight and getting 'beat up'. Vincent kept his eyes on the brawl in the yard-he stood still. By the time I looked out back again, good ole Aruba Joe was upright. I watched as his arms flailed wildly as he screamed at the much larger man. When I saw him knock Joe down with that punch, I just saw fire. I yelled to Crystal to get Jade under control. I told Vincent to go with Joe and I ran back to the bedroom to put a pair of shoes on. The back yard is full of these nasty two-inch thorns. The thorns are all over the island and the last thing I needed was to have one of them pierce my flip flops. The only thick soled shoes I had were a pair of three-inch heels. Dressed in shorts and a bathing suit top and those shoes I rushed out the kitchen door and start running down the hill toward Vincent and Joe–I lost no time getting to my men."

"Running in heels through the desert of thorns like a heroine," Jan said with a chuckle.

"I was feeling like super woman with all that adrenaline pumping inside of me. When I got there, the big man and Joe were still yelling at one another; two other men were on either side of the big man to hold him back. The other person, a woman, was standing off to the side watching. Joe had a busted lip and a huge purple

276

colored spot on his cheek. I planted myself in between the contractor and Joe and Vincent," Alex said. "I felt like a raging witch-seething with anger and prepared to get physical with this portly man if I had to."

"Great," exclaimed Rob, "first Joe gets slammed into the desert by some hot-headed contractor and you decide you want to get more of the same-Aruba Smack Down. The heat in Aruba must have broiled your brains."

"The only thing broiling that morning was my blood pressure," I said.

"Joe quickly caught me up to speed and told me what had been happening all morning," Alex continued. "I turned my attention to the contractor. I moved even closer to the man and looked him square in his dark brown eyes and told the fat-bellied man to get off the property *now*. I told him 'enough of your stuff' and stared him down. Apparently, he wasn't used to having a woman talk like that to him. I did not care-I had no fear of him. Now, I was spitting mad and ready to pounce on his lousy self. I gave him a look from his eyes to his dirty, rotten feet. He asked me why I was looking at him like that and to stop looking at him that way."

"Just at that time, the tow truck pulled up. Vincent pushed me to the side and he and Alex were both moving toward this guy and I'm thinking we were going to have a real brawl on our hands.

Just so you know, Vincent bench presses two hundred and fifty five pounds–he's in good shape."

"Good grief!" Jan exclaimed. "Vincent was not going to let his momma get hurt. He's the cub of a tiger."

"Vincent is certainly no sissy, and I could tell he was ready to have a piece of this dude. Alex was spittin' venom and I know she can throw me three-out-of-four rounds. Everyone had gotten totally out of control because of that idiot. The tow truck driver walked over to us. He calmly looked at us with a big, white toothy grin. It only took him a moment to realize something was not right. Pointing to the stalled truck I told the tow truck driver to pull the truck off my property. The driver could clearly see I wasn't a native Aruban. He hesitated for a moment and looked at the contractor for a nod of approval. After a solemn look from the contractor the driver began hooking up the chain to the rusty heap. The two other men helped him–I think they were happy to have the opportunity to get away from the situation. I turned toward the contractor and told him he was getting a visitor–I was calling the police. He shrugged his shoulders indifferently and walked back over to the neighbor's yard. In standard Aruban style the fat-bellied man slowly moved the dirt pile from my back yard; very slowly. I stood my ground and watched him. Alex and Vincent convinced me to walk back to the house. I called the police and Salvatore. Salvatore would help me– he knew everyone on the island. Salvatore got there faster than any

278

other Aruban I've ever known to move. I began explaining the situation to Salvatore. He knew how upset I was, and he agreed with me. Peering down the back yard, he said he recognized the contractor–he had seen him working in the community before. Alex went into the house for a cup of coffee while the three of us stood on the back patio. Two police officers pull up in the driveway–one was a woman. She wore aviator sunglasses and had a clipboard in hand. The male officer introduced them to us. I am not sexist, but I was thinking-'great'; what was she going to do with my backyard Brutus?"

Jan said. "I am picturing Popeye–you and Brutus–the contractor."

"Yeah," Rob chimed in, "with Olive Oil running in for coffee!"

The waitress came back to the table and replaced our empty breadbasket with a full, steamy one and another large chunk of butter. The young man was there with a pitcher and topped off our water glasses. The aroma was too much to ignore, and we each pulled off a slice, slathering it with butter. I savored every morsel before chasing it down with a gulp of pinot. "I initially thought nothing's going to get done–my neighbor had won again. I extended my hand and greeted each one of the officers with 'bon dia'. For the third time that morning I began explaining the situation about the contractor. Making sure the officers saw my bruise and cut lip-

I pointed to my face. The female officer nodded in silence as Vincent piped in and said the contractor had hit me several times. She took a few more notes entering our personal information–name and address–on her clipboard. When she got the gist of what had happened, she and the other officer walked down to the back yard. The two officers got details from the contractor and his crew; we could see the female officer writing them down. They were only with them for a few minutes. Alex came back outside. She can be a bit of an unhappy person when she doesn't get her morning java."

"You got that right," Alex said. "I looked forward to my coffee laced with Bailey's and whipped cream. Crystal and Vincent managed to console Jade upstairs. She had calmed down since the beginning of the back-yard brawl. I was glad of that. It hurt my heart to hear my daughter so upset. She's a bit of a sensitive sort."

"No wonder," Jan chimed in. "You can't blame the poor child for getting upset. Her mother and brother in harm's way one day and her mother's boyfriend the very next. It just sends chills down my arms. Look, Rob; see the chills and my hairs standing up."

Rob put his arm around his wife and pulled her a little closer to him. She tilted her head slightly, rested it against him, and involuntarily shuddered as if shaking off a cold chill. She was much smaller than he was. "Let him finish," Rob said. "I've got to hear what happened to Brutus."

"In the meantime, Salvatore had been listening to me and shook his head–half laughing at me." I looked over where the big football dude was sitting just a few tables away as he shot another glance in my direction. In the same situation, he probably would have tackled the guy and put him down hard–I figured that's what he was thinking. "Salvatore's brother, Dimitri, pulled up to the house behind the police car. Salvatore must have called him. Dimitri is this really big dude; tall with a solid muscular frame. As his name implies, he is a very happy man but, can be quite assertive. Dimitri built my house. We kept in touch regularly–he and Salvatore are more like extended family. After I gave Dimitri a few of the details, he couldn't believe what the contractor had done. Salvatore knew the other contractor–very well. Dimitri told us the other contractor was a real hot head; like we didn't know that. The two police officers walked back to the house and joined us. The policewoman told me she wanted me to file a formal report at the police station and visit the hospital first. I would need to take a doctor's report to the police station. In the meantime, she was working on pressing charges against the contractor, and it required a physician's statement. My word–I have not done anything like that before."

"Jesus, Joe," Rob said. "You are a drama magnet. From my initial introduction earlier tonight, you appear to be a clean-cut, rational looking dude, but you made all *kinds* of trouble in Aruba.

They probably won't let you get back on the island-all the commotion you made. More than likely, they've probably posted your picture in all the government and public places with the universal red line through it."

The people dining next to us were looking in our direction. Their plates showed they had barely eaten their dinner. By the looks on their faces, they were rather amused by our conversation. The entire back end of the restaurant had been listening to my tale by this time. Sadly, I thought, most people had only heard about Aruba through the media coverage after Natalie Holloway's disappearance–God bless her and her family. My audience probably never even knew Aruba existed prior to the notorious drama of this young lady-just two years older than Crystal. The prime suspect-Joran van der Sloot-was later convicted of the murder of a Peruvian young lady by the name of Stephany Flores Ramirez of Lima and sentenced to 28 years in the Challapalca Prison.

"Ahem; Jade finally came outside. She ran over to me crying, her eyes were red and bloodshot. When she threw her arms around me, I could feel her body was shaking. She said she thought the man was going to kill me. Crystal and Vincent came outside, too. I kept reassuring Jade everything was okay. She eventually calmed down-that girl *is* an emotional one. My main concern wasn't over the fight; I think Alex was mad at me. My ex would have gone ballistic over something like this. She'd fly off the handle if I didn't hang a picture to her specifications. Alex was right there with me but, at the time, wasn't saying very much. She's my rock. Vincent exhibited his strong side that day, too. Crystal is also one that doesn't say much either. You can look into her eyes and know she is always thinking."

"The police left. I explained to the kids what the officer had told me. Alex went inside to put on a shirt and get her purse, my wallet, and our cell phones. Cell phones are costly to use when you are out of the country but, in this case it was an exception to our rule to carry them. I told the kids to just hang out for a bit around the pool and we headed out to the Jeep. The son-of-a-gun started right up that time. As we backed out of the driveway, we looked across the patio to the back yard. The contractor and his crew had most of the dirt piles back on my neighbor's yard. Brutus seemed to work at a much faster pace shoveling dirt *after* the police arrived. Later, the kids told us Salvatore and Dimitri hung out for a few minutes longer after we left–I think they wanted to make sure the contractor didn't do any more stupid stuff."

"I dunno," Jan stammered. "I would have been too afraid to leave the house. Those men could've done more damage."

"The construction crew cooperated. I wasn't worried. The police meant business and they knew it. Alex reminded me–for the one hundredth time-we had to be at the airport by 4:30 to pick up John and Mary Lib. I had forgotten all about them with all the craziness of the morning. We found the hospital easily enough. The huge cement white structure could have been seen from practically anywhere from that part of the island. The emergency room was not as easy to locate. I had been there years before when my sister had a bad allergic reaction to a bug bite. Wasps are another insect to look out for. They'll give you a welt the size of Texas and make you some kind-of-sore, too."

"I have to tell you; I was not keen on going to the hospital. I didn't feel like I was really hurt. My ego and my pride were more bruised than my face and backside. But, Alex insisted I follow the instructions of the police officer. I think she was worried something horrible would happen if I didn't. I patted Alex's knee and gave her a quick smile. "I paid the intake woman ninety dollars-relatively cheap by our standards. She directed us to an air-conditioned waiting area. There was only one other person there. I was not looking forward to sitting in an emergency room for hours. I had a lot of gardening to do before her friends arrived. Surprisingly, we only sat about fifteen minutes in the waiting room. I was seen by a doctor from Holland. She mainly checked for any broken facial bones–wrote down my statement of what had happened on her incident report. And I noticed something a bit strange. She wrote the word 'abuse' and checked 'none' for broken bones. Alex and I chuckled at the term 'abuse'. In less than ninety minutes we were out of there. Rather quick by our hospital emergency room standards."

"I'd say," quipped Rob. "You can bet you'll have a four to five hour wait in the ER here-regardless of your injury or illness. We spent four hours waiting for someone to see Jan and me after we had a bad car accident. Jan had a broken shoulder and all they did was put an ice pack on it while we waited."

"That was horrible," Alex commented. "That must have been painful, Jan."

"Oh, it was," Jan said as she shrugged her once injured shoulder. "I feel it most when the weather gets cold or it's damp and rainy. And it just gets worse as I get older."

"We left the ER and got back to the Jeep in relatively good spirits. I was sure glad Alex was with me through the ordeal. I put the key in the ignition. I think you know the rest of the story. You've heard it enough before." I leaned in a little closer to the table. I didn't want to offend any of the other diners, so I said a bit softer, "that Jeep had to be female, because it sure was temperamental. I got out of the Jeep—the sun was getting hot—and I quickly got into a foul mood. Anticipating my next step, Alex got out and pulled the hood latch. Nothing appeared out of the ordinary—nothing had looked out of kilter any other time either. I walked around the Jeep and kicked one of the tires out of pure frustration. I decided to call the rental company. I was determined; that was going to be the last

285

time we would be stranded by that Jeep on our vacation. The rental car company agent started asking me all these questions. I paced around the Jeep while I'm talking to the guy–told him we were at the hospital. The guy on the other end was practically laughing at me. I kicked one of the tires again and half hoped it would go flat."

I raised both my hands as I saw Jan's face. "Don't ask me why I kicked the tire–I was just mad–and it made me feel better. And, I still had a lot of gardening to do. Alex grabbed the other set of keys from the glove box and tried the ignition. I looked under the hood again. I didn't see anything that appeared to be causing the problem. I'm sweaty and I had been aggravated most of the morning. Alex had pulled the key out of the ignition and put them in her purse. She thought the rental car company was going to come and tow the Jeep. I got back in the car using my set of keys I had in my pocket. The Jeep started. I looked at Alex-both wondering what had happened. Why now? We both laughed. Miracles never cease I tell you-or rather plain good timing. I spat into the phone a quick; 'never mind' and drove down to the police station. The one where the white fatality sign is-at the intersection just below the high-rise hotels."

"We walked into the building-anxious to get the ordeal over with. The receptionist told us we had the wrong police department to file an incident report. The one we wanted was downtown. There always seemed to be some sort of delay on this trip," Alex said. "It

286

took us another hour of driving around in an unfamiliar part of the island until we found the downtown police station."

"I thought you said you had been vacationing in Aruba for thirty years, Joe," Rob said with a sideways glance. "How is it you didn't know where you were going; especially, on such a small island?"

"Fair question. I tell you what, Rob. I never had to go to the police for anything before–here or there. That was unchartered territory for me. We walked into the cool entryway. A big, huge Aruban woman sat behind the desk. She must have weighed in at least three-fifty that morning."

"Her eyes were glued to an overhead television screen. She did not even look our way," Alex said.

"The woman totally ignored us like someone might ignore a lone spider walking up a wall-you see it and it's a pest but, not worth paying attention to. The woman watched her soap operas. We stood–directly in front of her and cleared our throats to get her attention. The receptionist's eyes did not leave the screen until the commercials came on.

"She must've gotten an advanced warning that two American heathens were coming in," Jan quipped. "Obviously, the soap opera was far more interesting than you two were. The receptionist was probably the wife of the contractor that hit you. I bet he called her earlier to be on the lookout for a 'tourista' in pineapple shorts."

"She told us to sit down and wait for a detective, picked up the phone, and babbled something in Papiamento–I just hoped she wasn't ordering lunch. Alex decided to go back to the house and check on the kids-Alex was particularly concerned about how upset Jade had gotten. I waited–seated next to a tropical palm plant."

"By the time I arrived back at the house," Alex said "the children were all smiles and had been swimming in the pool. Even in their young adult stage children are remarkably resilient. I explained Joe had gone to the hospital and was still at the police station and was fine. The girls wanted to tan and lay by the pool all day. They confirmed our thoughts. While he filed the incident report, Salvatore and Dimitri had waited around to make sure the contractor was cooperating. The trucks and dirt were gone. The only thing that remained was a long black trail where the truck had leaked oil in the back yard. Better to have black oil than Aruba Joe's spilled blood out there. It gave me shudders thinking the situation could have been a whole lot worse."

"Vincent, however, insisted on going back to the police station with me," Alex continued. "He said he wanted to make sure Joe was not hurt. Personally, I think he probably was just bored and didn't want to sit with his sisters around the pool. I was surprised I found the police station. It certainly helps when you know where you are going on that island."

"I was in the room with the detective when Alex got back. It was a somewhat atypical experience for me. You know the top 10 list David Letterman does on the tonight show? The detective had a top 10 list of his own behind his desk–in English–not Dutch. The top 10 question- 'what are the 10 things you don't want to ask your police officer if you don't want to put him in a bad mood' or something like that. The first item on the list was 'don't ask him how many donuts your police officer ate that morning.' They certainly have a sense of humor down there."

"After all, Joe," Alex said, "Aruba is just one happy island!"

Rob added, "After getting beat up in your own back yard earlier that day you needed a good laugh-my word."

"Laughing also keeps one young-my grandchildren will attest to that. We are always laughing at the crazy things Rob does," Jan added with a smile.

"It took an hour for the detective to compile his report. He asked me a number of questions and entered them–s l o w l y. He was a poker-used his forefinger of each hand to peck away at the keyboard when I answered him. He kept his face down toward it. With each answered question-I had gone over the details so many times that morning-I began to wonder what I was doing sitting at the police station. I was not physically hurt. I simply had a damaged ego. I wasn't wearing a watch–Alex had my cell phone in her purse. I kept thinking about my gardening, how the day was ticking away fast, and I had so much yet to do. The detective's face held such intensity as he struggled to enter my statement into his report. With a nod of self-satisfaction, he finished with a final hard peck on the keyboard, then the detective printed out the report. He sat turning his head from side-to-side and rubbing the back of his broad neck. He had a neck like a race car driver-they need a strong neck for protection from the G-force while driving and the weight of their helmets."

"As he handed the report to me to sign, he explained the contents of the report. I was filing a charge of 'abuse' against the contractor. Peering at the report I recognized it was printed in Dutch. I couldn't understand a darned thing. I handed the report back to the detective and told him 'I can't read it.' In disbelief, the detective looked at the report. His face no longer bore one of success. He became a bit perturbed at himself. Again, his head went down for the second time as the entire process began–one pecking finger at a time."

"But, I did see a bit of an advantage to the detective's oversight. I remembered and added a few more details the second time around. I thought it wouldn't hurt to embellish a bit either."

CHAPTER 21 – JOHN AND MARY LIB

"I finally had copies of both the hospital and police reports in hand. The detective told me the courts would deal with the rest. Probably arrest the contractor and put him in jail for thirty days. They take abuse quite seriously in Aruba. The big lady was gone– probably went and had her second lunch or ate one of the police officers. It was almost four o'clock."

Jan started fidgeting. Something was on her mind. "You didn't get to finish your gardening," Jan said. "What a shame, Aruba Joe."

"There was always time for gardening. Anyway, when I entered the lobby Alex and Vincent stood up from those hard, plastic chairs. They looked a bit anxious. Her friends were arriving in half an hour. We were only five minutes from the airport, and they had to get through customs. When we got into the Jeep, Alex at the wheel, I told Vincent what had taken place since I last saw him earlier. I also thanked him for coming down to sit with his mom and acknowledged his presence probably stopped the contractor from 'abusing' me even more. John and Mary Lib's plane arrived early- trade winds, I guess. It felt like the first 'normal thing' that had happened that day. John and Mary Lib were all smiles when they saw us. They hugged Vincent, then Alex. Vincent and I helped with the luggage; Alex helped with the introductions."

"Their rental car company was just across the street from the airport terminal. They also rented a Jeep; a bright red Wrangler," Alex added. "Mary Lib and John are retired; they are world travelers now. Anywhere in Europe is their absolute favorite destination. They like the old-world style of culture and architecture. She has deep English roots and his family is from Ireland. They had also been to most of the islands in the Caribbean, but this had been their first visit to Aruba."

"You probably should have held up a huge 'caution–pass with care' sign when they arrived because they were in the Caribbean with Aruba Joe," Rob said.

"Speaking of caution, Vincent decided to ride in the Jeep with Mary Lib and John as a quasi-tour guide," Alex added. "Traffic was a bit heavy, and he thought he could help navigate them through some of the roads. Several airlines had just landed. Luggage, people, and cars were filling the streets and sidewalks around the airport."

"The Sahara was parked right out front–I had John follow me. "I kept looking in the rear-view mirror to make sure John was behind us. Some of the lights in Aruba turn from yellow to red rather quickly. There are some unusual intersections in Aruba, and one must take caution. The traffic signs are European–a bit different from the US. At some of the intersections, there is a yield sign for one direction and the other direction has the right of way. If you are not familiar with the streets it can become a bit confusing if not downright dangerous."

"Sounds dangerous to me," Jan said. "I am very anxious in intersections. That's how I ended up in the hospital with a broken shoulder last year. Someone ran a yellow light and hit me in the passenger side while Rob was driving."

"At some of those intersections, even though you have a yield, you are supposed to stop if someone has entered the intersection. The Arubans enter with just the slightest hesitation. Anyway, it was at one of those intersections where I must have lost John. Even though Vincent was with them Alex was worried whether they would find the house."

"How could someone not find your house? The island is barely twenty miles long," Rob responded with a chuckle.

"Since we were driving through some of the side streets, I drove a little slower and kept looking out for them. Alex looked out her side window for the red Wrangler when suddenly, Alex spotted them, 'there they are!' Yep, John was headed right toward us from the opposite direction. He passed by and we waved to one another."

"Vincent sat in the back seat," Alex said. "I saw him shrug his shoulders and put his hands in the air. John is one of those manly types. Mary Lib later told me he got hot under the collar every time Vincent told him he was going in the wrong direction."

"There was no room for them to turn around or for me to pull over and wait for them. Traffic is busy at that time of day. The side street we were on was rather narrow. I decided to just keep going toward home. I had confidence they would meet us back at the house at some point in time. We had plenty of daylight left."

"A bad omen," Rob said.

"You can eat those words because, when they finally arrived, they both had huge smiles on their faces," Alex said. "I can assure you, Rob; they *never* had a vacation like they did with us."

"When we got back to the house, the girls were getting ready to go to the casinos. Ten minutes later the red Wrangler was in the driveway. Vincent and I helped John get their bags inside to their room while Alex showed Mary Lib the grand tour of the house. I gave them the large master suite upstairs."

"Vincent and the girls traipsed off to the casinos in the Sahara–started right up for Crystal. I knew the children couldn't wait to get out on their own. Can't say that I blame them," Alex said. "Mary Lib and I sat on the patio overlooking the ocean and waited for the guys."

"When we joined the girls on the patio, John said he was starving. We decided to drive along the coastal road and figure out which restaurant to go to. We rode down to this amazing restaurant on a pier in John's rental. "The sunset was spectacular that evening. The air over the water was just a bit cooler. Everything about that

294

night was perfect, including our meals. We told John and Mary Lib all about our Aruban adventures prior to their arrival. I thought John was going to choke on his grouper when I told him about my brawl with the contractor earlier that day. He told me he had wondered about the cut on my lip and bruised cheek."

"I think it was really Alex's description of my legs sticking out of my pineapple print bathing suit–lying upended in the dirt-that tickled him most."

"The moon followed soon after. We spent the rest of our dinner catching up with one another and trading vacation stories. John and Mary Lib talked about all their past exploits on Caribbean trips and cruises," Alex added. "Except for misplaced baggage they never experienced any trauma. They usually traveled first class. Life had been very good to them. Mary Libs father had grown a clothing chain somewhere up north and sold it in the late eighties. I think he had some thoroughbreds, sold his farm, and ended up a very wealthy man. Mary Lib was his sole heir. And John; he was an investor all his life. Started at a real young age around Wall Street types. Mary Lib says he works six days a week when they are not traveling. Sits on his computer all day long; reading and investing."

"The next day, John was the first one up and he concocted a breakfast feast for everyone. We discovered John is a bit of a culinary expert. The kids were feeling adventurous. They decided they wanted to go four wheeling. I made a reservation for the three of them and figured the rest of us would enjoy one great day by the pool. Alex had known John and Mary Lib for years–I was just meeting them for the second time. As a matter of fact, the first time happened to be in the same restaurant Alex and I rekindled our relationship."

"How did you come to know John and Mary Lib, Alex?" Jan asked.

"Let's see," answered Alex. "About twenty years ago I met Mary Lib when I had volunteered for a committee. We worked on putting together a shelter for displaced women and their children. The core program was to rehabilitate, counsel, and get the mothers into a college or technical training. Mary Lib was one of the co-founders of the program. John was helpful in doing some of the construction for the shelter-one of his other talents."

"Mary Lib and John sound like good people," Jan said. "It's nice to hear about people helping and caring for others."

"The kids wanted to see more of the island on four-wheelers. Alex and I took off in plenty of time to get to the four-wheel rental center by one o'clock. Mary Lib and John stayed at the house. My God, you should have seen the paperwork just to rent those things. It was like signing your life away. Alex must've signed ten pages just for the kids to ride four wheelers around for a couple of hours. The woman at the rental place led us to the back of the building, through a rusty metal door, and onto a large ceramic tiled patio.

They had a seating area in the back. There were some colorful wooden benches along the perimeter of the porch under an aged, wooden pergola. An old Harley was next to the farthest post. Thirty minutes went by. Alex went inside to find out what the delay was. The woman told her a large group had gone out earlier that morning and was to return any time. A squeaky fan slowly spun above our heads barely keeping the air moving."

"Another hour went by before we heard the loud engines in the distance. The group started pulling in; must have been thirty of them. The back lot filled with four wheelers, people and dust; lots of dust. Several young Aruban men appeared out of nowhere and took the four wheelers to a lean-to shed in the back of the lot," Alex said "and left three of them behind. The young men were quite efficient and, in an instant, everyone was gone; except the five of us and two of the young men. They showed the kids how to operate the four wheelers. Jade, my little motor head, seemed a bit nervous about how to ride hers at first.

"The three of them took off to fill their gas tanks at the neighboring gas station-they waved a hand and grinned toward us. Alex and I walked around front to watch them drive until they were gone and the sound of the four wheelers disappeared."

"It certainly sounds like your group did a lot of waiting," Rob said. "Waiting at dinner, at the police station, at the patio...,' his voice trailing off.

"Aruba '*island time*' is kind of like that of our slow southern style back here but, the islander's conception of time is slower still. Building a house in Aruba takes years–not months; the wait in a restaurant is hours–not minutes. And you must ask for your receipt when you are done because it is considered bad manners if they approach you first. Alex and I jumped back into the Sahara; anxious to get back to our guests. The Jeep wouldn't start. At this point, I knew without bad luck with that Sahara I had none. I wasn't waiting another minute and called the rental company. I think it was the same guy I spoke with the day before and he argued with me; for the second time. He told me no one ever had a problem with the Jeep before and they would send someone out right away. I hung up on the idiot. He was still talking to me but, I didn't give a monkey's butt. I was sweating bullets. I don't know if I was sweating from the heat of the sun, or my blood pressure was escalating again. I sweat when my blood pressure goes up. We looked under the hood–only because we knew we were going to wait awhile and had nothing else better to do. I had been bound and determined not to have the vehicle win the war even though I felt defeated. I pulled out the other key set from the glove box. I looked at the two sets of keys again. I realized there was a difference between the two keys on each set–something I had not recognized prior to that very moment. Each key was a bit different."

"Oh my God," Rob quickly added, "you were using the key that didn't have the chip in it. The car could not start because the one key only opened the car door–not start the ignition!"

"Rob, it was like one of those light bulb moments–you know. I got back into the Jeep–put in the one key–nothing happened. I put in the other key and the Jeep started right up. I had been using the wrong key half the time. I dialed the rental company and cancelled my previous call for help, explaining about the two keys. The tone of the guy completely changed, and he became quite apologetic to me. I wasn't about to contradict him. Could've saved one heck of a lot of grief if I would've recognized the two different keys sooner. I felt extremely foolish. Alex didn't laugh at me. She was decent about it. For that, I was glad. On our way home, we stopped at the local grocery store. The air conditioning felt so good. We picked up some lunch meats and cheeses. A nice dip in the pool was going to revive us. Turning into the driveway there was one of the four wheelers with a flat tire. I could hear some loud engines beyond the back of the house. Curious as to what was going on, Alex and I walked to the back patio. Beyond the backyard, where the incident with the contractor occurred the day before, we saw John and Vincent doing donuts behind the house on the unfinished road; brown dust flying *everywhere*."

"Crystal was on one of the lounge chairs and told us Jade's four-wheeler got a flat right after they got gas. Jade was laying on a raft in the pool. Mary Lib was reading a book and laying on one of the lounge chairs on the other side of the pool. Alex went about preparing lunch and put away the groceries. The kids had already called the four-wheel company and they pulled in a few minutes later to fix the flat. I hadn't realized it before-the wheels on the four wheelers were not in the greatest shape. The water never felt as good as it did that day. I did ten laps and sat on the corner cement bench in the pool. I was famished."

"Mary Lib and I just wanted to enjoy our lunch poolside and exchange some girl talk," Alex said. "I put a large tray of fresh fruit, cheese, and lunch meats on the patio table. The pool, the palm trees blowing in the crosswinds, and the green parrots flying overhead made a perfect backdrop for a relaxing day. Mary Lib prepared a few rum drinks and brought out a pitcher of water."

"It all sounds so lovely," Jan said.

"I decided to test the four-wheeler in the driveway. I examined the tires before I took off. At a closer inspection, they looked really bad-all cracked and dry rotted and filled with a black, rubbery textured compound that looked more like dog poop with grass sticking out of it. Apparently, that is their method of fixing tires, fixing them with some rubbery, poopy looking goo. I caught up with John and Vincent in no time. The unfinished roads in the new phase were perfect for popping wheelies and doing donuts. The building lots of the subdivision are mostly hard, compacted dirt with a few cactuses and shrubs growing about. Construction had just started on one of the new houses. Other than that, it was totally open territory for a good run. When we got back to the house, Alex reminded the kids the vehicles had to be returned by six o'clock. They got out of the pool. Got their gear back on, straddled the seat on the four wheelers, and took off. The four of us had the pool to ourselves; to relax and enjoy the sun and water. I did a couple more laps. I got out of the pool and laid next to Alex on the lounge chair. Mary Lib and Alex were jabbering away about kids and birthdays. I enjoyed listening to Alex's voice and the sound of the dolphin fountain spitting water into the pool."

CHAPTER 22 – THE MUD BOG

"We sun bathed, swam in the sun, and played Scrabble. We nibbled on the cold lunch plate while sipping on some mighty good alcoholic concoctions. The girls came bustling in. All I could think of at the time was' 'what now?' They had been crying and were still pretty upset. Vincent was not with them. Alex got Crystal and Jade to calm down and talk clearly. Vincent had gotten his four-wheeler stuck in the lake in the center of the island. Alex thought he had an accident or was hurt. The girls reassured her Vincent was fine but, the four-wheeler was a mess–covered in mud in the middle of the island. I was rather surprised to hear that. Usually, the lake is dried up. The girls said other people were four wheeling on the lake and they decided to join them; it looked like fun. John and I had to be all macho and rose to the occasion to help Vincent. The couple of shots of Patron had clearly given us an additional infusion of manliness. Wasting no time getting ready, I grabbed a shovel and some hemp rope from the garage closet. I had every intention of pulling Vincent out quickly to get back to the game."

"I suggested Mary Lib and I go since John and Joe had been drinking all afternoon," Alex said. "John told me it was 'man's work' and to enjoy the sun. I had about enough of problems and was embarrassed John and Mary Lib had to witness our latest island dilema. I was becoming angry we traveled so far to have so many problems. And not just at Vincent. I was angry I gave in to a vacation when I knew we were fine without one."

"You didn't say anything to me, Alex. I'm just now hearing about this; how come?" I was really surprised to hear this from her. Alex used to be able to tell me everything that was on her mind.

With a sigh Alex answered, "would it have really mattered? My son was the latest victim to another problem on our vacation and in front of my friends. I thought it was best not to say anything when I was really fuming."

There wasn't anything I could have done to change things. I could talk to Alex about it later as we drove home from the Cafe. With a bit more thought, perhaps it was one of those things I needed to avoid altogether-silence is golden.

"As we backed out of the driveway, Crystal and Jade were still arguing over whose fault it was that the four-wheeler had gotten stuck. I genuinely think they were more worried their mother was going to be mad about their brother and were relieved when she acted calm. The girls jumped in the Sahara with me. John followed in the Wrangler. As we approached the lake, Crystal pointed to the dirt ramp for access onto the lake. I immediately spotted Vincent and his red four-wheeler–partially buried in the middle of the huge, dried up lake. He looked so small out there and no one else was around. In the past, I have seen plenty of people riding around on the lake and never saw anyone stuck in it."

"Like I said," Alex added as she slowly emphasized each word, "everything seemed to go wrong with us." She swallowed a huge gulp of wine.

I hadn't realized it until now but, I think she was had become a bit tipsy.

"I did a quick visual survey of the lakebed. The surface appeared hard, and I saw tire tracks-plenty of them. There were a few damp spots. I drove right onto the dried lake without issue. The whole time I remembered thinking 'how in the world did Vincent get himself stuck.' John was going at a steady clip just behind me- I peered at him over my left. That's when I noticed there wasn't any dust kicking up behind us. We were moving at a fast pace-almost to the point where Vincent was standing when the Jeeps tires began catching a bit in the mud and I started slowing down. Crystal told me to look out for the deeper mud ahead and to steer away from the center of the lake. I hadn't seen the mud when we got on the lake. Vincent had his arms on his hips watching us. We were about fifty feet away from him. As wet mud flew everywhere I began sinking down. I stepped on the gas, the engine got louder, sounding like it would burst. My only thought was to make it to my destination and to drive a little faster. In a fraction of a second, I drove that Jeep deeper into the mud. Crystal had laughed at me, and I failed to see her humor. Vincent had his hands on the top of his headshaking it from side-to-side. I looked over my shoulder again and there was

304

John–about a hundred yards or so behind us. He tried driving in the center of the lake–exactly where Crystal had said to steer clear of-his Wrangler had nose-dived in the mud. The rear end was flat on an angle. You could hear John cussin' and his engine revving loud. Sounded like both he and the Jeep were going to blow up. As mud flew from the back tires, the front end of his Jeep just went deeper into the gray mud."

"I asked Crystal to move over to the driver's side as I climbed out. Our situation was bad, but we weren't as bad as Johns. I told her to wait until I told her to step lightly on the accelerator and hold it steady. Once I got positioned, I yelled at Crystal to start. I began pushing the Jeep from the back of the Sahara and it moved a little." A quick look of disbelief in Jan's expression made me add; "we started making some headway. For some silly reason Crystal let up on the pedal-a mistake when I specifically told her not to. I yelled to her, again, to hold steady on the gas. Once she finally listened to me, we got some momentum. When we had moved about three feet, the back end slipped out of my hands, tipped upward, and the front end of the Jeep went down in the mud. Jade got out from the back seat and joined me to push. The two of us were on either side of the back of the Sahara and we gave it everything we had. She's a muscular girl and is quite powerful for her size. John came over and threw his shoulder against the Jeep with us–absolutely nothing happened-I nearly broke my back. I asked Crystal to just get out of the Jeep-her additional weight wasn't helping the situation. I noticed the position of the tires were sideways. I leaned inside, grabbed hold of the steering wheel, and straightened the tires using all my muscle power. I tried everything I could think of; rocking the Jeep back and forth didn't work. We knew we needed a different strategy. Our feet sunk in mud above our ankles; it would have pulled the sandals off my feet if I didn't have strong straps. John admitted he thought driving in the center of the lake was the better place to be–was he wrong. The kids were easily frustrated, and Vincent shook his head. Jade blamed Crystal for getting the Jeep stuck.   Crystal was just about in tears. Our mud-splattered bodies were far from the four wheeling images found in vacationer magazines."

Stretching my arms open while I looked at the other diners, "we were not to be defeated by the mud bog."

I changed my focus back toward my table of wide-eyed faces. "We looked around the lake for something to wedge under the tires. I found a wooden plank from the side of the lake, took out the shovel and rope from my jeep, and we managed to get Vincent's four-wheeler out of the mud. We were triumphant and five very happy people. I told the kids they might as well leave. They needed to return the four wheelers back to the rental company and I did not have to ask them twice. John and I felt like we had everything under control. I felt a bit more energized. We carried the wood plank and the shovel over to the Wrangler. We figured his Jeep was lighter than the Sahara and could easily get it out of the mud."

"A few minutes after they had left, Salvatore pulled into the driveway," Alex said. "He said he wanted to make sure Joe had recovered from his back yard brawl with the fat bellied contractor–those were his words. Salvatore also takes care of several other houses in the neighborhood and was just up the road. I filled Salvatore in on our latest island escapade. I told him John and Joe were still with the children at the lake. He told me he had noticed people on the lake and had wondered what they were doing. He laughed out loud at the obvious predicament Joe got himself into. Like the gentleman he is, Salvatore offered his assistance–asking if there was anything he could do. As we were talking, we heard the four-wheeler pull into the driveway–it was Vincent. My God–he was an absolute mess. Vincent was covered in a mixture of gray wet and dry mud on his hands, arms, feet, and legs. The four-wheeler was too. I turned on the garden hose and rinsed the mud off the vehicle and into the side garden. Vincent sprayed himself off in the outdoor shower-my handsome boy was a mess. Salvatore laughed at us calling us 'wild Americans'. Vincent told us Crystal and Jade were coming back to the house. The girls arrived about twenty minutes later. They explained what had happened on the mud bog and gave us directions to enter the dried lake-forewarning us about the wet mud–saying it was like quicksand where the Jeeps were stuck."

"Now, it was getting hotter and late into the afternoon. The children were worried about how they were going to get back home after they dropped off the four-wheelers. We certainly weren't going to be able to pick them up," Alex said. "I told them, 'When I was younger, I found a way to get where I needed to be in a difficult time. That we had used a cab before on this vacation and they could use a cab again.' Once the girls sprayed off the mud, they all spun out of the driveway wasting no time."

"I asked Salvatore if he would mind driving Mary Lib and I to the lake. Grabbing my camera and cell phone; we took off. Salvatore drives a white utility van–the back end is like that of a flat-bed for hauling things around. The cabin doesn't have any air conditioning and it was hot and stuffy with the three of us in the van; Mary Lib owns a rather abundant rear end. During the ride, I filled him in on all the details about the hospital and police station visits from our previous day. He shook his head and smiled. He's not necessarily a man of many words. When we arrived at the lake, I was in disbelief. Salvatore did make a few comments-something about how crazy Joe's trip to Aruba had become. When we pulled up to the edge of the lake, I lost all concern over his comments and my jaw dropped. The Jeeps were parked midway on the lake, about a quarter of a mile from the roadside. They were sunk up to their axles in mud; only half of the tires were visible. There were deep impressions in the mud not too far from Joe's Jeep. Assuring Salvatore we had everything under control, Mary Lib and I got out of his truck, and half ran to Joe and John."

I watched Alex's face-some hostility was still visible as she described the 'mud bog' escapade.

"The situation didn't look very good. They had gotten themselves into one heck of a mess." Alex added.

"John and I were trying to use the old board to wedge under the Jeep's tires and maneuver the Wrangler out of that gray gunk. By Jiminy; all we managed to do was sink the Jeep deeper into the mud. As we wrestled with our manly strategies and that gray mud, there was a huge sucking sound as it sank. Glancing around the perimeter of the lake, the gray dirt was lighter in color-compacted-and appeared solid to ride on. Judging from the tire tracks, the perimeter must have been where the kids originally started riding. Once I stepped back and evaluated more of the lake there were a lot of lumpy areas. I quickly realized-we were not the first group to get stuck out there. Mary Lib and Alex arrived and walked between the two Jeeps looking at them from every angle-assessing the situation."

Turning toward Alex, I added, "Okay, so it didn't look good. But, you have to remember where our minds were at the time. We had quite a few drinks at the pool before we had arrived; thus, giving us the manly confidence to conquer any task. John and I put our physical strengths together and as hard as we pushed, the Jeep didn't move–not an inch-embedded in that thick mud. We were covered in mud up to our knees. A couple of other four wheelers came out on the lake. We all stared toward them. It wasn't a bunch of kids. For a few moments, we stood watching them-half expecting them to sink in the muck."

"I told Joe the lake was a huge mud bog," Alex said. "Clearly, the reason the other four wheelers didn't get stuck-they knew how to ride. They got closer to us; circling around the area of the Jeeps and popping wheelies. We could hear them laughing at us. John had no appreciation of their laughter-he was quite miffed. He was also worried the Jeep wouldn't start once we got it out. I had never seen him angry like that before."

"John's a big dude, too. He's about six-foot four and carries a good two hundred and fifty on his bones. He works out a couple times a week and is in pretty good physical shape–a former college football player, Rob," I said. "The more the guys on the four wheelers rode around us, the angrier he got. Mary Lib tried to reason with him–to calm him down-and he would not hear one word."

Flashing her an appreciative smile, "Alex, on the other hand, the woman that likes everyone to get along decided to walk toward this one guy. We watched her talking to him and wondered what in the world she was doing. The man got off his four-wheeler and the two of them walked over. As they got closer, I could read 'S-W-A-T' in white letters on the front of his black t-shirt. I was curious about this muscularly buff younger man. I'm thinking to myself, 'now what'? Feet spread shoulder-width apart, Mr. SWAT extends his hand to John and me. Our hands were covered in mud bog grit—he didn't seem to even notice—and shook our hands firmly. His eyes never strayed from ours. He said he was an Aruban police officer—Mike was his name. He explained his buddies were also off duty Aruban police officers. He also pointed to his brown house on the road just outside the lake."

I stopped for a moment and turned my head, deep in thought, and looked through the restaurant's window. The sun had pretty much gone down for the day. The staff busily turned up the overhead lighting and reset some of the few vacant tables left from the departure of early diners. Outside, the artificial, yellowish glow from the tall metal light posts replaced the light Mother Nature had previously supplied. I made a brief visual scan of the restaurant as a younger man walked toward our table. His white chef's hat perfectly centered on his head; a white apron covered his short-sleeved black t-shirt and black pants. He wore black Adidas Sambas with white leather strips.

"This is Angelo," Jan said as the younger man bent toward Alex and me-extending his hand in greeting. Jan and Rob beamed proudly as their son-in-law approached us. "Alex is a good friend of

311

mine and this is her wonderful, handsome man, Joe." Her tone was proud.

"Please tu meet chu both," Angelo responded with a pleasant smile accompanied with a rather strong Italian accent. He rested his hand on Jan's shoulder as he stood talking with us for a few minutes–asking us how we like the entrees we had ordered. He also explained entrée in most countries is actually an appetizer but, in the States we use it to define the main meal. Leave it to the Americans to reinvent the wheel. You could tell he loved his mother-in-law as much as she did him–he gently rubbed her shoulder. "I change up menus for my regulars. It makes so happy." His annunciation on menus was spoken more like 'man-use'.

Angelo was a man of few words. He left with a 'caio bella' to Jan and a raised palm to the rest of us. He was obviously quite busy as he hurriedly exited toward the kitchen.

"Angelo is a perfectionist," Rob said. "Everything has got to be just so. He keeps his people in line and has a great manager here. You'll never get a bad meal or send anything back."

"That is nice to know," Alex said. "I'll be back for sure."

I looked at her wondering if she realized she hadn't said 'we'll'. While Angelo had been talking, I took advantage of the brief hiatus and began spreading some butter on the fresh bread–more like lathering it on my bread–that's how much I like butter. Satisfying my palate, I was anxious to start talking again. Perhaps due to my nervousness, my right knee involuntarily started bouncing up and down. Patience is also not one of my personality traits.

"Anyway, Mike further explained he had been watching the whole thing from his garage while he changed the oil in his car. After an hour of watching us, he said he could see we weren't making any progress. He'd called a couple of his buddies to help us out. By that time his two 'buddies' had joined us. John had been silent other than a low grunt when he shook Mike's hand. He stood beside Mary Lib with his arms folded–taking in the conversation. He kept looking at the two Jeeps and I wondered if he had been listening to what was being said. I guess he had been mentally working on a strategy to get us out of the mud-like he would have done in a scrimmage in his college days. The sun was beginning to go down over the ocean and I knew we would miss watching the sunset from my house."

"Instead," Alex spoke with a bit of attitude, "we spent the next couple of hours on a mud bog."

"Mike offered the assistance of one of his friends to tow us out of the mud bog. He said his friend had a big truck that could pull any vehicle out of *anything*. It sounded like a simple and was a much-welcomed solution. John and I both accepted the offer. My objective was to get the heck out of there and back up to a nice glass of wine-poolside. We felt a bit of relief to have some local connections on our side."

313

As she leaned into the table, Alex spoke up, "I just couldn't understand how the whole thing had happened in the first place. Granted; Vincent-so young and inexperienced-but, Aruba Joe and John? I still don't understand what made them think they wouldn't get stuck. Men are supposedly logic driven-so they keep reminding us-right Jan?"

Jan spoke with a resounding, "yes! That happens to you, too? Rob often tells me how I get too emotional and how women don't think logically."

"Precisely my point," Alex said while she stomped her foot on the floor-her tone quite firm and matter of fact. "If Vincent got his four-wheeler stuck-what made them think the larger vehicles wouldn't get stuck in that nasty, mud bog. Where was the logic on the mud bog that day? After all, the Jeeps were far heavier than the four wheelers."

"Simple;" Rob answered with a knowing smile in my direction, "testosterone and alcohol."

Rob reached his arm across the table to give me a high-five. I answered his all-too-true comment with a full palm slap and a jovial reply. "Truly, I thought the Jeeps would get through anything. Haven't you seen the off-road commercials? That's why I had rented a Jeep in the first place and why John did the same. We wanted to be able to cruise the island and enjoy the sights. Speaking of sights; we looked like one interesting sight to the locals."

"I can picture that image, Joe," Rob said with a sly smile. "You sure did give something for the Arubans to talk about. They must think Americans are absolute idiots with people like you messin' up on their turf."

"And there is some responsibility and skills needed when driving off-road. It was blatantly obvious you and John had neither," Alex said as she crossed her arms.

Admittedly, our adventure had been rather unique; of that I am certain. Alex was not going to get the best of me. She had been angry in Aruba that day and far into the night-I was not going to accommodate her in a repeat performance-not tonight.

"While we waited for the truck to come to our rescue, this old guy walked out the back of his house located a few hundred yards from us. Many homes line the perimeter of the lake. The old man carried a lawn chair to the lake–just along the edge of the dried-up part. He wore bright plaid shorts and a straw hat, sat down, and waved to us. We couldn't see if he was Aruban or not but, we smiled and waved in return. Crazy ole' man; I suppose our situation proved to be adequate entertainment for him. I doubt we were his first view of foolish adventure seeking vacationers from his back yard. Americans stuck in the middle of the 'mud bog', Arubans finest police officers popping wheelies, and driving circles around the Jeeps-stuck axel deep in mud."

It reminded me of a scene from an old western; the Plains Indians surrounding a herd of buffalo. We were the 'meat' of the day. Those officers were just passing time riding their four wheelers before their tow truck buddy arrived. A huge Safari truck pulled onto the mud bog; one of those colorful tourist type trucks-looked like a large, colorful school bus. The truck had animated South African wild animals painted on the sides and covered by a colorful, striped canvas canopy. He drove through the mud at a steady clip and slowed to a stop. We had high hopes of our rescue and watched the truck; waiting for him to come over. I had wondered what he was doing for such a long time. Mike rode over to his friend; muttering something about how his friend should've known about the mud. The driver got out of the colored bus, and we watched them. Mike rode back to us–shaking his head from side-to-side. I didn't take that as a good sign. No-I did not. The Safari truck driver ended up getting the Safari truck stuck. We all turned our heads toward the Safari truck when we heard some raised voices. Sounded like someone was mad but, we couldn't understand what was said."

"Holy crap!" Rob said with his fingers scratching his chin. "Your day and your luck just kept getting worse. I guess I can see how it had to have been entertaining for the old guy in the lawn chair. I probably would have done the same thing-with a nice cold one in hand and a bucket full beside me."

316

"Oh, yeah," Alex added. "Our situation accelerated to ridiculous, and I was not a happy girl to say the least. The tally of inoperable vehicles had increased. We were back to having three vehicles stuck in the mud bog; scattered in different locations and embedded in the gray mud. We weren't any better off than we were before the Safari truck arrived. I thought the Lone Ranger had arrived to save us and it turned out goofy had arrived.""

"You sure did give the locals something to watch. I bet that was a sight and a half," Jan said. "Sounds like the old man had a good time watching the antics of the stupid Americans on the mud bog in a front-row seat."

"Mary Lib felt sorry for the Safari truck and walked across the mud bog to meet the unlucky driver," Alex added. "Oh, it got better. John and Joe had been debating on whether to call our rental companies, leave the vehicles for the next morning, or call a tow truck. Leaving the vehicles did not seem to be too good of an option. Who knows what the Arubans would have done to the Jeeps; they'd probably strip 'em down to their rims."

CHAPTER 23 – LONE RANGER MEETS NUMBER ONE AND TWO

"We were in a different country; not in the U.S. for goodness' sake," I said. "As much as we hated to do it John and I called our rental companies. We thought that was our viable option as we swallowed our pride. We had started to sober up. A half hour later we heard the low hum of large truck engines. Houses on the west side of the lake hid our view. For a few minutes, there was a bit of a lull. Then, two tow trucks came onto the mud bog and stopped side-by-side. The liberators had arrived. One tow truck was somewhat gray and battered looking-the other one was much larger and painted sparkling white. The white truck really stood out against the darkening night sky and mud."

"The Aruban sky was beginning to host a full moon–cooling temps were coming over the lake–gray mud was everywhere and on everyone. The guy from the white truck walked over to us and introduced himself as Mark. He said he was from the rental company John had used. Mark and John walked over to the Wrangler. Mark is a twenty something attractive looking guy. He walked back to his big, white tow truck and flipped on the overhead lights; they filtered over us and proved to be an excellent light source. The two other guys got out of their truck–leaned against the back of it and stared toward us as if making a strategic assessment.

318

Mark saw us looking at them and explained the others were there to help us with the Sahara."

One of the hecklers from the table across from us decided to chime in. "Doesn't surprise us, Aruba Joe. You were like a magnet-stuff was just attracted to you."

"I know. Thank you for the encouragement, sir," I responded half-jokingly.

"The white truck looked like one from the seventies. A rather macho beast," Alex said. "Mark said he bought it in pristine condition from the states. The truck was a huge over-sized monstrosity. John described our futile attempts to get the Jeeps out. They began spinning some sort of strategy to pull the Wrangler out of the mud bog. Other than the low humming sounds of the truck motors and our low voices there was no other sound on the lake. I was at the mercy of those strange men to get us out of our predicament. I could barely see the outline of the Safari truck. With a flashlight in hand, Mark walked over to the Wrangler and got down on all fours and was careful not to get covered in mud. I could tell he had done this before, 'cause when he stood up, he barely had any of the mud on him–unlike the rest of us. He impressed me with that alone."

"Mark returned to the white tow truck–pulled the winch lever, walked the cable toward the Wrangler, and hooked it to the Jeep," I said. "The thick metal cable slowly tightened until it was about a foot off the ground. The night wasn't quiet any more as the loud whirring sound of the motor revved up. Mary Lib walked over to Mark. Gosh darn; that woman can get people to talk about anything. She found out Mark had bought the tow truck from the states from some guy he knew in Miami. Mark had it shipped to Aruba. He said the cost to ship was almost as much as the truck. Everything must be imported to Aruba, of course. Mark said it was his livelihood now. He found out he could make a far better living towing vehicles on the island than selling car parts."

"Mary Lib came back from the Safari truck earlier. The driver and his pregnant wife had come to help. Mike's brother-in-law was on his way to dinner with her when he got the phone call. His wife did not want him to help. She's into her ninth month and didn't want to have any stress. He convinced her they would only be about 30 minutes. Mary Lib is one of those chatty types that could virtually strike up a conversation with anyone. Her white hair must have something to do with it. I think it gains trust for all those she meets. She also wears her age well," Alex said.

"We're standing off to the side of the Sahara watching-Alex had her fingers crossed. The Wrangler slowly came toward us through the mud. It was a long, steady process. The Wrangler literally inched its way across the mud bog. The front end pushed through the mud with loud baritone sucking sounds as the Jeep moved forward. We finally saw some progress. The Lone Ranger arrived on his white steed to help the victims of the mud bog. Mary Lib clapped her hands and jumped up and down."

"Alex cheered Mark for his heroic deed. I can tell you John and I were just as happy. We were exhausted from all the digging, pushing, and pulling we had done earlier. We had spent about six grueling hours on that mud bog. What a beautiful sight-to finally see that Jeep in motion-half covered in gray mud-the other half in muted red. But we didn't care about that."

"Hell," Alex added, "even the old man sitting on his aluminum chair stood up and whistled. We barely made out his silhouette in the dark. I had forgotten he was there."

"Mark pulled the Wrangler onto solid ground. John was hoping the darn thing was going to start; that worrisome thought kept crossing all our minds. Those Jeeps had been so deeply embedded in the mud. Reaching into the Jeep John turned the key in the ignition Amazingly, the Wrangler started right up. He smiled a huge toothy grin in our direction."

"We sure were glad we had rented a couple of Jeeps. Those things are remarkably durable. Any other vehicle would have been torn apart and would have been no match for the mud bog. Mark settled with John; cost him three hundred dollars but, he gratefully peeled those fifties into the palm of Mark's hand," Alex said.

"Hey, John and I both felt that way. If three hundred dollars was the extent of the cost for the damage of the day's antics, we gladly paid it just to get the dickens out of there. John was ecstatic at that point," I said as I looked toward Alex. God, she looked beautiful. Her sapphire blue shirt seemed to enhance her natural blue eyes to a deeper intense shade. I had myself a good woman.

"Anyway, Mark finished putting his gear away and walked over to the other tow truck. They all know one another on the island. Mark and the two oversized Arubans held a discussion for a few minutes. Judging by the looks on their faces I gathered the Sahara was going to be a far greater challenge than the Wrangler."

Alex said, "the Sahara... was stuck even deeper in the mud than the Wrangler had been. We were worried."

I hadn't noticed before now, but the waitress was standing next to Jan and Rob's side of the table. Her hand rested on the top of the mahoghany back of their side of the booth. She was looking straight at me–intently listening as I talked about the mud bog. "I'm so sorry. I didn't even realize you were there. I was so engrossed in my story."

"No," the waitress said, "you are fine. I couldn't help *but* listen. I hope you don't mind. I just wanted to know if you were finished with your dinners. I came to pick up your plates and see if you wanted any dessert or coffee or tea."

"I would like some Earl Grey tea," Jan said turning to the young girl.

The rest of us asked for a cup of coffee. Alex asked if she could have some fresh whipped cream on the side for her coffee; I requested Bailey's Irish Cream. We waited quietly while the waitress removed our plates-retreating quietly to the kitchen. My comfort level with Jan and Rob had changed; I wasn't feeling anxious. Or perhaps the glasses of wine were having their calming effect on me. However, I was not sure about how Alex was feeling. I still sensed a bit of tension-yet at other times.... It was time to move on to my story.

"The moon had a hazy white halo surrounding it and the stars were so bright they sparkled like distant diamonds on a dark canvas. The evening sky could have been quite a romantic backdrop for another time if we had been somewhere–anywhere–on the island doing just about anything. The trade winds had diminished–a slight breeze replaced them. The tow truck drivers realigned the spotlights toward the Sahara. The residents of the houses surrounding the dried-up lake had begun turning off their interior lights; only a few were still on. The homes appeared as rectangular shaped silhouettes in the darkness. I had wondered if the old guy was still sitting on his chair watching us. We could no longer see that far. We heard some screeching noises from somewhere on the other side of the mud bog. The noises were intermittent and then became totally silent. I assumed some wild dingo or snake must have cornered prey–then quietly dined on the unlucky victim."

"Oh, my God," Jan screeched. "Wild dingos and snakes?"

"There are wild dogs all over the island, just like the wild donkeys down at the Natural Pool. They don't bother anyone. Occasionally, you can see a herd of goats on the hillside behind my house. As for the snakes, I never saw one but the driver to the Natural Pool said they were there. Animals can't get their food from a grocery store, Jan. They must get it somehow."

"I know," Jan replied, "I guess I just don't like thinking about it–that's all. It sounds so brutal. I mean-animals killing one another–it's too gruesome for my mind."

"Jan," Rob explained, "doesn't handle the thought processes of the food chain too well. She squirms and squeals when we watch animal shows. The mental imagery is just too violent for her."

"Got it. I will make a note for future reference."

"I had decided to walk over to the other tow truck to see what the game plan was for our Jeep. The two, big Arubans spoke little English. I could decipher a bit of the response when spoken in Papiamento mixed with English. I did get the gist of it-they would only take a few minutes to get the Sahara out of the mud. I was relieved to hear that and said as much to Alex. She had been looking for a flip flop she lost earlier. Big Aruban Number One pulled the wench from the back of the truck. Big Aruban Number Two unhooked the latch for the wench. It was the first time either one of them moved since they arrived. They sat there the entire time Mark worked on pulling the Wrangler out of the mud."

"Kind of like Dr. Seuss's Thing One and Thing Two! So funny, Aruba Joe," Jan said.

"We joked about the two hefty Arubans. Perhaps they had been the sons of the woman at the police department. They were just as disengaged that night from us as she had been the day before. Most Arubans are related to one another. If not to someone on the island, to one of the other islands nearby. My encounters with Arubans have been pleasant and accommodating; nice people."

"Big Aruban Number Two, the one standing by the tow truck, walked slowly over to the Sahara and spoke to Joe. Through the tow truck lights, we could see his fleshy arms swinging by either side of his rotund body as he walked directly in the light from the trucks following its path of light on the mud bog. The Arubans walked around the Jeep a couple of times, kicking the tires, and talking amongst themselves. I wondered if they had ever towed a car before," Alex said.

"I let those guys work on the Sahara and went back to stand with Alex. She had given up the search for her flip flop."

"The main issue about my flip flop was it was navy blue suede with rhinestones. I loved them. You know I love shoes, Jan, just as much as you do. Parting with them was a huge disappointment; so hard to see in all that gunk," Alex added.

"I feel your pain," Jan said in response. "Once, I lost a good pair of my favorite yellow colored patent leather sandals in Ocean City. The tide came in and before I could grab them, they floated away."

"Big Aruban Number One spoke to me in a blend of Papiamento and a butchered bantering of the Queen's English. He confirmed he had hooked the winch up to the axle and was going to drag the Jeep out. That much I understood. Mark and Mike had walked over to the far side of the lake and had just come back from the Safari truck. Mark had known the Safari's driver a long time. The Safari driver's wife was still pitching up one heck of an angry storm at the poor Safari driver for getting stuck. Now, at least, we knew the source of the screeching noises earlier."

"Thank goodness," Jan said "at least it wasn't because of a snake or some other critter dining on some defenseless creature. Just hearing you talk about that possibility earlier gave me the shivers." Jan shrugged her shoulders in a jittery sort of way.

"Mike said he might as well leave since there wasn't a whole lot he could offer other than some moral support. He also said he recently became a new father and hadn't been getting much sleep lately. He removed his wallet and proudly displayed a recent picture of the baby boy and his wife. She was a beautiful young woman. After we shook hands and the girls gave him a huge hug for all his help, Mike and his four-wheeler disappeared in the dark. Looking

326

around us, I noticed his other off-duty friends weren't around. I had forgotten all about them."

"Mary Lib had gotten all kinds of island gossip from Mike earlier," Alex said. "She began sharing some juicy island gossip after Mike left. Mike told her the Arubans were mad at well-known television personalities as well as the American media. Specifically, he had told her by name the ones that were not welcome on Aruban soil after their derogatory tales of the notorious and internationally known story of a young American tourist. Of course, we all knew Natalie by name. Mike also told Mary Lib the Aruban police were always on top of the investigation; far from the media coverage we heard on the news channels."

"Fortunately, *you* didn't have such a serious situation down there. God bless. I hope none of us ever have an experience like that–home or abroad," Rob said. "That kind of thing is something I wouldn't wish on my worst enemy."

Alex continued, "Mike also educated Mary Lib about what his job in Aruba entailed. He spoke about the ongoing training of the Aruban police. Those people travel all over the world to visit foreign police departments, S W A T, medical, and governmental agencies. They exchange their ideas, experience, and tactics. That's how he had gotten the S W A T t-shirt. Apparently, the officers exchange uniforms and other paraphernalia with one another during their international training. Mike told Mary Lib the Americans and

Israelis had the 'best protection' and the 'most trained security personnel.' From my viewpoint and experience the Aruban police were a great bunch of guys."

"The Safari had to wait for one of the tow trucks to become available to pull him out. I felt bad for not going over to the guy to help him and his wife but, I was preoccupied with our Jeep. Once the winch was attached to the Sahara, we all clapped as the loud truck motor started pulling the winch cable tighter; we were getting out. We were going home to the pool and a nice glass of wine-finally. I had visions of getting back to relaxing in the pool mindful I would need to visit the outdoor shower first as the mud was caked all over my body. John's Jeep had come out so swiftly; however, that was not to be the case for us. The cable snapped with a 'zinging' sound as it went flying past us."

"How dangerous," commented Jan. "If one of you would have been in the way of that metal wire it could have killed you!"

"We weren't standing in between the truck and the Jeep in harm's way," Alex answered. "The large fog lights from the tow trucks gave us plenty of light. But you are so right Jan. That wire was thick."

"The two larger Arubans walked over to the cable, let it out a bit more and tied it back together with their large, bare hands. They started reeling in the cable and hooked it back up-the same thing happened again. I decided to walk over to them-to see what

328

they planned to do next. I got an eyeful of tanned, plumber cracks as the Arubans bent over to tie the cable together again. I never did get their names," I said.

"Mark talked to One and Two in Papiamento. He interpreted their response back to me and said they never had this problem before. It was a bit hard to believe. We watched them again. Again, the same thing happened. We had been out on that mud bog since late afternoon and we were getting tired. I asked Mark to help us out. He did better than those two jerks. Mark seemed far more experienced and equipped and he had a much better-looking tow truck than the other two Arubans.

"One and Two walked over to us; John came back over to join in. He and Mary Lib had been leaning against the red Wrangler watching the duo and their non-productive performance. Two made a phone call to their boss. I guess he needed to find out what to do since the duo certainly couldn't figure it out. John and I began our own conversation. We felt we needed to take things into our own hands. We offered the butt-cracking twosome $300 to call it a night and offered Mark $200 to pull the Sahara out. One and Two looked offended with my offer—I just wanted to get my Jeep out of the mud bog and get home. A nice glass of wine was waiting for me at the house and had my name on it. It was blatantly obvious the Jeep was not getting out of the mud by *that* tow truck with *those two guys*. Mark intervened for us. He knew we had enough of their shenanigans. He said a few undecipherable words and One and Two began pulling in the cable. I walked over and gave them the money and could not have been happier to watch them drive off. Mark expertly positioned his tow truck on the dry dirt in front of the Jeep; being careful to angle it just the right way. The other two guys had been trying to pull it out sideways. Once the wench was snug, Mark started his motor and began the process of pulling out the second Jeep. Initially, we did not see any movement at all. Then, the Sahara began moving slowly with a sucking noise much like the Wrangler."

"Mark had to angle the tow truck in a few different directions in order to get the right leverage. The mud kept folding back in front of the Jeep sinking it deeper into the mud every time he pulled making it impossible to proceed. Mark wasn't the type to give up. He kept repositioning the hook underneath the Jeep. Suddenly, we heard this big moaning sound of air popping from the sunken beast as it started to rise upward through the mud bog. There was a big 'harumph' sound like some prehistoric animal getting ready to charge its adversary. Alex came back to join me; she had found her flip flop somewhere. Her cheeks were full of dried mud. Mary Lib had already gotten in the driver's side of the Wrangler and John was standing beside it–they didn't want to leave us on the mud bog until we were completely out."

"We were a team throughout the entire trip," perked up Alex as she raised her hand-the index finger pointing upward. "That's one positive thing I can say about our trip."

"Mark pulled the Sahara real slow and steady. The mud would pile high then slide off the front of it as he pulled the metal beast through. We began to see more of the green hood of the Jeep and less mud. The front tires finally reached solid ground. Mud covered the tires–at least six inches of the gray mud was up the side of the Jeep. I felt a huge surge of adrenaline when I saw all four tires."

"We could hear and just barely see the old guy in the lawn chair as he stood up and clapped his hands, his body a partial silhouette against the darkness. Since the evening's entertainment was over, he must have decided to go in-we could hear the metal clinking of the lawn chair. We sure gave him a couple of good hours of amusement to pass his time," Alex said. "Not only that, but he also had a great tale to tell his friends at the senior center in the morning."

"Alex, that is too funny," Jan said laughing.

"Sakes alive, Joe" Rob said. "Did the thing start?"

"It's a Jeep, Rob. Of course, it started. What a great commercial we would've made for Jeep. Nothing, even the Aruban mud bog, can keep a Jeep from running."

"That is, as long as you use the right key," Alex added with her beautiful smile.

"Mark got us out of that nasty mud like a true pro. John shook his hand and told him 'He was the man'. I pulled the hook from the frame. All of us were thankful to be finished with that ordeal. We were exhausted, a bit sun burned, and covered in wet and dried mud. Mark finished reeling in his winch and secured the large metal hook in the back of the tow truck. I shared the same feeling John had when he gave Mark his money earlier-relief. Alex climbed into the Sahara. Remarkably, none of the mud had seeped inside. Mark led us through the opposite side of the lake from where we had entered earlier. We were mobile once again. We watched as Mark drove back onto the perimeter of the lake in the direction of the Safari. He had more work to do. We honked our horns and drove to 'home–sweet–home. The moon was full and bright."

CHAPTER 24 – SHE'S A DANCER

Everyone seated around our table began laughing and a couple of them clapped their hands. "God, I am so funny," I whispered to Alex. "I sure do know how to entertain people with my story."

Aloud I said, "This is one Aruban vacation my family never experienced. They couldn't believe what happened when I told them about it."

"Oh yeah! Your family was lucky Aruba Joe wasn't with them," Alex responded.

"When my family has traveled to Aruba, it has always been a good time at the beach, pool, dining at all the best restaurants, and doing outdoor water sports. Admittedly, the most excitement we had in several decades was during a poolside wet bathing suit contest. My other sister signed up for that event. Alcohol may have played a bit of a part in that one. That was tame compared to what Alex and I did in just a couple of days in Aruba. And, somehow, I don't think anything like that will ever happen again."

"Were the kids home when you got there," Jan asked. "I bet they were worried sick about all of you."

"They were fine Jan," Alex said. "They watched television and swam in the pool."

"Our work was not completely over when we arrived back at the house. John and I parked the Jeeps out front along the curb rather than in the driveway. We thought it best to hose them down-before the mud dried like concrete. God only knows what it would've done to the paint and the under carriage. And I certainly didn't want that gray mud in my driveway. The kids came out and helped–brought us a couple of beers. I crawled under the Sahara and hosed the undercarriage–it was thick with bog mud. Vincent scrubbed the exterior and John was doing much of the same. The Wrangler wasn't as bad as the Sahara."

"Now," Alex added, "while the boys rinsed the Jeeps, I stood watching a stream of gray traveling down the hill along the curbside. There were huge clumps of mud-one and two feet deep in the road. I didn't know where Joe's Road went to, but I was hoping the mud found its way down some drain into the ocean. Joe was not a bit concerned about it. I figured it was his house and his neighbors."

"Alex was the only one worried about all the mud. I wasn't. My worries had been getting those Jeeps on solid ground and cleaned up. No one got hurt. The kids had a blast touring around the island earlier. John, Vincent, and I had a good time doing donuts out back. Hey; it turned out to be a good day in Aruba. And we got a bunch of laughs watching those two clowns trying to pull us out. It was as close as you could get to a three-ring circus on the lake that night. The only thing missing was a circus tent."

"Did you ever find out anything about the Safari truck?" Jan asked.

"No, we never did. I think they were in good hands. The next day I drove down-the only remnants of the mud bug adventure were the huge clumps of grey mud and deep ruts. We were worn out by the time we finished spraying and washing the Jeeps. You couldn't even tell they were even in a lake when I was done with them. I may have found myself a new profession–car detailer."

"Seriously now, they looked good by the midnight moon. Jade even dried them with a couple of beach towels," Alex said.

"By the time we got inside the house, the air conditioning felt wonderful. The kids were watching Michael Jackson on CNN and playing Scrabble. Jackson had died the Tuesday before we left on our trip. I stopped for a moment to watch Michael on the screen-doing his infamous version of the 'moonwalk'–rather apropos for that evening and our moon experience on the lake I'd say. It wasn't the most romantic or scenic time I've experienced down there-under the moon but, it sure was the most memorable. A good shower put us back in paradise mode."

"The next morning, I decided to engage in the more simplistic pleasures of our vacation; like we had intended. A morning workout seemed like a viable option. A nice walk to the clubhouse and a relaxing day by the pool was in order. Mary Lib and John joined me. They both had a morning exercise regimen at home. They were all about physical fitness-even at their age-I was impressed. However, Alex and her girls-hmmmm. Vincent was the one that enjoyed working out but, he couldn't get his butt out of bed each day."

"Yep," Alex started in again. "The three of them headed off to the gym. The girls and I sat on a couple of lounge chairs around the pool, which was a good enough work out for us. We were surprised by an early visit from Salvatore."

"That poor man had his hands full watching after all of you," Jan said. "I bet he couldn't wait for you to leave so he could have some peace and quiet."

"He came to check on us. He was curious about how long it took us to get the Jeeps out of the mud. While we were talking, a white Cadillac pulled in front of the house. The driver honked the horn to wake the dead," Alex said. "I heard a woman's voice as she shouted for Salvatore. The woman must've recognized his white truck in the driveway. He ran out front. We heard her shrill voice demanding to know who was responsible for all the mud in her driveway and on the white marble floor in her garage. We could not hear Salvatore s response."

"The woman had a white marble floor in her garage?" Jan asked. "My goodness. A nice floor in the garage here is a painted floor. That must have been some garage."

"We knew who the culprit was; so, did the woman screaming at Salvatore. There was plenty of evidence in front of Joe's house," Alex continued. "He promised Mrs. Caddie he would get it taken care of. He climbed in his truck and took off down the road. She gunned her engine and peeled off in the opposite direction; she was in a bit of a mood."

"Just so you know," I said to Rob and Jan, "Mrs. Caddie, as Alex calls her, owns the largest and most exclusive estate in Aruba. They have several buildings, a huge pool house, and white marble statues on the grounds; just down the end of the cul-de-sac."

"My word," Jan said, "you all got yourself into a real pickle again; with your neighbor this time."

"Let's put it this way," Alex began. "The woman was screaming at Salvatore even while she drove off. The girls and I waited for her to disappear. We kept out of sight on the back patio. We found a shovel, bucket, and the hose out of the garage and started working on the mess in front of the house. And I mean to tell you— it was still one helluva mess. There were mounds of gray mud all over the road. Somehow, they seemed bigger in the daylight than they had the night before. We shoveled and carried mud one bucket full at a time and dumped it in the back yard."

"By the time John, Mary Lib, and I got back from the gym, Alex and Jade were sweeping up the last of the mud. The remains of our evening from the mud bog were reduced to nothing but some dry, gray dust. Alex told me about the woman I know exactly whom she was talking about. The road was just about spotless after I got done with it."

"Yeah, Joe really helped," Alex chided. "That is after the girls and I nearly broke our arms and backs carrying all that wet mud down the slope in the back yard. I don't know how many buckets of mud we carried. We worked for hours."

"Salvatore came back to the house. He is such a good sport. By that time, all of us were sitting around the pool. He was smiling a white grin and waved a newspaper in his hand. He called out to me. 'Hey, Joe; you made the papers.' Sure enough, there was an article about the contractor and me, right on the inside of the front paper. The article was typed in Papiamento. We huddled around him at the table on the patio–looking over one another's shoulder–anxious to hear what was written about me. Salvatore read it out loud for everyone to hear. He pointed out the part that all of us could read; 'the American called the Aruban contractor an 'a..hole''. When he got to that part his voice became shrill with the word 'a..hole! He repeated it several times and said a last 'A dot–dot–hole'. He gave us all a good laugh. Never had I made the papers. Not in the good ole U S of A and certainly, never in Aruba."

"Salvatore left to finish cleaning up the neighbor's house-smiling and shaking his head. I felt bad for him; that he felt responsible to clean up the neighbor's garage floor. I caught up to him and tried to persuade him to let me help. As he got to the truck, he gave me a sideways glance– 'she wouldn't want you to do it. It would be like an insult to have an American clean her floor. An Aruban could–yes; an American–no'. After twenty some years, I am still learning about the Aruban culture. It made sense. By that time, even Vincent had woken up. I showed him the newspaper– emphasizing the 'a..hole' like Salvatore had."

"We all agreed to lay around the pool; have a 'pool day,'" Alex added. "We also agreed no one was allowed to leave the house and do any physical activities and just chill for the day."

"I don't think you guys knew how to chill", Jan said. "Not in hot Aruba, anyways. It seemed everywhere you went Joe, and whomever you were with-things just got totally out of control. It doesn't sound like you had one normal day so far on your vacation in Aruba."

I thought about what she said for a moment and was just about to speak when the waitress came back to our table with our tea and coffee. I noticed the streetlights outside of the restaurant and how they lit up the sidewalk and street. Several of the tables in the restaurant had emptied and then filled again. However, the diners at the tables around us were still there listening to my tale of Aruba. I acknowledged them with a smile and a low nod in their direction. I normally did not have such an opportunity to be at the center of attention. Don't get me wrong; I thoroughly enjoy being the center of attention. It's just the opportunity didn't present itself. We took a sip of our beverages; mine was delicious as always.

"We really had a lot going on while we were there." I thought for another moment. I wasn't quite sure how I was going to respond to Jan at first. I didn't want to appear defensive–none of the events were really *my* fault. After all, I didn't cause the initial problem when we checked in our luggage. The woman behind the counter was the one with the attitude. And I didn't ask for the upgrade to first class. Yes, I knew I was entitled to an upgrade due to my mileage points. It wasn't my hand flipping off the power switch on the island causing the kids to lose their twenty dollars in the slot machines. I didn't put Alex's foot between some rocks and mess up her foot. And, I only had the best of intentions for a special dinner at the Divi."

"I didn't throw a punch at the contractor, and I certainly wasn't the one who instigated the four-wheeler event in the mud bog. I did mess up on the rocks at the Natural Pond. And even then, I had just wanted another wonderful Aruban experience on our vacation. The Jeeps and four-wheeler on the mud bog were shared by several participants–not, just me! The Sahara and the keys–that wasn't my fault either. The mud into my neighbor's garage was a bit unfortunate. Granted-a lot of weird stuff had occurred. And then it hit me. Oh God-what were these people thinking about me? After all, I had just met Rob and Jan. I wasn't worried about the other

340

diners; chances are I would never see them again. I decided to give my best answer without sounding too aloof or arrogant.

"It was just a series of unique circumstances that had, quite frankly, spiraled out of my control." That made me feel good. I decided to just forge onward with my story. The look on Rob and Jan's faces was all the encouragement I needed.

"A series of 'unique circumstances'," Rob repeated. "Hey Joe, I somewhat like that summation."

"Certainly, a day at the pool seemed safe enough. John, Vincent, and I had bruised egos to mend. Everyone agreed to a day of total relaxation. But first; John and I took off for the nearest car wash and made sure the vehicles were spotless underneath. They have a special bay to lift the vehicles just for that purpose. We were back home and in our trunks in less than an hour. By midday, the entire group was either reading or sunbathing. The girls laid up top on the balcony upstairs. I didn't want to even look. I think those girls are a mirror image of their mother when she was their age. Throughout the day, three wild, green feathered parrots flew overhead in a race-like manner. They are beautiful parrots. Now, that's something you do not see here at home. Since the day we built there, they have flown over the house; racing one another and chirping noisily. It is moments like that, which make me so appreciative of Aruba-just a great day."

"Alex and Mary Lib prepared a nice lunch of meats, cheeses, and veggies. Perfect for the afternoon around the pool. John disappeared from the poolside. He came back out with a couple of glass tumblers filled with Patron tequila. He had sliced lime wedges all around the rims. In the pool, there are a couple of cement ledges on two of the corners to sit on. We sat in the pool and enjoyed the tranquility of the Aruban, afternoon sun. Vincent and John sat together; sharing conversation on world events and the stock market."

"Vincent seemed to hold his own with the sixty something year-old man. John was enjoying the younger eighteen-year-olds youthful views," Alex said. "They sipped on the tequila–engaging in some male bonding that day. We were all getting so tanned. I loved sitting around the pool as long as you use the right suntan lotion. It was perfect weather each day. The palm tree branches swayed in the breeze and tropical birds sang to us from the wild back yard cactus. Except for our second night when we had that horrible storm the weather was great."

"We swam laps, read, and napped. One of the books Alex brought with her was 'Venus and Mars'; Mary Lib really got into reading that one. It didn't take long to discover John's elaborate sense of humor. He is a rather funny fellow. John was full of tales from his boyish college days. We heard all about his football plays and his charming stories of the gorgeous girls he dated. Vincent

342

became a bit bold and started reciprocating stories and told John about all the girls *he* dated."

"That pool conversation began to sound more like 'locker room' talk," Alex added.

"Vincent fired stories right back at John and both provided entertainment. I'd say they did a lot of *male bonding*. John insisted on giving Vincent shots of tequila; Vincent shared his Jägermeister. John told one tale–Vincent told his. I never did those kinds of things in high school or college. One joke John told really stood out from the rest. You know, Alex, I can never remember how to tell a joke. History is what I can remember–jokes I must write down. Remember the one about the Indians honey? The faw-quar-wees?'"

Before Alex could answer I suddenly remembered the joke. "John stood up in the pool. He'd consumed quite a bit of Patron, Jagger, and some dark vodka–Van Gough I think it's called. He held his hand over his eyebrows, moving his body at the waist from side-to-side; like he's looking for something." I stood up at the side of the table as I imitated John from memory placing my hand over my eyebrows and turned my head from side to side. "John said, 'you know the faw-quar-wee Indians–you ever heard of them? The chief of the faw-quar-wees–when they're out on the plains–leads his tribe in search of buffalo." As I felt the eyes of the other diners, I felt a bit of pressure "The male Indians of the tribe are very brave hunters. For several days, the Indians rode across the hot, dry plains in search of the buffalo. From a single hunt, buffalo meat supplied food and clothing materials to the tribe for months to keep them fed and warm. Well, the Indians had now been out on the plains for a week–and there was not a buffalo to be found. The Indians were covered in dry dirt from head feathers to moccasins. Their mouths were dry from the dust. Their water supply was low. The painted ponies they rode were barely able to walk and lathered in white foam under their forelegs and chests-their heads hanging low."

I paused as so many heads and eyes had shifted in my direction. Here was my moment; this was it. Tonight, I wanted to deliver the punch line better than John had in Aruba. I sought to deliver belly laughter. I could see Rob and Jan were very much interested in hearing the joke. Alex was probably hoping I wouldn't mess up the punchline; her eyes grew in size, and she pursed her lips together. "Well, the chief stopped his pony and all the other men stopped their ponies, too. They were standing atop a high canyon overlooking the plains. The heat was unbearable. The chief puts his hand over his eyes to narrow his search across the vast plains looking for a sighting of buffalo." I did the same with my best look of intensity. "From upon his mighty painted steed, the Chief yelled; 'where the faw-quar-wee?'"

At first, there was silence. Alex chuckled inwardly. "I don't get that joke at all," Jan said. "What's the punch line again?"

"You have to understand," Rob said, "Jan is a bit slow when it comes to jokes. Don't worry honey," he said to Jan, "I will fill you in on the way home tonight."

Jan took it good naturedly and shrugged her shoulders. "I don't get many jokes–it has nothing to do with you Aruba Joe."

"Alex and I thought it was funny. The kids laughed. Mary Lib had just shrugged–an indication she'd heard that joke quite often. Oh, weellll." I guess it's just one of those things that you must be in the right mood for-in ARUBA!

A few of other diners chuckled or smiled; no belly laughs. They had no sense of humor either.

"John and Vincent got blitzed by the pool. There were no injuries–other than a little sun burn. That night, we decided to have dinner at Texas de Brazil. Ever heard of them?"

Rob and Jan looked at one another and shook their heads 'no',

"Well, it's this Brazilian franchise restaurant–have a bunch of them like it here in the States–very nice. Lots of food and have a great salad bar. They serve you as much as you can eat–different beef cuts, chicken, and pork. I'll have you know we had one terrific dinner followed by one beautiful evening going to the casinos. Not one person got hurt or lost that night either."

"I can't believe you made it through one entire day and one entire evening without some sort of crazy experience happening to you guys, Aruba Joe," quipped the big guy over at the table by the window.

"Exactly my thoughts. You must have felt like something had gone wrong when it went right," Rob said. "Like your luck had changed and you were actually in paradise after all."

"Say what you will–both of you. We had an absolute blast. Now, I know this vacation sounds a bit absurd. If I had been with anyone else besides Alex, then this vacation would have been viewed as a catastrophe. Perhaps it had something to do with the moon, I don't know. Alex's birthday was the next day–she was turning fifty-two in Aruba. I was determined to make it the most memorable birthday of her life. It was-wasn't it, sweetie?"

"That was a special and rather unique birthday. You did a good job–I sure have that day to remember for a long time. No one can take that away from you," Alex said with an exaggerated tone and a killer smile to compliment her tanned face.

"Uh, oh," Rob said. "By the tone of your voice, Alex, I can't tell if it was a good birthday. But my instinct says I think we're going to hear something rather amusing in the next few minutes."

"Shush, Rob," Jan said. "Let Joe finish telling his story about Alex's birthday. I just love birthday celebrations!" Jan clapped her hands together. She was not hard to please.

By now, we had finished our coffee and tea. I didn't want to get into the birthday story until the waitress took our cups away. The

346

Cafe had some pretty darn good food and service. I stretched my arms over my head and looked around the restaurant. The football dudes were still there—the restaurant staff were busy. It had become quite crowded for a Saturday night in August. A good sign even though the economy was starting to wane.

"I woke up a bit earlier than usual on her birthday. I wanted to make the day special for her. Alex had wanted to go horseback riding. We had planned on going horseback riding from the very first day we had arrived. Horseback riding in the morning and dinner in the evening. Alex used to have a horse when she was a teenager. I bet you didn't know that about your friend, Jan."

"I did not but, I bet she looked beautiful riding on it," Jan said with a smile at her friend. Alex smiled a 'thank you' back.

"The kids woke up with other ideas for the day. They came up with going to the Venezuelan side of the island, to the calm beach side of the island. Alex thought there were too many ideas for one day and decided her and I could go riding another day-giving in to the beach. John and Mary Lib loved the beach. They had the darkest tan. Skin was a bit leathery-know what I mean? Like I said, they do a lot of traveling. I never saw her three kids move to get ready so fast. I made dining reservations for eight o'clock at my favorite restaurant thinking that would give us a full day on the beach. We packed a cooler full of water-didn't need anything else. There is a pier bar next to the beach area. Alex grabbed a bunch of beach towels and lotion. Mary Lib packed some books, and we headed out the front door. The day could not have been more perfect for the beach. As we drove along the beach toward the high rises, I noticed a flock of wild pink flamingos standing on a sand bar. At first, I don't think John realized what I was doing as I pulled the Jeep off the side of the road. Alex jumped out of the Sahara and pointed to the wild birds. Mary Lib followed suit with her camera in hand. She's a semi-professional photographer."

"I only saw flamingos at the zoo," Jan said. "It must have been wonderful to see them in a natural habitat."

"Other cars pulled alongside of us to view the birds. One old guy had a booklet in his hand. He was vacationing and told us he was from Holland. He spoke fluent English and explained he was on sabbatical, a college professor from Amsterdam. Mr. Holland said he enjoyed his vacations in Aruba every summer and took pictures of the wildlife on the island. Some of them were good enough to win awards in contests and he was rather proud of his skills."

"The children stayed in the car. They were not the least bit impressed by the flamingos and just wanted us to hurry up," Alex said. "Jade said she wanted to gamble. That girl has gambling in her blood. I think she dreamt of numbers, sirens and whistles, and lights."

"Mary Lib managed to get some nice pictures of the birds before we got back in the Jeeps. Saying 'caio' to Mr. Holland we drove to one of the hotel garages. Jade convinced Crystal to go to the casino with her; the rest of us found some beach chairs along the water next to the pier bar. They serve good drinks as well as sandwiches and appetizers. Our plan was to be off the beach by four o'clock; we arrived about eleven. The sun was warm. The trade winds had picked up their momentum across the island as per usual but, not enough to blow sand all over you. Sometimes, that can happen down there making a beach day somewhat unpleasant. That is why I usually stay at the house-at my pool. I don't like sand sticking to my lotion. The winds also reduce sweating and keeps the flying insect population down."

"The sky was the most beautiful shade of blue, a shade of periwinkle. The five of us finally got a chance to read and relax the first couple of hours," Alex said. "Vincent didn't want to 'waste' his money in the casinos like his sisters. He sat right along with the 'adults' soaking up the sun and reading. On our vacation, I learned something about each of my children that I really didn't know before. It's uncanny what you find out about people when you spend a lot of time with them." Her voice trailed off as she looked down into her wine glass-swirled its contents-took a sip-and then sat back against the booth. I only could hope what she had learned about me was my truth and love for her; more than life itself.

"It was one of those beach days when you sunned, took a couple of dips in the ocean, read and then did it all over again throughout the afternoon. About one o'clock, John offered to buy Alex a birthday round and walked over to the pier bar. Alex accepted saying 'only one drink, John,'. He came back with his big hands full of plastic cups. Once we finished our drinks, John took off again for another round. Instead of only drinks this time, he had a variety of appetizers on a tray."

"John had some wonderful coconut shrimps, little quesadillas, and some fried potatoes," Alex said. "They were delicious."

"John explained the pier bar's happy hour was from four to five and wanted to buy Alex a birthday shot before we had dinner. Alex agreed to accept one, *just one*, melon ball. Note: she just wanted ONE. She knew John and his alcohol. Mary Lib had also emphasized that they limit the time at the bar. I reminded *everyone* about our dinner reservations, and we could not stay at the bar too long. The plan seemed reasonable and would fit into a fabulous birthday dinner at Windows On Aruba for my sweetie. Windows is on the top floor of the clubhouse at another golf course community. The view of the ocean sunset is magnificent from every table in the restaurant."

"Seems to me, if you didn't have a good dining experience at the clubhouse why experience another one?" Jan said. "I would have stopped at the great appetizers."

In defense of my manhood and the fact I take pride in showing guests and family a good time I had no choice in the matter. I responded. "No, I can assure you the birthday dinner location was right on que. Windows is the perfect place for a special dinner. Don't get me wrong; Del Sol's restaurant is usually very nice, too. We just happened to pick the day their chef decided to pull a 'no-show'. That was a rather unfortunate and unique situation and could happen with any restaurant. I won't hold that against them."

"Seems to me you had a lot of '*unique*' situations in Aruba, Joe," Rob commented. "Although, I remember we attended a golf-course wedding. The clubhouse chef had a heart attack just after they served appetizers. And the staff *finally* decided to let us know as the ambulance sirens started blaring."

"Duly noted, you guys. The girls came over from the casino to join us and swim in the ocean. The gentle and warm water just heightens your sense of relaxation. We spent the day watching different types of boats passing by the beach–catamarans, speedboats, sail boats, cruise line ships, and huge cargo carriers. There are times when the navy fleet shows up-when Venezuela gets rambunctious. The beach and the ocean weren't too crowded. I am content to just watch the blue green water. The surf is gentle on that side of the island. You can walk out a hundred to two hundred feet or more and the water is only up to your chest. When we got too hot, we just walked in, swam around for a little while, floated on our backs, and went back to the beach. The beach is a white, fine sand-stays cool, too."

"It all sounds so dreamy," Jan said with her head slightly tilted.

"By four o'clock we did enough worshipping of our bodies to the yellow ball in the sky. We could hear happy hour had just started at the pier bar. The music was playing louder than it had during the day," Alex said. "The music was calling my name through the salty, Aruban air; '*Alex come play.*' I didn't quite realize it then but, the alcohol had already begun its wanton effect on me."

"Crystal and Jade decided to run into town. They wanted to shop for something special for their mother's birthday. The girls asked Vincent to join them, but he declined again. I think Vincent rather liked hanging out with the adults; he's more mentally advanced for his age than the average young person. He didn't share in his sister's interests in the casinos either. We packed up our towels, books, and cooler. John and Mary Lib were used to having a drink before dinner and wanted to stop for one drink before we went home to shower."

Just the memory of that evening made me smile involuntarily. None of my previous trips to Aruba had similar

352

memories. I should be thankful to God for that. I don't know of any family vacations that could remotely compare.

"I really didn't see any harm in going for the happy hour drink," Alex said. "We had plenty of time, at that point, before our dinner reservations. We put our beach bags by one of the tables closest to the bar. There were only a few other patrons scattered about the restaurant and bar area."

"By the time we finished coordinating our stuff at the table, John had ordered the melon ball for Alex. And John ordered a melon ball for me. And John ordered a melon ball for Vincent and Mary Lib. And, of course, John had to order one for the bartender and himself. Singing a rather out-of-tune version of '*happy birthday*' our elbows headed north as the melon ball met our esophagus. That John sure was a quick one. He had the bartender line up the next round of shots-before we finished the first one; before any of us realized what was happening. I counted them. There were fourteen shots lined up at the bar–B52's I think John called them. Michael Jackson's voice crooned through the speakers scattered about the pier blasting the satellite radio station. Seemed like Jackson's music was playing everywhere we went on our trip. By about the fifth shot, I think it was the Lemon Drop, this guy had joined us from the other side of the bar. He was all alone, and Alex had signaled him from across the bar to join us. Now, I just want you to note something because you probably don't even know this

353

about your friend, Jan. But, when Alex drinks, several things happen to her. One; she gets intoxicated rather easily. Two; she gets extremely lovable. Three; she'll get total strangers together to dance and drink right with her. And, her eyes," I said holding my forefinger and middle finger in the shape of the letter 'v' toward my eyes, "turn a brilliant shade of violet. I'll tell you; by the time she's through, she'll get the whole place having a great time. It is truly amazing to watch Alex in action. She hates to see anyone not having a good time when she is having fun. She wants everyone to be on their feet– to the point of exhaustion-not sitting in their chair. I don't know where she gets that kind of energy. I love to dance, but I'm not about to go up to some stranger and invite them to dance with *me*; that's for sure. Alex has little inhibition when she's sober and virtually none when she's drinking alcohol." I looked at Alex for a moment, took a sip of my water glass, and went on.

"This one guy could have passed for Robin Williams' double-he had all the physical attributes including hairy arms. Mary Lib encouraged Alex to do that sandwich dance with him. They debated on who was in front and who was in the back of '*Robin*'. If that guy didn't have a good time before he met us, he certainly did that night. The man grinned from ear-to-ear the entire time he was dancing–between Alex and Mary Lib. Robin wore a camera around his neck and took lots of pictures; probably put them in his album when he got back home. John, on the other hand, stood at the bar

354

the entire time-ordering shots. There were at least fourteen more different shots of one concoction or another–lined up and ready for the taking. I realized we were definitely not going out to dinner. The evening had gotten off to a different path. I knew showing her the view of the ocean from the semi-circular dining room at Windows was not going to happen. She would not see the view of the ocean, a view of the city and it kinda made me mad. My plans were negated by John's desire to drink-a lot."

"I get your disappointment, Joe," Rob said. "I hate it when I plan a special evening for Jan, and something goes sideways-not quite like that. One time I had planned this elaborate, romantic dinner at our house. Just the two of us. We had barely put a fork in our salad when her sister came by. Her sister lives over an hour away and we usually see her on holidays. She doesn't like to drive to the country, you see. No sirree; I certainly would not have liked what happened on Alex's birthday either."

"Rob," I answered rather matter-of-factly. And, truth-be-told, I would have been truly miffed under any other circumstances. "For some strange reason I ended up being okay with the way the day had turned out. Initially, Alex had wanted to spend time during the day horseback riding– we went to the beach. I had wanted to take Alex out to dinner–we ended up getting extremely drunk with a group of people we didn't even know. A soccer game was playing on the television."

"The entire bar, including the bartenders, were engaged in an international celebration of her birthday with our group from America. Even the Aruban security guards came by to watch. Everyone at the bar knew the words to the Michael Jackson songs. It was an amazingly peculiar time. Somehow, I knew we would get to the restaurant-eventually. I wanted to show her the chandelier hanging in the entranceway made of vibrant colored blown glass globes. It was created by a student at Rhode Island School of Design–RSDI–aka 'riz-dee'. The entire restaurant is colorful and the food; just as unique. They hold an auction gallery of local artists to display their items periodically. I think they raise some serious money."

"A Brazilian soccer player, a Holland auto rep, a couple that was on their honeymoon from some South African town, and even these two girls from Maine had a great time with us. Vincent got into dancing with the two girls. I think they were in their late twenties. John and Alex made sure everyone was having a good time. John kept the shots lined up at the bar and Mary Lib kept everyone dancing. The bartender asked Alex to dance behind the bar. I think she even got up on the bar at one point although she won't admit it."

"I don't know why you keep telling everyone I was dancing on the bar," Alex said in a defiant tone. "I was dancing '*behind*' the bar!"

356

"Oh, hush," Jan said in response to her friend, "like there is some sort of significant difference, my dear. Sounds like you are splitting hairs there, my sweet. And, honestly, I think Joe's just jealous he can't do the things you do at age fifty something. You're the party girl-he's the romantic. That much I have learned about the two of you tonight; Venus and Mars."

Sometimes, it pays to listen. Jan sure did have us figured out. It didn't take her long, either-just a few hours.

Alex added, "for some reason, '*Beat It*' and '*Thriller*' put me in a very happy mood."

"I think it sounded like the shots of alcohol put you in a 'happy mood'," Jan said with a giggle, "while on '*one happy island.*'"

"Yes, Jan," Alex answered, "we were on one happy island!"

"While their mother was finishing her international performance, Crystal and Jade came back from their shopping trip. They found all kinds of Aruban trinkets, including, a beautiful pearl necklace for their mother. In all the excitement, I completely forgot to cancel our dinner reservations. Quite frankly, I was a bit too embarrassed to call the restaurant and cancel. My entire family is known at the Windows. At one point, I did wrestle with what to do. And I knew ending our celebration and taking a bunch of drunkards to the restaurant was not an option either."

"Could you imagine, if you would have taken that drunken crew to the restaurant? You would have been kicked off that island for sure, Joe. Your family name ruined," he added with a chuckle.

"Perish the thought. You are right on the money with that one, Rob. I'd have been the ultimate bad guy and my mother would have been furious with me if I would have taken them to the restaurant. She knows the entire staff on a first-name basis. Besides, we were sharing only one more night with John and Mary Lib. There was no way I would have left that island without taking my sweetie out to celebrate her birthday dinner in Aruba."

"By eight o'clock, we had enough of the sun, fun, and certainly beyond our limit of alcohol. It took over an hour to get everyone to leave at the same time. They were like herding cats. I'd get the group toward the front and then someone would disappear, and I'd have to go back after them. Jeez! I had stopped drinking long before everyone else had–someone had to get sober. Mary Lib had also stopped drinking at some point. Judging by some of her comments during their stay John had always been an over indulger of libations. Although she didn't make a public display, I think she was mad at John. She confided in me; said he drank excessively and really didn't know when to stop. John had given Alex a birthday kiss and that just pissed her off even more. I think the woman had a trickle of jealousy in her veins. I convinced John to have the bar tender prepare our bill. It totaled more than six hundred dollars!

And that was the second bill he had paid while we were at the pier bar. We made it back home-Maryland Lib and I drove. Naturally, I didn't want anyone in our party to become the next number on the alcohol statistics board at the police station. John was in no shape to drive. John and the kids went out to the patio. Mary Lib was the first to turn in to bed. Alex and I followed not long after."

"Since Mary Lib's mood didn't change John stayed up and kept drinking," Alex said. "Can't say that I blame her. He has several health issues, just had gastric bypass surgery a few months before, and was on some medication. But I told her he was a grown man and could make his own decisions. I certainly wasn't going to tell the man what to do."

"The next morning, big John moved rather slowly around the house. He wasn't in the breakfast making mood. I don't think the man's stomach could have handled the smell of food cooking. He looked pretty rough when he came out and sat at the patio table, on the other side of Mary Lib. She was a bit slow to talk to him. Alex did her best at making her usual idle chatter to keep conversation rolling. I decided to make good use of my time and trim a few of the wild grasses around the back side of the pool. I've had my fair share of domestic quarrelling."

"Apparently, John decided to bite the hair of the dog that bit him the night before and poured some of his Van Gough vodka into his coffee. By the time I was done my work, John seemed a bit livelier, and Mary Lib had returned to her talkative state. We wore ourselves out that week. I don't ever remember getting that plastered before. Must've been all that sun and the beach. You've heard the movie *'Blame it on Rio'* I think Mary Lib blamed her husband's drunk on Aruba. I noticed she sure did like to nip at John's heels every so often; probably kept him from doing serious injury to himself. He had good intentions–like Alex–of getting everyone around him in a good mood. John also enjoyed getting everyone plastered.

I did manage to call Windows later in the afternoon. I half expected them to be upset with me but, they were most gracious. I apologized for not making our dinner time the night before and told them Alex was a bit under the weather. By the time I finished the call, the entire group was lazing around the pool. I noticed the bird of paradise on the back wall looked a bit piqued. I clipped some of the dead blooms to stimulate newer growth and discarded the dead branches. That was the extent of my work that day.

The palm trees had grown so much since the previous winter months and provided a bit of shade in the early afternoon. The wild parrots flew around the house. The white Grecian cement columns looked like they could use some paint, another job for my next trip. I heard a squeal from Alex. I nearly dropped my trimming shears. She had jumped off her lounge chair. Her bathing suit top–which she had untied–fell to the ground. I was looking at her free breasts until I noticed the look on her face. She began pointing toward me and screamed to 'move away' from the back of the house. I looked down at my feet just as a four-foot iguana sauntered within just a couple of inches from the heel of my shoe. I have never seen an iguana as large as that one. My feet came off the ground as I sprinted out of the way of the lizard's path. In turn, his body rose as he extended his legs, giving him a height of at least 3 or 4 more inches from the surface, and ran across the patio with his tongue darting in and out of his mouth. He stopped for a minute; spun his head in my direction as if to challenge me, jerked his head up and down a few times and took off again. Mary Lib ran into the house to get her camera. The girls pulled their feet up off the patio and sat crossed legged on their chairs. Vincent ran over to me to watch the iguana and get a closer view of the creature. John looked at us from across the patio in amusement. And, just as he got to the other side of the patio, the iguana raised his head toward Vincent and me exposing his large fan-like neck. Iguanas do this to warn potential predators. Mary Lib clicked her camera making sure she caught the gullet of the animal in her lens. She got some great pictures of him."

"The lizard had triumphed in obtaining his throne on the wall around the Bird of Paradise," Alex said. "He was letting you know he ruled in the back yard. It was his way of warding off the backyard intruders. I certainly wasn't going to challenge him. His lime green skin on his body was beautiful. He had a long, black ringed tail tapered to a thin end nearly a foot and a half behind him. His tail rested along half of the stone wall and his body covered most of the other half."

"Alex finally realized her top was lying at her feet; not before everyone had an eye full. I enjoyed the view; complete with tropical flowers, a cool pool, an iguana, and a nice pair of boobs; *my* idea of paradise. Jade wanted me to get rid of the iguana. I rather liked having a lizard guest at poolside. He keeps the insect population down. From my perspective-he was an asset. Vincent started doing cannon balls in the pool trying to splash his sisters. The iguana eventually sauntered off, wriggling through the grasses behind the patio. I think we caused too much commotion for his afternoon sunning; amazing how they disappear in the back yard blending in with the colors. Once the girls knew he was gone they relaxed."

"My goodness," Jan said. "I would have been scared to death. I would have gone into the house after seeing something like that in my back yard."

"Jan," Rob said, "you are such a silly woman. Joe said the iguana left. They don't attack humans."

"I don't care," Jan responded, "I would not have been able to relax knowing something like that was crawling around me."

Alex laughed at Jan. "Oh, Jan, iguanas don't attack people. They prefer insects and vegetation. It is a common sight to see them sprawled on the concrete walls and rocks in the community. I rather enjoyed watching them."

"Jan, you would probably like the wild, green parrots; racing around the rooftops and between my neighbor's homes. After a full day of sun and dipping in and out of the pool, we got ready for Alex's belated birthday celebration. The two girls wore sparkly dresses. The rest of us were a bit more casually dressed. John and I wore our Hawaiian shirts and long pants. John looked rather dashing in his red, floral print and white linen pants. Vincent wore a pair of shorts and polo shirt. Mary Lib and Alex decided on cocktail dresses. That's Aruba-you can dress any way you like down there. We were an attractive looking group. We climbed into the Jeeps and drove, once again, along the familiar coastal road toward the Divi Links to dine at Windows on Aruba."

"I rather like the sound of being able to choose between getting dressed up or wearing shorts," Rob said. "I like to have those kinds of options. I don't always want to wear a suit and tie to dinner–makes me uncomfortable after a full meal. Besides, I must wear a tie to work every day. Been doing that for twenty years or so."

"That's because every time we go out to eat, you stuff yourself with dessert," Jan commented as she poked Rob in his side. A knowing smile lit up his face.

"The girls got excited when we entered the restaurant; there is a low-lit bar with a few tables and bar stools. When we arrived, the maître'd led us to the bar for a few minutes–just long enough for them to prepare our table. The back of the bar is designed with blue and green colored square glass panels encased in wood. Some of the glass is 'sea glass'-the sharp edges rounded due to the constant movement against sand in the ocean. They have an extensive collection of liquor bottles sitting in front of the lit panels creating a rather eye-catching display. That's where the chandelier with the blown glass art hangs. The restaurant boasts its international interest in artwork. Local artists display their creations for visitors to view, too."

"Wow," said Jan. "You know I am always looking for new pieces of artwork for my house."

"Table lamps sit on top of teak wood tables. The dining tables were covered in white linen; lightly wood-stained chairs surround the tables. We were seated at a table against the window overlooking the pool and golf course. The entire restaurant has a panoramic view of the ocean and resort grounds. Everyone selected their favorite dish. We had a variety of pasta, fresh fish, and steak with salads. I ordered a couple of appetizers for everyone to share-the appetizers are impeccably created by the chef each night. John, of course, made sure we had plenty of wine to drink with our dinner. The groups tummies were a bit squeamish. There was still some daylight at seven oh-five. I got up from the table making the excuse to visit the men's room. Locating the maître'd, I reminded him about the reason for our dinner celebration. Not long after I had returned to the table, several of the other waiters and waitresses joined in to sing a nice rendition of 'Happy Birthday' to my sweetheart. She beamed at me as the group sang to her. Just like you are looking at me now." Alex spoke to me with her eyes-they said 'happiness' from the memory.

"It seems your birthday dinner turned out wonderful after all," Rob said. "You did a good job, Aruba Joe."

"My compliments to the staff at Windows. They made the evening perfect for all of us. Everything was good; from the cocktails before dinner to the last sip of Baileys after dinner."

"The next day was a bit gloomy–not because of the weather. John and Mary Lib had a flight out of Aruba in the early afternoon. We were sorry to see them go. The group had formed this family unit while we were there. Everyone helped one another and played hard together. Alex and Mary Lib had known each other for years and had the chance to catch up on the latest news and gossip. They enjoyed their female talk. John had been quite entertaining. The kids really like them, too. Alex looked up to Mary Lib like the older sister she never had. I can see why; Mary Lib is a woman of grace and rather artsy. She enjoys going to museums, the theatre, and is a world traveler. And she knows her history. You can listen to the woman tell her tales of her experiences and vast knowledge of many subjects. She has this warmth about her that draws you in–makes you feel you can trust her, and she really shows an interest in you. You would never know that she is an heiress to a vast fortune–big money from up north."

"It was our last day before we had to go home. The crosswinds were blowing a mild fifteen miles an hour. Jade decided to detail the Jeep. The girl is crazy about keeping cars cleaned. She wanted the Jeep to sparkle and shine when we dropped it off. She cleaned it down to the last grain of sand; hand buffed the exterior and practically spit-shined the windows–inside and out. Alex had gotten tanned during the week. She wanted to go for a drive. I was eager to do whatever she wanted. Alex put on a bathing suit cover up and we decided to travel to the southern end of the island. We told the kids we were headed out for a ride. They were content to play the radio and enjoy the pool."

"That sounds nice," Jan said. "The two of you actually got out for a night together by yourselves."

"As we drove along the coast, the combination of the warm air and smell of the ocean had a unique calming effect. I was driving with my sweetheart and that's all I cared about. The drive along the island coast is so scenic. Some people were laying on the sand; some enjoyed the blue green waters in the surf."

Alex added, "don't forget the people on the jet skis. They were having so much fun."

"We decided to stop at one of the open-air restaurants for a drink and a sandwich. Just as we were getting ready to order, another couple stopped at our table. They introduced themselves and asked if they could join us."

"Ned and Suzy were from Washington, DC. They were a nice couple. Yeah, he was some sort of business partner of a burger retail franchise and Suzy was a real hoot."

"Ned and Suzy were an adorable couple," Alex added. "Ned is blonde and tall; Suzy is just a little over five foot and is just a sweet person. Cute as a buttercup."

"They had never been to Aruba before. We talked about real estate in the Baltimore and Washington area. It seems Ned liked to dabble in real estate investments. Suzy talked about going four wheeling and asked if we would like to join them. Alex wasn't much on the idea. Especially after what we had experienced with the kids and the mud bog." In the back of my mind, I wondered if Alex had told Jan about that day, too.

"Can you blame her, Joe," Jan said with a giggle. "You already had one very expensive four-wheeling day."

"Yeah, that's what we told Ned and Suzy. We gave them all the details about our four-wheeling experience. But Ned said he really would prefer renting a motorcycle. He had seen a place near their hotel that rented them by the hour. I haven't been on a motorcycle for over twenty years. Let's see, the last time I rode one was on a business trip in Las Vegas with my brother-in-law."

Alex said, "I had ridden on the back of one the year before, but I would rather stick to a four-wheeled vehicle with doors, a roll bar, and seat belts."

"So, you see what I was up against? Suzy made a proposition. She suggested Ned could rent the motorcycle. He and I could take turns riding on it and she and Alex would be content to ride in the Jeep. It was a workable plan. We finished our Balashi beers and downed our sandwiches. I followed Ned to the rental place. I was fired up about riding a motorcycle."

"Well, I'm glad you two met some people to have some fun with," Rob said. "You and Alex seem like a friendly, fun couple."

"Rob," Jan said, "Sssshhhh. Maybe you ought to listen to Joe finish telling his story about their motor cycling." Jan stopped speaking as she took a sip of her glass of water. Rob looked at her quizzically. "Go on, Joe-finish telling Rob about your ride to the other end of the island."

Yep; Jan knew something. How much I was uncertain.

"Good God," Rob said. "Don't tell me something else went wrong."

"Well, the rental was cheap enough and I *was* looking forward to a ride on the bike. But I never even had the chance to."

"What do you mean," Rob asked. "Wouldn't Ned let you take a turn on the bike?"

I cleared my throat. I had told this story so many times but, tonight was different. I wasn't exactly sure where to begin. Suddenly, I didn't know how to put into words what happened. I had no saliva; my tongue was stuck to the roof of my mouth. This version was in front of Alex; in front of her friend whom she adored. And, in front of so many strangers. So, I just sipped my Pinot and slowly began.

"I told Ned to follow us in the Jeep. I knew all the beaches on the south side of the island and how to get there from the rental office. Traffic was starting to get congested. Ned was keeping up with us. The girls and I got to talking. Suzy was a lively one and had so many stories to tell and told us how she and Ned had met; just rambled on about anything and everything. I realized I hadn't been paying much attention to Ned-hadn't heard the bike either. When I looked in the rear-view mirror, he was no longer behind us.

I told the girls I had lost sight of him; Suzy immediately got upset and spun around looking for Ned. Holding on to the roll bar, Suzy stood up in the backseat; looking for any sign of her husband."

"I told Suzy the island wasn't that big, and we would just turn around and go look for him. Maybe he ran out of gas. You know sometimes they do forget to fill them up when they get too busy," Alex said. "Naturally, I wanted to reduce her anxiety because Suzy really started wigging out."

"I backtracked toward the rental office covering the same roads. We looked everywhere for Ned and the bike. There was no sight of him. It was as if Ned had disappeared. We weren't driving fast. There are no highways on the island; not like there are here."

"Suzy kept trying to call Ned from her cell phone-no answer," Alex said.

"We drove all the way back to the rental office and there was no sign of Ned. For the second time, we retraced our route traveling much slower than we had gone before. There was no sign of Ned anywhere. We looked at the gas stations thinking maybe he had stopped to fill the gas tank. No Ned."

"And do you remember what Suzy did?" Alex asked.

"Good gracious woman. How could I forget?"

"All of a sudden, there was this bone chilling scream from the back seat of the Jeep. Suzy was in hysterics. I looked in the

371

mirror and saw her looking over toward the center of the roadway and to all our amazement and absolute horror; there was Ned."

Judging from the look on Jan's face she didn't know what I was about to say. Alex hadn't filled her in on all our vacation details; Rob was clueless, though. His eyes were bulging as he looked at me to finish.

"What happened to Ned? What in the world did Suzy get so upset about?" Rob asked.

"We *all* got really upset when we saw Ned. Here is this couple we had just met. All Alex and I had wanted to do was go for a nice ride that day. All Suzy and Ned wanted to do was enjoy the countryside of Aruba. But sadly that was not what happened at all. In the middle of this huge cactus, and I mean it was probably one of the biggest cacti in Aruba, was Ned. I spun the Jeep around to the side of the cactus and we all hopped out toward Ned. It was like some horror movie, some horrific image from a Stephen King scene. Ned was spread eagled in the middle of the cactus. His arms and legs were entwined with the branches of the cactus." One of the ladies at the table near us gasped loudly.

"Oh my God!" Jan said in a high-pitched voice. "How in the world did it happen? Did someone hit him, or did he lose control of the motorcycle? You know I have had some bad accidents myself."

"I had no idea what had happened to Ned. The bike was lying on its side in front of the cactus; fuel was leaking from a hole

372

in the middle of the gas tank and the rear tire was bent sideways." I still carried the image of that day in Aruba; a far too vivid one. I cannot forget what I saw. And I don't think I ever will. "Now, I can tell you this; the sight of Ned imbedded in that cactus was one of the scariest things I have seen in my lifetime. I saw a dead person in the woods when I was a young boy. Guy had a heart attack. But it didn't affect me like Ned did."

"Suzy was still screaming. My ears had never heard those sounds before," Alex said. "Cars drove by slowly and looked at us. A few of them pulled over on the side of the road to help. They asked what had happened to the man in the cactus and like Joe said, we were clueless at that point."

"One of them, a paramedic, ran toward us with his phone in his ear. He spoke rapidly in Papiamento. I did understand him when he spoke the word 'stat'. He picked up the motorcycle and pulled it away from the cactus, clearing the area in front of Ned. The good thing, if you could possibly say anything about the incident being good, was Ned appeared to be unconscious. Small trickles of blood were coming out of him from everywhere. The paramedic scanned his body. No bones were showing but, his limbs were in a contorted fashion among the cactus branches." I still experience anxiety about those visions.

"I told Joe to call the hospital. He still had the number in his phone from our visit. Just as he started to dial the number, we could hear the sound of a siren coming toward us," Alex said.

"Yeah, the paramedic-that's what he was on the phone for-I bet he called," Jan said.

"We were glad they arrived so quickly. He must have been in the cactus for twenty to thirty minutes by that time. Suzy was still half out of her mind, the poor girl. There was no comfort for her at the time. There was nothing we could even do. The ambulance crew and some other paramedics that had randomly stopped to aid Ned sprung right into action. Another ambulance arrived and two more paramedics got out and ran over to help. It took six of them to maneuver Ned from the cactus. They pried him loose; three or four of them on either side. Together, they lifted him onto a standing stretcher. A couple of police cars had also stopped. When you're in trouble in Aruba they sound out the troops. Alex stayed with Suzy; she had a firm grip on her. Both her arms surrounded her. Suzy shook from head to toe like she was freezing."

"I had both my arms around Suzy because she was so out of control. I physically held her tight against me to restrain her. I didn't know what else to do and I was afraid she was going to try to pull Ned away from the Cactus," Alex said. "We just watched in absolute horror while Suzy's husband's body was lifted off the cactus.

374

"It was an absolute nightmare," I said shaking my head as the memory drifted back to me; a sight that would affect all of us for a long time. "Suzy could never have helped Ned alone. Physically, she was just too small."

"You know," Rob said, "I'm just finding it difficult to picture the situation in my mind. It's just something I cannot fathom here. Not to mention, the pain that poor guy must have been experiencing or the fright he must have endured from that accident. Furthermore, this was not something you did. But I don't think I would *ever* travel with you." A twinkle in his eye confirmed he was not to be taken seriously.

"Rob, give him a break," Jan said as she leaned in toward me and looked right into my eyes. "It all sounds like such an incredible situation; the beautiful island, the cray-cray things you did. And this accident. I had no idea." Her arms dropped to her side. Then she added; "you must have all felt so helpless."

"Once we found Ned everything went so fast. Within minutes, there was all kinds of people helping him. "

"Next thing I can remember," Alex added, "was seeing Ned's limp, long body being hoisted by all those big men onto the metal stretcher."

"The paramedics strapped Ned's body on a white vinyl board. I saw his body shaking from head to toe-he was in shock. One of them placed his head inside of a restraining collar and secured him tightly. His eyes were closed and all I could focus on was the blood leaking out of him," Alex said.

"Now, that's not true. He wasn't a bloody mess Rob and Jan. There were just a lot of pin holes; not deep punctures on the front of his body at least. He did have a couple of deep punctures on his back and shoulders. The top of his body must have gotten the greatest impact as the thorns of the cactus were thick. I was standing behind Ned when the paramedics hoisted him off the cactus and got a good look at his back. Suzy was screaming for the men to help her husband. For a woman of her size, her voice screeched over top of the blaring ambulance sirens."

Alex added, "Ned just laid there; motionless." She closed her eyes, slumped her shoulders, and relaxed her arms by her side as she spoke. As if she was reliving the event. "I think his brain must have decided to put him in some sort of coma. I was thankful for that. His face twitched or a finger would move. But, other than that, the man was in a virtual deep sleep."

"All of those men around him were moving at high speed and obviously well trained; I can tell you that. Ned was hooked up to a bag of glucose by one guy, some other guy was cuffing him for his blood pressure, and all the rest of the men were tending to some other details."

"One of the policemen spoke to the paramedics. The Aruban paramedic pointed in the direction of Suzy and me," Alex said. "The

376

policeman walked over to us-it was Mike from the mud bog. We were standing about twenty feet away from Ned–watching everything the men were doing. At first, Mike nodded at us as if he remembered us but, couldn't quite place where he knew us from. Then, he broadly smiled-leaned back and pointed to us and said- 'the Jeeps on the lake, right?' He began asking Suzy questions, who was he, how did he get in the cactus-that sort of stuff. Suzy just kept screaming."

"Instead, I answered for her and told Mike everything we knew. Suzy couldn't speak a word. Mike did his best to ask her questions. I think his line of questions were for two purposes. One; to get as much information for his police report. The other purpose was to get her mind away from her husband's injuries and get her to calm down. He was trying to get Suzy to focus on something other than seeing Ned-must've learned that in his American training. A couple of other officers came over to Suzy, too."

"Well, if it would have been me," Jan interrupted, "I would have been doing exactly what Suzy was doing. I can't imagine being in that situation."

"Oh, Jan it was just horrible," Alex said, "they got Ned into the back of the ambulance and one of the paramedics came over to Suzy. He gently took her hand, looked into her eyes. She stood staring at the younger man-like in a trance-seeing but not. She gasped for her breath–tears were streaming down her face. The man was amazing. He put his arm around her waist, still holding her hand with his other hand, and gently guided her toward the back of the ambulance. He looked back at me and gave me a nod. He jerked his head toward me as if to tell me he wanted us to follow them to the hospital. He was very handsome. I knew Suzy was in good hands."

"Those men in uniform sure look sharp. A uniform makes a man handsome," Jan added with a knowing twinkle in her eye.

"Joe and I got back into the Jeep and left the motorcycle on the side of the cactus. I could see the wet blood spots over the cactus where Ned had lain just moments before. The blood-stained cactus held the image of Ned's body. It looked weird-like one of those chalk outlines at a crime scene," Alex said. "For the first time, I noticed a camera man taking pictures-must have been from the local tv station. Images like that are quite powerful to the public audiences."

"A tow truck had come by and half-walked/carried the motorcycle up the ramp; and strapped it in place against a wire rack. I drove over to the truck and told the driver the name of the rental company we had gotten the bike from. He said he knew of it and would take the motorcycle there on his way back down the road."

"All of us were deeply affected by what had happened to Ned," I said. "Alex and I had just met this couple and we had bonded immediately with them. There were so many connections; not just that they were Americans."

"I called my children. I told them we were having a good time and wouldn't see them for a couple of hours. I didn't want them to worry about us," Alex said. "They were sitting by the pool, and I wanted them to keep having a good time. There was no sense in upsetting them; especially, Jade."

"Tell me the guy didn't die. Please tell me that everything turned out okay with Ned," Rob said in a deeply caring tone. A look of anguish consumed his face.

"To put you both at ease, no, Ned didn't die. I wish we would never have gone with Suzy and Ned that day. But it happened; it was horrible. Our hearts were so torn up for them. As we pulled up to the hospital, the ambulance was already parked at the emergency room entrance. We knew that door all too well. Alex and I parked the Jeep in the parking lot. We wanted to be with Suzy as quickly as possible. She really needed us."

"You know, it is amazing how events bring people together: horrific as all of this may sound to the two of you. It was almost as if we had always known Ned and Suzy. We felt so incredibly close to them. Our lives shared such a monumental ordeal together. I wanted to be right by her side; as much as I would someone I knew for a very, long time." Alex added reinforcing my exact thoughts.

Her voice became faint. She was a bit tearful. If I could take away one of the crazy incidents from our vacation, it would have been Ned wrecking his bike. The sheer memory of Suzy's tear-stained face still shook me up. "When we walked in through the emergency room's entrance doors, she practically fell into my arms. The three of us just held one another until Suzy stopped sobbing and shaking."

"I could barely make out what she was saying. When she was able to speak somewhat coherently, my ears strained to hear her words; I think she was saying 'thank you, God'," Alex said. "We stood there for a long time with our heads bent toward one another. It felt like we were glued together; deep into our own silent prayers."

"I couldn't understand what she was saying at all. My heart was beating so loud I thought you two could hear it."

"Where was Ned?" Rob and Jan asked in unison.

"The poor man could have been dying somewhere in that hospital at that very moment!" Jan exclaimed.

"Slow down. Ned was in the emergency room with the doctors. I don't know what they sedated him with at the scene of the accident. Whatever it was I was sure it was some good stuff and he was not feeling any pain. I mean he wasn't dead or anything. He had lost some blood; those cactus thorns had to have been incredibly painful. I had stood close to Ned and watched the paramedics as they wrapped his left arm and leg with the splints to immobilize his

380

limbs. The left side of his body appeared to be the most affected. I could see none of his injuries appeared to be life threatening. Like I said: I think Ned had gone into shock at some point right after impact; a very good thing. I don't know what Alex and I would have done if both Suzy and Ned would have been screaming. A woman screaming is one thing, but a man is yet another. A bit unsettling-if you know what I mean."

"The nurses had asked Suzy to stay in the waiting room as they rushed Ned into their x-ray department," Alex explained. "Sometimes, things appear far worse than they are. Granted; the accident was a horrific experience, but the man was very much alive."

"Whew!" Rob exclaimed. "I couldn't imagine having to go through all of that and so far from home–in a foreign country and a foreign hospital-for goodness' sake!"

"Then what happened?" Jan asked. "When did Suzy get to see Ned again?"

"I think it was about an hour after we arrived at the hospital. When they brought Ned back from x-raying his body, one of the nurses came to the waiting room area. The nurse led Suzy into the ER. The doctors told her he was resting calmly and quietly. They told her he had a concussion-not sure what he hit his head on-and had multiple fractures on his left arm, leg, and a few minor fractures in his ribs."

I looked at Rob and Jan's contorted faces; their brows furrowed. The look in their eyes. Jans were full of tears.

"Jan, the fractures weren't bad ones. Ned must have had strong bones, because the way the doctor had described it, the fractures were hairline fractures," Alex said. "I guess it was because the cactus wasn't hard like a tree but, filled with cactus juice.

"Guys, Ned is okay. We've spoken with them since then. He's okay," I said.

Jan looked at me and then at Alex. "I don't know how you two handled that. I would have fallen apart. I wouldn't have known what to do. That girl, Suzy, would have had to comfort me."

Alex looked kindly at Jan and said, "You know, Jan, when there is an emergency like that, your mind goes into a different gear. It is like there is some sort of subconscious, manual override. Almost like an out-of-body experience. You just 'do' rather than 'think' about what to do. I really can't explain it other than that."

Alex continued, "Suzy needed our help. As bizarre and ugly as you can imagine-Joe and I focused on her-that is all I can tell you."

"What happened after Suzy met with the doctors?" Rob asked. "What was his prognosis? My God, how did the man get back home?"

"Well, the doctors kept Ned at the hospital for two weeks, and just released him last week to come home. He's resting in his

DC home with Suzy by his side. As a matter of fact, she called me this morning to tell me Ned was sitting up in his favorite Lazy Boy chair with his feet up. Of course, he's got some mending to do. Suzy said they will never step foot in Aruba again."

"How in the world did the accident happen?" Rob asked.

"I don't know. We never did figure it out. When I asked Suzy how it happened, she told me Ned didn't know; that he couldn't remember."

"I've heard about that before," Jan said. "Sometimes, people never remember how an accident, or a bad experience took place. Maybe, it's God way to protect us from having the bad memories and keep us from remembering so we don't suffer or feel pain."

"When we left the hospital that evening, we arrived home and the kids were still out by the pool. It was good to be home. We never did tell them what had happened. Alex and I agreed."

"We took the kids to one of the local eateries for our last night in Aruba. After eating pizza, we strolled over to the Occidental hotel for one last visit to the casino. Jade sat at the penny slots. I strolled over to the craps table. I'm not much on slot machines. The casino was full of people."

"I went with Joe. Crystal and Vincent planted themselves on either side of Jade. Suddenly, we heard a bell dinging wildly from the slot machine area. Someone must have gotten lucky," Alex said.

"I lost my twenty bucks at craps, and we walked back over to the slots. As we approached the line of slots, Jade was jumping up and down. She had just won over three thousand dollars on the daggone penny slots!"

"My word," Jan exclaimed. "Three thousand dollars-on a penny slot machine. I have never heard of such a thing! Jade must have been excited."

"Excited," Alex said, "Jade has always had good luck, but she had never seen so much money before our Aruba trip!"

"I made her cash in before she decided to spend another nickel. We were going to leave the casino whether she was ready or not. The cashier gave her thirty, one-hundred-dollar bills! Jade counted the bills again before she left the cashier's window. She could barely fit the money in her purse. We walked out of that casino with big grins on our faces. On our way back to the Jeep, Vincent made Jade buy us all ice cream to celebrate. Jade took the cash and counted it all over again."

"Woo hoo!" Rob said. "Your daughter must have felt like a rich young lady."

"That she was, Rob," Alex said. "When we got home, Jade locked it in the house safe. She wanted to make sure that money wasn't going anywhere. Joe and I started packing up and we got ready for the next day. I began cleaning and washing all of the beach towels and Joe vacuumed the entire house. It was kind of like a therapy session for each of us."

CHAPTER 27 – THE COLOR RED

"Sunday was our last day. We did the hustle in the morning. There wasn't one piece of dirty laundry. I packed up the Jeep. It was a far different sight from the day we arrived. We had room for our feet. Departure from Aruba is always bittersweet. I hate when I must leave."

"I thought we were plenty early enough to enjoy an ocean side lunch. There's this little restaurant only a few miles from the airport. Lizards wander all around the patio. They crawl right up to your feet. I think those little buggers know when the food arrives because as soon as it does, a couple more lizards appear. Their skin is in shades of fluorescent green and blue. You can feed them right from the table."

"We were a bit somber as we left the restaurant and, at the same time, anxious to get back home. I knew Alex and Crystal had not wanted to travel on Sunday. They both have early morning Monday meetings. I wanted to savor every minute in Aruba and insisted on traveling on Sunday instead of Saturday. We'd get home by ten o'clock and there is plenty of time to sleep. After all, you don't get to go to Aruba every day."

"I dropped them off in front of the airport–helped them with their luggage–and took off to the car rental. We had plenty of time before our flight departed. When I got to the rental center the guy rang up my ticket. I handed him the keys–both sets–and decided to look down at the receipt. Good thing I did. They had charged me an additional six hundred dollars! I told them they made a mistake and must've charged me for an extra week or something. The guy looked at my bill and asked me if I was the guy that got stuck in the mud on the lake. I told him 'yes'. He said the salt had damaged the undercarriage and they had to charge me a fee to clean it. For forty-five minutes I argued with the guy."

"I was madder than a hornet by that time. Those guys held me up from getting to my seat in first class. When you travel from Aruba to the US, they recommend arriving two to three hours prior to your departure. If you get to the ticket counter less than an hour before departure, no one will help you. I stood my ground. There was no way I was walking away. I demanded they were to take the additional money off my ticket, and they refused again. They told me I ruined their Jeep. 'Ruined it'," I said. 'How can you ruin an old Jeep like that?' Gooey rubber plugs were in the tires, plastic pieces just crumbling apart; how could I have ruined something that came back to them in better condition than when it was leased to me? At least it was clean."

"I threatened to contact the credit card company and dispute the charges. They couldn't have cared less. By this time, I was worried I was going to miss my plane. I grabbed my luggage and insisted they take me to the airport right away or they were going to pay for another ticket *and* my next rental when I returned in November. Several other people had come in the front door of the rental car company. At that point, they had the upper hand with me– we both knew it. They gladly drove me to the airport to get me out of the office before I made another outburst."

"When I got to the airport entrance, I looked toward the ticket counter. The place was desolate. That was not a good sign. One person remained at the US Air baggage claim. I ran up to the counter. Slammed my single bag down on the scale and the woman looked at me kinda funny. Thrusting my ticket across the counter at the woman dressed in navy blue with a white buttoned-down shirt. She said the ticket counter was closed. I told her about my problem with the rental car company. She just shook her head and continued counting something in the register drawer."

"I called Alex right away. She was not answering her cell."

"Oh, God, Joe," Jan said. "I would have been in tears if I were to miss my plane. Alex must've been so worried."

"I was half a lunatic standing there arguing with the woman. I interrupted her again and asked her to call the US Air desk–to call security or to call Customs. By that time, I was yelling at her, and she stood calmly as she told me I had to check in two hours before departure. I bet she repeated that at least ten times."

"I was thinking Alex is sure gonna be mad at me, now. If she was mad at me when we left home–about the first-class ticket–I

388

knew she was going to really be mad at me for missing the flight back home. I grabbed my bag and looked everywhere for someone to help me. There wasn't even a sky cap standing by. When I turned back around and faced the ticket counter, the woman I had been talking to was now gone. I tried calling Alex again. The phone disconnected. Her phone had horrible service in Aruba."

"Alex, what were you thinking? Were you worried about Joe missing the flight?" Jan asked.

"I kept looking for Joe every step of the way. There is this huge room for customs–people stood in that room like a herd of cattle standing in a stock yard. Much like the cattle stockyards in downtown Fort Worth, Texas," Alex said. "And every time the phone rang from Joe I answered it. And each time I answered-there was no sound. The phone would blink a few times and shut off. I became anxious as I moved my luggage forward in line as people were moving."

Alex was in deep thought. The three of us waited. I knew she had been worried about me.

"People just kept looking at me; knowing I was upset," Alex said. "I tried to be calm for my children and yet, I was so worried about where Joe was. I found myself getting mad about him missing our plane. I had enough of the peaks and valleys of our vacation. My mind was overloaded worrying about work the next day, keeping my children in sight and constantly picking up and putting down my luggage. It was so stressful."

Alex looked over at me as she finished her statement. I could easily see the emotion in her eyes. She didn't express her emotion with tears. She didn't need to. Her eyes told me so much in that moment.

"Well," Alex started again. "All those people around me knew I was living a vacationers' worst nightmare. Losing one of the people in your party is not the way to end your vacation. I was still a bit numb from Ned and Suzy. My mind just wasn't thinking clearly. All this stuff was coming at me from all different directions. I felt such turmoil. I felt deceived. I did my best toward calming my children. Jade, my emotional one, kept asking me why Joe wasn't with us yet. She is the one who always fears the worst about everything. She is also the one who thinks negatively about everything. All I could make out during one of his calls was Joe saying something about his luggage. I thought they might have confiscated it for some silly reason. You just don't know about that sort of thing these days. I felt like we were treated like criminals during the boarding process. First one customs-the Aruban-then the US Customs. Everyone is a suspected terrorist. And, when you are out of the country, they have different standards in Customs. In a half an hour our flight was leaving. I expressed my concern to the guy at customs. Americans work in customs and live in Aruba. At least he spoke good English but, he wasn't much help. He said there was nothing he could do. I made the decision to keep going and kept looking toward the entrance of the cattle room–turning my head constantly to look for Joe through the double doors. Just wanting to see his handsome face."

"Alex had no idea how hard I was trying to catch up to her. My hands hurt from clenching them so tight. I was sweating. My head pounded with the frustration at the rental car place and the desire to meet up with her. It was apparent she couldn't hear me over the noise at customs. I tried to tell her to get help–tell someone I was stranded. I don't know what she heard 'cause the phone just kept cutting off. I wanted to be with her to help her. She had never done that before–not with three kids. I wanted to make sure she was okay. I felt like I had let Alex down. Adrenaline ran through my body to do something and yet I was helpless to do anything."

"We got through both customs and the children, and I ran to the baggage conveyor belt," Alex added. "I told Vincent and Jade to take our luggage and put it on the belt while Crystal and I ran toward the US Air gate. Jade looked frantic and Vincent did his best to be 'the man'. Once they got the luggage on the belt, they caught up to Crystal and me. I had to take off my flat sandals trying not to break my stride. Crystal was in front of me. She's a fast little girl. My heart pounded–I'm not the most physically fit person in the world. We got to the gate, and I rushed over to the desk. There were several people in front of us. I was torn between getting on that flight and waiting for Joe. It wouldn't have been such an ordeal if he would have made our return flight on Saturday; like I had wanted him to do. After making a few phone calls, the woman at the desk finally acknowledged me and told me there was nothing she could do. Seeing the look on my face, the wench asked me 'what did I expect?' and told me we should have arrived two hours prior to our departure like we were instructed. The plane started boarding passengers. I looked in desperation around the gate waiting area. Joe was nowhere to be seen."

"I looked at my cell phone. It was almost three o'clock and realized I was not going to board that plane–not with Alex. My heart sank. I felt doomed. I damned those guys at the rental place for making me late-after all my years of loyalty. I figured I would fight the extra charge with my credit card company when I was home the next day. I was equally upset with myself. The only thing left to do was wait for the check in to reopen. There was one more flight leaving Aruba on Sundays."

"You could have just gone back to your house–stayed another week in paradise," Rob said.

"You know, for a fleeting moment or two, I did consider doing just that, Rob. I quickly eliminated that option. There didn't seem to be much point in staying in Aruba alone. I was determined to get on a plane that day."

"My cell phone rang. It was Alex. I thanked God she was finally calling me. She told me she tried to get the airline to wait for me. They simply would not help. I told her to go ahead and to drive the van home from the airport. That seemed to be the only viable option at the time. And told her the keys to the van were in her purse. I figured my sister could pick me up at the airport and take me to Alex's house to get the van later. As I hung up, I told her I would see her soon. A quick glance at the flight board showed the next flight out had a layover in Charlotte for an hour. I figured I had a good shot at getting on board. If you have ever been in a situation where you felt helpless or lost, then you can certainly understand how I felt. Standing in an empty airport really is an odd feeling. I decided to take out a book and read while I waited for the ticket counter to reopen. That hour was one of the longest hours of my life."

"I don't know what I would have done if that would have happened to Rob and me," Jan said. "I just couldn't imagine how you felt; you poor thing."

"Believe you me, it was one of the worst feelings I've ever had. I was at the point of exhaustion and I did get on the next flight. My only sense of accomplishment was managing to get another first-class seat home. I had a couple of Bloody Mary's to ease my frustration. A little vodka did wonders. When I arrived in Charlotte, I checked my emails. I reached in my pocket for my key fab to hook up to the internet. It was at that moment I realized I had the set of car keys with me. Alex and the kids couldn't get home; I had the friggin' keys to the van with me. I also remembered with additional dread; Alex didn't want to travel on Sunday in the first place. She had emphasized the importance of a meeting she and Crystal had first thing on Monday mornings. My heart sank to a new low as I realized I had to make *that call* to Alex. I called my sister first just to put her on stand-by in case I needed a ride from the airport. My sister was cool about the situation—she understood my predicament and was willing to help me out if I needed her. She also offered to pick up Alex and her kids if that's what needed to be done. There was nothing left for me to do but, endure those next couple of hours. Alex called me as soon as they arrived at Dulles. I gave her my flight number and suggested she drive home with my sister; that I would join her later."

"When I called Joe," Alex said, "we were seated at this little restaurant inside the airport. I thought about his backup plan for a moment and told him I'd call him back. I told the children what was going on. We were all so tired. It was a 'school night'. And, in our world, that meant to be in bed by ten. We had gotten up extra early that morning to finish packing, wash laundry, and cleaned the entire house. We had been through so much in Aruba. Part of me wanted to leave him stranded. The children pleaded with me to choose to go home with Joe's sister. My heart was torn. I wanted to do what was best for my children and me. I called Joe back and told him we had done everything else together during that trip and we were going to finish the trip together. My children's faces drooped. They were not happy with my decision at all. Vincent muttered something under his breath-I dared not ask him to repeat it. I was in absolutely no mood."

"That is Alex; what an amazing woman she is. She is all about doing things as a team, sticking together no matter what. I knew that night in Charlotte as I know right now that she would always do the right thing; for all of us. I called my sister again before boarding the airplane and told her what was going on and thanked her for agreeing to help on such short notice. I updated her on our decision."

"After we ate," Alex said, "we dragged our luggage and our bodies down to the baggage claim area. Let that be a lesson to anyone traveling to the Caribbean; take only half of what you think you need. You stay in a bathing suit, shorts, tee shirts, and flip flops most of the time. And you end up wearing the same thing over and over again. We sprawled across the seats and half slept waiting for Joe. The time could not have gone by slower. Crystal kept complaining about how tired she was. There was nothing we could do but wait."

"Oh, baby," I said as I wrapped my arm around Alex's shoulder and pulled her closer to me. "I did not know this. I'm sorry."

I could feel Alex's body stiffen against me.

"You got to see things from my point of view, Alex. I offered the seat to you. You decided you wanted to sit in coach with your kids. Now, true or false?"

"Yes, Joe, you offered the seat to me. But it should never have been an issue in the first place," Alex snapped. "You should have just done the right thing and turned it down. You could have used that ticket another time, when you weren't with me. You should have wanted to be with me. Need I also mention the stewardess?"

Well, I could tell there was no winning that argument and I didn't care to comment further. I needed to change the subject real fast and can't understand why I even brought it up again. I would find some way to make up to Alex later tonight.

"Anyway," Alex started. "I heard an announcement on the overhead speaker. Joe's plane had finally arrived. I told the children I was going to find Joe. I got up and headed toward the escalator. I knew what I was going to say, and I wasn't going to let him change my mind-no sirree. I was determined. He was going to get it right between the eyes with a shot of words I would use to impale him. When I got to his baggage claim area, a steady trail of travelers

396

headed toward me. I did not see Joe. I thought I must have missed him. I strolled over to the baggage claim area. Those people moved out quickly; there were only a couple of people left there. Everyone's faces were tired. It was a long travel day. I noticed his brown suede hat first as he stood looking down at the conveyor belt for his bags. I tapped him on his shoulder, and he spun around."

I had to interrupt. "I was so glad to see Alex again. It felt good to put my arms around her and hold her. We had been apart for most of the day, and it felt like an eternity. We picked up my bags and went back to the kids. They weren't the only ones that were tired. Together, our team headed out of the airport and began the ride back home. We were exhausted."

Alex let out a big sigh. I think she resolved to end whatever she was going to say. She had to have realized just regurgitating her emotion from that late night was no longer significant.

The Cafe had emptied out by this time. The patrons around our booth were still listening to my story. The man who had spoken earlier, stood up to leave and crossed over the aisle to our booth.

He looked in my direction and held out his hand to Alex and asked, "what happened to you? I thought you were going to give it to the bum at the airport and let him know what a klutz and fool he was."

Alex looked into the strange mans' eyes for a moment and then back into mine. "You know it was a strange thing but, I figured

I better take care of Aruba Joe and the children. They all needed me that night."

"Hmmm. Makes sense. And," the stranger added with a smile to the two of us; "I hope you get back to Aruba someday and have a really quiet visit in paradise."

The other patrons got up as well. They waved and thanked us for the entertainment. The big football player got up, shook his head and said, "you could have killed it Aruba Joe. I was pulling for you. I know what it is like to be an underdog." He fist bumped me as he nodded to our table and turned his back and walked out; a full smile on his face.

The lights had dimmed in some of the dining room area. The staff was re-setting tables for the next days diners. We gathered our things and headed toward the entrance.

"I am so glad to have met you two," I said to Jan and Rob as I took Alex's arm. "What an amazing meal. After you," I nodded.

"And, what an amazing story. So much happened to the two of you and Alex; your kids! My word." Jan responded. "I for one hope you two get back to Aruba soon. Rob and I will look into a trip ourselves although I think we will stick with sunbathing and more activities at a hotel." She smiled at both of us.

As we walked toward our cars, we embraced one another and said our farewells. Rob appeared a bit in thought and added, "You have come a long way. You have some rather interesting memories. I hope you two make many more together."

We drove home in a semi-silence. We chatted about the meal, the wine, and chuckled about the people at the other tables. I knew she had been married twice before and didn't want to make any more mistakes. Both of us had a lot to think about.

Alex said, "I have a trip to Virginia. I am leaving early Wednesday morning to my aunt's. I will be away for a few days- taking her to Ft Lauderdale to visit her brother Scott. I like visiting my oldest Aunt Connie and highly value our time together."

She had mentioned her uncle's health before and how it had declined. I was surprised she was taking so much time away from her job. Perhaps Alex had changed a bit and was beginning to experience the value of taking time away from her job.

Alex added, "I couldn't bear to let my aunt take the trip alone. My mother used to go with her and can't travel any more. Work has slowed down, and I thought I would take full advantage of the situation."

I didn't have much planned that summer. I had spent more money than I had intended in Aruba. I wasn't broke but, needed to be a bit more conservative with my spending to refill my coffers.

The air conditioner was still working. Its steady hum kept the silence from becoming deafening as we traveled the thirty-minute drive to Alex's house. Perhaps, we were a bit emotionally drained from the evening and the heat of the night. It would be the longest thirty minutes in my life-much longer than waiting in the airport had been. I pulled into the cement driveway; the front porch light was on. When I put the car in park, I leaned my arm over the steering wheel and stretched my arm toward the back of her seat which, supported my hand. Alex turned and smiled.

She hesitated before she spoke, "thank you for dinner and I really thank you for remembering our plans. You saved me on that one."

"I had a great time tonight. Jan and Rob are such nice people. I can tell she thinks the world of you."

I wanted to grab her. I wanted to tell her how I felt. I was twenty-one all over again-I had nothing planned to say to her. Instead, I opened my door and walked around the front of the van and opened her door. I was a gentleman. She stepped down-being careful not to catch her heel on the rubber lined step outside the passenger door. She grabbed her purse, and we walked arm-in-arm. The light sensor facing the driveway caught us and lit up the side and front corner of the house as we stepped up on the front porch. Alex turned toward me when we got to the door. The soft light barely captured her face-she leaned toward me and kissed me. A gentle kiss as her hand lingered on my shoulder.

"Thank you again. I am so tired. I think wine does that to me," she said.

I could sense she wanted to say something to me. She didn't. Both of us short of words-afraid to let down our invisible shields to expose our vulnerabilities. I gave her a firm hug and knew we weren't there yet. Perhaps we would be someday soon.

As I walked away and opened the van door, I looked toward Alex-she had already gone inside. The door was still halfway open. 'I love you,' escaped from my lips-a single tear fell-an involuntary shudder swept over me as I climbed into my seat.

She heard the night voices of some frogs and the lone sound of a dog's bark in the distance. She had left the two side screens open on the bay front window before she left. Did she hear a voice or was it her imagination playing tricks on her? The dark night always carried sounds from afar. Turning off the front porch light, her mind drifted back to a warm November evening the previous year-when it began. There was time. A couple of weeks from now. Maybe next spring-they would meet again. Maybe at the next awards event. Her mind was incapable of processing the details from the evening. She slowly walked to her room, kicked off her sling back black leather shoes, and slipped under the covers without taking time to undress. She was exhausted. Her mind needed to rest-to recover from so much emotion. Something she was not used to. Not for a long time. The last thought before she drifted off to sleep was 'goofy never gets better.'

I didn't know if I would see Alex any time soon. I would give her time. Give her some space. She had her three children to focus on and I had two cats. One of which, stayed outside most of the time and was quite self-sufficient. I drove with some music playing-turned down low-the entire way home. Nazareth's song 'Love Hurts' came on. Ironic, isn't it? That song was out-quite popular-back in the day around the time I first met Alex.

Traffic was light. The side roads were dark save for the lights of the residential areas I passed. I crossed a well-lit major intersection and plunged back to the darkness of my journey toward home. Pulling up to my driveway off the stretch of back country road, I noticed the front porch light was on. I couldn't recall if I had turned it on before I had left for dinner. I usually left it off until I went to bed. After grabbing the pile of the last couple of days mail from the mailbox, I proceeded up the long steep driveway. I made a mental note to install a few solar lights alongside it before fall.

I was tired. My eyes were dry. But, it was hard not to miss the red Cadillac parked at the top; in front of the garage door like it had for so many years.

ACKNOWLEDGMENTS

I am deeply humbled by the support I have received from family and friends during the more than thirteen years to complete this book. My core group: my husband Joe and my children Lindsey, Tara, and Anthony have never lost faith in me and my ability to publish Aruba Vacation. I also want to give special thanks to Cindy, Debi, Lindsey, and Sandy for taking hours of their time and expertise to critique the book and provide much appreciated comments. Their devotion and commitment have given me the strength and reinforced my passion to write my very first book.

I hope you find the book equally entertaining and interesting enough to make your next vacation plans to *ONE HAPPY ISLAND – ARUBA!*

Aruba ta dushi! (Aruba is lovely!)

ARUBA PICTURES

ARUBA SIGN

AERIAL VIEW

BACK YARD VIEW

ISLAND VIEW-LIGHTHOUSE-ROUGH SIDE

ARASHI BEACH

NATURAL POOL

SUNSET 1

SUNSET 2

MUD BOG

MUD BOG SAHARA

BIRD OF PARADISE   WHITE FLOWER

ORIOLE BIRD

WILD DONKEYS

IGUANA

AIRPORT BAR

MS. KITTY

Bibliography

*Cameron, J., (*1997) *Titanic,* 20th Century Fox.

Dahl, R., (1964), *Charlie and the Chocolate Factory,* Alfred A. Knopf, Inc. 1964, and in the United Kingdom by George Allen & Unwin 1964.

Dion, D., (2007) *Celine Dion: A New Day - Live in Las Vegas (DVD),* Legacy Recordings December 11, 2007.

Donen, S., Director, Peters, C. and Gelbart, L. *(1984) Blame* It on *Rio,* Sherwood Productions.

Diamond, N.,1970 Cracklin' Rosie *Tap Root Manuscript* Uni Records , Tom Catalano, August 1970.

Geisel, T., (1957), *The Cat in the Hat,* Random House, Houghton Mifflin.
Gray, J., (1992), Men Are from Mars, Women Are from Venus, HarperCollins.

415